CHICKEN SOUP FOR THE TEENAGE SOUL ON TOUGH STUFF

CHICKEN SOUP FOR THE TEENAGE SOUL ON TOUGH STUFF

Stories of Tough Times and Lessons Learned

Jack Canfield
Mark Victor Hansen
Kimberly Kirberger

Health Communications, Inc.
Deerfield Beach, Florida

www.hci-online.com
www.chickensoup.com
www.teenagechickensoup.com

We would like to acknowledge the many publishers and individuals who granted us permission to reprint the cited material. (Note: The stories that were penned anonymously, that are in the public domain, or that were written by Jack Canfield, Mark Victor Hansen or Kimberly Kirberger are not included in this listing.)

I Kiss Like a Horse; The Last Song for Christy; and *Cookie-Cutter Hands.* Reprinted by permission of Rebecca Woolf. ©2001 Rebecca Woolf.

Have You Ever. Reprinted by permission of Tiffany Blevins. ©1999 Tiffany Blevins.

I Am Loni and *Friends to the End.* Reprinted by permission of Cynthia Hamond. ©2000 Cynthia Hamond.

Again; I'm Sorry . . . ; and *Seize the Day.* Reprinted by permission of Shari Henderson. ©1999 Teal Henderson.

Why I Have to Take U.S. History Again and *The Purse.* Reprinted by permission of Tal Vigderson. ©2001 Tal Vigderson.

Good-Bye My Angel Dear. Reprinted by permission of Tyler Phillips. ©1999 Tyler Phillips.

(Continued on page 341)

Library of Congress Cataloging-in-Publication Data

Chicken soup for the teenage soul on tough stuff : stories of tough times and lessons learned / [compiled by] Jack Canfield, Mark Victor Hansen, Kimberly Kirberger.
    p.   cm.
    ISBN 1-55874-942-X (trade paper) — ISBN 1-55874-943-8 (hardcover)
    1. Teenagers—Conduct of life. I. Canfield, Jack, date. II. Hansen, Mark Victor. III. Kirberger, Kimberly, date.

BJ1661 .C296 2001
158.1'28'0835—dc21

2001039354

© 2001 Jack Canfield and Mark Victor Hansen
ISBN 1-55874-942-X (trade paper) — ISBN 1-55874-943-8 (hardcover)

Publisher: Health Communications, Inc.
          3201 S.W. 15th Street
          Deerfield Beach, FL 33442-8190

Cover design by Andrea Perrine Brower
Typesetting by Lawna Patterson Oldfield

With love we dedicate
this book to our teens: Jesse, Christopher,
Melanie and Elisabeth.
We love you!

Contents

9. EATING DISORDERS & DEPRESSION

10. DEATH & DYING

11. GROWING UP

Acknowledgments

They say it takes a village to raise a child. The same is true of compiling and editing these books. There are so many people whose generosity of spirit and hard work are reflected in this book that it is difficult to express the depth of our gratitude to each and every one of them. This is our best and most heartfelt effort to do so.

Our deepest and heartfelt thanks to:

Jesse Kirberger, Kim's teenage son, for his wit, his kindness and his ability to continually inspire all those who know him.

John Anderson, Kim's husband, for assuring that Kim doesn't lose her sense of humor and for loving her even when she does.

Inga Mahoney, for loving Jack and bringing out the very best in him.

Christopher Canfield, Jack's son, for being such a creative and caring teenager. We love you so much.

Kyle and Oran Canfield, Jack's older children, for all their love and support. If we could bottle your creative genius and spread it around, the world would be a better place.

Patty Hansen, Mark's wife, for loving him, for loving teens and for being such a big supporter of preteens. (Kim thanks you for being so much fun to dance with, too.)

Elisabeth and Melanie, Mark's daughters, for being the cool and wise teens that you are.

Kim and Jack's mother, Ellen Taylor, for loving us, putting up with us and always giving us the room to be ourselves.

Fred Angelis, Kim and Jack's father, for his love and support and for teaching us a strong work ethic.

Mark's parents, Paul and Una, for all the love and support they give him.

The amount of hard work that goes into a book like this is tremendous. Each time we compile a *Chicken Soup* book, we are amazed by how many people it takes and how many people step up to the plate with a smile on their faces and love in their hearts. The following people have contributed not only hours and hours of hard work, but have also contributed their love, energy and compassion. For this, we are extremely grateful to:

Mitch Claspy, the president of I.A.M. 4 Teens, for his creativity and strong work ethic. We hold Mitch in the highest esteem for his ability to oversee the production of these books. Kim is so grateful for your commitment and your dedication. Thank you, Mitch, for your brilliance at being able to do so many things to such perfection.

A huge and heartfelt thank-you to Tasha Boucher, senior editor of I.A.M. 4 Teens, for your dedication, your hard work and your amazing capacity to attend to all the details of these stories with such grace. Kim has said numerous times that she feels so lucky to be able to work with someone who has so much integrity and does such a good job at everything. We also thank you for the friendship you share with Kim. It means the world to her.

Lisa Wood-Vazquez, Kim's assistant, for keeping Kim's life running smoothly and for doing it all with such a great attitude. You are a highly valued addition to her staff. Kim is extremely grateful to you and so are we.

Nina Palais, you are a true gem. We thank you for running the Teen Letter Project, for keeping Kim's office together, for being mom to everyone and for having a heart of gold. We also want to acknowledge all that you have done for Soup and Support for Teachers.

Sharon House, who has gone to great lengths to promote this book and make sure it gets into as many hands as possible. Thank you for all your efforts.

We want to extend a big heartfelt thank-you to the following teenagers who worked especially hard on this book:

Christine Kalinowski, for having such a great maturity in your work and for being wise beyond your years.

Hayley Gibson, for your important feedback on the stories and your dedication to this job.

Jenny Sharaf, for your reading, writing and editing skills. We are also grateful to you for your efforts in keeping the Teen Letter Project running smoothly and being so good at multitasking.

Lia Gay, who remains one of Kim's dearest friends, for continuing to support us in whatever way we need. Thanks for all the editing and the incredibly valuable feedback.

The rest of our amazing staff of teenagers who put so much effort into making this book so special. Thank you Rose Lannutti for keeping things together and for your tons of hard work.

We also want to thank some teens who are new to our staff: Caitlin Owens, Lily Lamden and Ashley Fisher. We appreciate your input and your hard work.

Colin Mortensen, for your continued friendship and inspiration. You will always be part of this team.

The following teenagers took precious time out of their lives to read the original manuscript, help us make the final selections and make invaluable comments on how to improve the book. A huge thank-you to: Katrina Mumaw, Pamela Rizzo, Karen Groth, Britney Graham, Kelsey Walt, Katie Conner, Blaire Tacquard, Jill Muschinski, Jessica Turner, Jenna Ahlberg, Cara Wells, Emily Pember, Laura Bauer, Erin Downey, Michelle Andoniello, Berni Donovan, Lauren Mee, Maribel Antonio, Patricia Ochoa, Anna Meyer, Meghan Deppenschmidt, Shaina Swedburg, Cassandra Sarenco, Brian Chan, Laurel Walker, Kelly Kitts, Helen Scammell, Carolyn Rae, Theresa Galeani, Jenny Merlo, Suzi Bonnot, Chris Ingram, Dominic Donovan, Maxwell Li, Hayley Gibson, Jenny Sharaf and Christine Kalinowski.

We want to thank the staff of our wonderful publisher Health Communications:

Lisa Drucker and Susan Tobias, our amazing editors at Health Communications, who give it their all. This book is of the quality it is because of their expertise, patience and genuine kindheartedness. We love you.

Peter Vegso, our publisher, for being supportive and open to new ideas and inspirations. Thanks for continuing to publish books that make a difference.

Kim Weiss, our talented publicist at Health Communications, who is not only a great friend but an absolute joy to work with.

Maria Dinoia, of the Health Communications awesome publicity team, whose hard work continues to keep these books on the bestseller lists.

Terry Burke and Kelly Maragni, who continue to shine at what they do. Without their brilliant sales and marketing skills, the success of the *Chicken Soup* books would not be what it is today.

Randee Feldman, for her masterful coordination and support of all the *Chicken Soup* projects.

Thanks to the art department at Health Communications, for their talent, creativity and unrelenting patience in producing book covers and inside designs that capture the essence of *Chicken Soup:* Larissa Hise Henoch, Lawna Patterson Oldfield, Andrea Perrine Brower, Lisa Camp, Anthony Clausi and Dawn Grove.

Teri Peluso, Christine Belleris, Patricia McConnell, Karen Ornstein and the rest of the Health Communications staff, who give so much of themselves in order to make these books a success.

A huge thank-you to everyone in Jack's and Mark's offices:

Patty Aubrey, for her constant leadership, love and support.

Heather McNamara and D'ette Corona, for their meticulous and insightful edits that made this book even stronger. Your hard work and dedication is treasured by all of us.

Leslie Riskin, for being so instrumental in obtaining permissions and for always offering her assistance.

And the rest of their amazing staffs—Nancy Autio, Veronica Romero, Robin Yerian, Teresa Esparza, Cindy Holland, Vince Wong, Sarah White, Patty Hansen, Trudy Marschall, Maria Nickless, Laurie Hartman, Michelle Adams, Tracy Smith, Dee Dee Romanello, Joy Pieterse, Lisa Williams, Kristi Knopp and David Coleman—who made the process of doing this book so much easier. We appreciate all of their hard work and dedication.

Claude Choquette and Tom Sand, who manage year after year to get each of our books translated into over twenty languages around the world.

Ron Carnell, whose Passions in Poetry Web site *(www.netpoets.com/)* has been a constant source for amazing poetry.

Because of the immensity of this project, we may have left out the names of some people who helped us along the way. If so, please accept our apologies and know that you are appreciated.

Introduction

Dear Teens,

Six years ago we had the idea to write a *Chicken Soup for the Teenage Soul* book for teenagers. As you know, it was very well received and millions of teens have found comfort and support in the stories that were written by their fellow teens. We received thousands of letters requesting that we compile more books for teens. These requests, combined with the deluge of stories that were being sent, gave us the needed motivation and resources to continue the series.

Every week we continue to receive hundreds of letters and stories from teenagers around the world via the Internet and through the mail. As we read the mountain of mail, we began to notice that the chapter on tough stuff was the most popular chapter in the books. After a while, we began to get requests for an entire book on tough stuff. Our response to these requests is the book you now hold in your hands.

For those of you who might be new to the *Chicken Soup for the Teenage Soul* series, Tough Stuff has been a chapter in all of our previous books that included the more challenging issues and experiences of being a teenager, such as drugs and alcohol, rejection, loss of friendships and relationships, death, suicide, divorce, physical and emotional abuse, and eating disorders.

Although the content of these stories is often disturbing and sometimes even tragic, the potential for insight, learning and "growing up" is enormous. We believe this is the reason for the overwhelming response to these types of stories. For example, we have had stories in previous books that dealt with the death of a parent. This is one of every child's worst fears and one might question the benefit of including such stories. However, we have repeatedly heard comments such as these from our readers: "After reading that story, I immediately sat down and wrote my parents a letter apologizing for giving them such a hard time." And, "Though my mom and I still have our little arguments, it is different now. I appreciate her so much more and I KNOW that everything she does is because she loves me. I didn't really understand that before reading that story." We rarely print a story unless the person writing it has learned or realized something profound from their experience. Hopefully, this lesson gets passed on to you, the reader, and will spare you similar pain. At the very least, it will let you know that you are not alone in the world with your challenges.

One of our most important criteria for including a story is that it leaves the reader a better person for having read it. An example of this is the much-loved poem "Somebody Should Have Taught Him" from the first *Chicken Soup for the Teenage Soul* book. In this poem a young girl is killed by a drunk driver on her way home from a party where she chose not to drink. It is an extremely emotional poem that still makes us cry when we read it. The response this simple but powerful poem has evoked from thousands of teenagers is a newfound commitment to never drink and drive. Many teens have written letters promising this to their parents; others have designed contracts that they have signed with witnesses, while in other cases some teens simply made a promise to themselves that they have written about to us. The most gratifying part of all of this is that years later we have received follow-up letters informing us that they have kept their solemn commitment.

Another subject we touch upon in our Tough Stuff chapter is eating disorders. There was a story in *Chicken Soup for the Teenage Soul* about a girl and her difficult, but ultimately successful, recovery from anorexia. Several months after the book was released, Mark Victor Hansen was approached by two people in tears at a booksigning asking if they could have a minute of his time. They told him that their daughter had received the book as a graduation gift. She was about to leave for college and everyone was excited. When she spent the entire week-end before her departure alone in her room, they became upset. The parents thought their daughter should at least find some time to spend with them before she left.

Sunday night she came downstairs and asked if they could talk. She sat down with them and announced she would not be leaving the following day for college. She went on to say that she had an eating disorder and now, after reading *Chicken Soup for the Teenage Soul*, she was able to find the courage to be honest with them about it. She said she felt weak and scared for her life. She asked her parents to take her to see a doctor first thing in the morn-ing. They did and her fears were confirmed. She was on the brink of death and, had she not come forward when she did, she would have died. At the time they told Mark this story, she was still in the hospital.

There are no words to describe what we feel when we hear this kind of story. We are grateful and we are humbled, but more than anything, we are certain that as long as these stories are changing lives, we will continue to compile these books.

Guidelines for Reading This Book

Be aware that this is an entire book of stories about difficult and often tragic events. Although a *Chicken Soup* story always contains something that is inspiring, uplifting or life-changing, the most positive element in some of these stories might be your response to do something different in your own life more than the content of the story itself.

Read this book one story at a time.

It is not necessary to read the stories in the order they appear in the book. In fact, you may find it preferable to skip around and read the stories that you are drawn to as opposed to reading an entire chapter from beginning to end. Trust your intuition.

Parents of younger children (as well as older brothers and sisters) should be aware that many of these stories may not be appropriate for children who are not yet teenagers (ten- to twelve-year-olds). We suggest you read the stories first and then decide which ones are suitable for your child (or younger sibling).

We started this book with a chapter on self-acceptance because we feel that this is the most important issue facing teens today. These are stories about embarrassment, harassment and teasing, and were rated very highly by our panel of teen readers. The story "I Kiss Like a Horse" uses some strong language when describing the cruelty that was inflicted upon the writer. We debated long and hard about changing some of the words (like *slut* and *whore*), which we felt might be offensive to some readers, but in the end we felt it would detract from the impact of the story. Sadly, this is a very common situation that teenage girls are faced with, and we felt it was very important to leave the story as it was written in the hopes that it would help other girls facing the same kind of verbal and emotional abuse, as well as sensitize teenage boys and girls to the incredibly damaging power of their words.

In an effort to provide as much support as we could to those of you who are facing similar tough stuff in your lives, we have listed some useful hotlines and Web sites at the end of many stories and in the back of the book. If you are facing a challenge similar to that addressed in one of the stories, we encourage you to reach out for help. We also hope you will encourage your friends and brothers and sisters to use these valuable resources as well.

Keep in mind that part of growing up is learning how to deal with difficult issues, and the benefits can be great if you have the courage to ask for help. Human beings are not designed to go through life alone. No one has to bear the burden of the tough times all by themselves. There are thousands of dedicated professionals (teachers, counselors, ministers, therapists and psychologists) as well as competent and caring volunteers who have devoted their lives to helping teens through the tough stuff. Have the courage to reach out to some of them and let them help you.

Our hearts are with you as you read these stories and as you confront the unique challenges of your life. We pray that each and every one of you find comfort, hope and inspiration in the courage, strength and faith of the teenagers who have bravely shared their stories with you on the pages that follow.

All our love,
Kimberly, Jack and Mark

To everything there is a season
And a time to every purpose under heaven:

A time to be born, and a time to die;
A time to plant, and a time to pluck up that which is
   planted;

A time to kill, and a time to heal;
A time to break down, and a time to build up;

A time to weep, and a time to laugh;
A time to mourn, and a time to dance;

A time to cast away stones, and a time to gather stones
   together;
A time to embrace, and a time to refrain from embracing;

A time to seek, and a time to lose;
A time to keep, and a time to cast away;

A time to rend, and a time to sew;
A time to keep silence, and a time to speak;

A time to love, and a time to hate;
A time for war, and a time for peace.

Ecclesiastes 3:1–8

Share with Us

Most of the stories in this book were written by teens like you. We would like to invite you to send us stories you would like to see published in future editions of *Chicken Soup for the Teenage Soul.*

We would also love to hear your reactions to the stories in this book. Please let us know what your favorite stories are and how they affected you.

Please send submissions to:

Chicken Soup for the Teenage Soul
P.O. Box 936
Pacific Palisades, CA 90272
fax: 310-573-3657
e-mail for stories: *stories@iam4teens.com*
e-mail for letters: *letters@iam4teens.com*

Come visit our Web site:
www.iam4teens.com

You can also visit the *Chicken Soup for the Teenage Soul* site at:
www.teenagechickensoup.com

We hope you enjoy reading this book as much as we enjoyed compiling, editing and writing it.

1

ON SELF-
ACCEPTANCE

*. . . And you help each other realize that
all the things you want to be . . .
you already are.*

Gretchen, Dawson's Creek

I Kiss Like a Horse

Forgiveness means letting go of a hurtful situation and moving on with your own happiness.

Amanda Ford

He was the first boy to ask me to prom. He was also the first boy to dump me two days before the dance. My dress was scarlet, and I spent every afternoon after school on my tiptoes, dancing before the mirror with my hair in my hands, daydreaming about a slow dance under blue lights and perhaps a swift caress under falling stars.

Max was a junior, and I was a freshman. Max had a car, and I had a bike. Max hung out with girls who were, in my opinion, straight-up mean. These girls liked Max and hated me. I was too young to be with Max. I wasn't cool enough. I didn't scream and fight and smoke weed at high-school parties. A week after our breakup, I awoke late in the night to the shrieks of girls' voices and the horns of several cars.

"You slut! Max never liked you. Stay away from our guys from now on. . . . He was just using you! You're so-o-o-o stupid!" I didn't move. I didn't even look out the window. I was afraid they'd see me and keep yelling.

"Come on guys, let's go," one girl shouted. And then they were gone.

I just lay there dumbfounded. I woke up early the next morning and surveyed the damage. Toilet paper wasn't that big of a deal. I had been toilet-papered before. But the chocolate syrup on the garage door wasn't pleasant. "You Kiss Like a Horse" it said, and the stains lingered long after I tried to hose them down. The driveway was painted with half a dozen cruel phrases describing untrue details of my nonexistent sex life. I kept my mouth shut, though, and laughed it off. They were all lies, so what did it matter?

Everyone knew the next day at school.

"You must be so embarrassed," she said.

"I feel so sorry for you," he said.

"So what does a horse kiss like?" he asked.

"Did you really have sex with him?" she asked.

"Shut up, who cares, whatever," I said. "And, no, I didn't have sex with him."

Max was one of the only boys I had ever kissed, and I guess I wasn't a very good kisser. I bit his tongue once or twice, and he bled. At the time, he was sweet about it.

"It's cool . . ." he had said, wiping the blood from his lip. "It doesn't hurt. You can bite me all you want."

I guess when the game is over all bets are off, though.

The taunting didn't stop—it only got worse. A few weeks later the older girls had a "list" photocopied and circulated around school. Not only was my name associated with biting and horses, but now I was number one on the "High-School Whore List."

"I'm not a whore," I sighed in the girls' bathroom as I was washing my hands. The paper signs were taped everywhere. I tore them down.

All I did was kiss him. And I didn't even do it right. "I'm not a whore!" I screamed at two dozen eyes stripping me of my innocence. I was disgusting to them. I was disgusting to everybody. I was even starting to believe that I was all the things they said I was. It's funny how easy rumors are to believe, even if they are about you. I carried myself differently. I went to parties and kissed all the boys. I wanted them to tell me that I wasn't a sloppy kisser, that I wasn't a horse, and that I wasn't a bad person. No one ever cleared my name, though. Instead, they all tried unsuccessfully to bring me home with them. After all, I was the "easiest and cheapest date in school."

I was never able to fulfill my prom fantasy, let alone wear my gown or get my hair done. It was hard enough staying home the night of the prom, barefoot on the couch between my parents watching *I Love Lucy.*

The dress was still hanging in my closet the night the phone rang, my beautiful never-been-worn shoes still neatly in their paper box. I answered the phone.

"Neighhhhh."

"Huh?" I couldn't believe it was still going on.

"Neighhhhhh."

Click.

Whoever it was hung up. Was Max behind all of this? What had I done to be treated this way? Did I miss something? Would it ever end? I couldn't take it any longer. This wasn't going to stop until I did something about it. I needed to find Max and talk to him. I needed to do something.

I found him at his locker. I had purposely avoided that hallway for the past couple of months. I didn't want to see him. But today was different. I was tired of avoiding confrontation. I wanted my life back.

He ignored me at first, and I grimaced.

"I have to . . ." he began.

I interrupted. "So why? What did I ever do to you? You broke up with me. You spread rumors about me. I don't understand. What did I do to you?"

"... get to class," he finished.

"Why, Max?"

"Listen, I don't know what you're talking about, and even if I did, it's not my problem." He didn't care. He didn't want to.

I don't know what I expected; maybe an apology or an explanation. I guess I hoped that he would take it back. I wanted him to tell me that he was sorry and that he would undo the rumors and set me free. I wanted him to tell me that, after all was said and done, I really didn't kiss like a horse. He didn't say a thing.

It turned out that I didn't need an explanation after all. His silence spoke words that he could never muster. Max was afraid. He couldn't be with me. He wasn't supposed to. His friends hadn't approved and so he got rid of me, even though I know he didn't want to. He had to convince himself that I was a monster or the worst kisser in the whole school. He had to convince himself that he didn't like me anymore, and for that reason, I felt sorry. I felt sorry for him and for all the pathetic souls who believed him. I felt sorry for the girls who wasted their baby-sitting money on toilet paper and their weekends fabricating degrading lists. I felt sorry for all of them. And for the first time in months, I felt relieved. I knew who I was, and the rest didn't matter.

Max was just some guy—some guy who needed to grow up. And I refused to be just some girl. So what if I was a lousy kisser? It took me years before I was steady on my Rollerblades. And so what if the older girls didn't like me? It wouldn't be long before I myself was an "older girl." And so what if there were rumors? They weren't true. I held my head high, defending my morality and reputation with a string of confidence. I wasn't the only one.

Lies and rumors, hate and envy fly like bullets every day in high school. I got hit, like many unfortunately do, and I was ready to get back out there, shielding myself with the truth and a force field of confidence I forgot I had.

About a week later, a boy at school stopped me in the halls and asked, "So, is it true that you kiss like a horse?"

I smiled. "You know what, I've never kissed a horse before, have you?" He shook his head, embarrassed, as I turned around and walked away.

Rebecca Woolf

Have You Ever

Have you ever lived my life?
Spent one minute in my shoes?
If you haven't then tell me why
You judge me as you do.

Have you ever woken up in the morning
Wondering if this was your last day on Earth?
Have you ever left your house
Unsure if you'd return?

Have you ever seen your friend get shot
Outside his favorite store?
Have you ever seen a friend die
From drugs he'd never used before?

Have you ever seen your mom get beat up
By your stepdad messed up on booze?
Have you ever had an unwanted pregnancy
Forcing you to choose?

Have you ever sat beneath the stars
Hoping God will hear?

Have you ever seen your friend drive away
After way too many beers?

Have you ever had a friend
Experiment with weed?
Have you ever covered up guilt
By doing a good deed?

Have you ever considered suicide
As the only way?
Have you ever tried to hide yourself
Behind the things you say?

Have you ever wanted to protect
Your friends and everyone in sight?
Have you ever felt such pain
That you cried yourself to sleep at night?

Have you ever lived my life,
Spent one minute in my shoes?
If you haven't, then tell me why
You judge me as you do.

                                        Tiffany Blevins

I Am Loni

To be nobody but yourself in a world that's doing its best to make you somebody else is to fight the hardest battle you are ever going to fight. Never stop fighting.

e. e. cummings

Why do I even try? If there's one thing I should have learned, it's, try or not, I'll probably screw up. Mom says, "Loni, a lady shouldn't say things like 'screw up.'" That just proves my point. I even screw up how to tell you that I screwed up.

I know, I have so much going for me. Don't even go there. Dad brags about my grades, and Mom's proud of the person I am and all my activities. Grandma goes on and on about my pretty face. *Yeah, too bad about the rest of me,* I think to myself.

I'm not, like, big enough to be featured as The Amazing Amazon Teen in *The Guinness Book of World Records,* but I am big enough not to like shopping with my friends. "How cu-u-u-u-ute!" they squeal over every rack of clothes. They know they'll fit into anything. I can't commit until I scan the plastic circle dividers to see how high the sizes go.

I pretend that clothes don't matter to me. That explains my semi-grunge look everyone takes for my chosen style. No outfit is complete without a sweater, flannel shirt or sweatshirt tied around my waist to cover up . . . oh . . . everything.

So, when we go to the mall, I'm the designated shopper. You know, like the designated driver who goes to a party but doesn't partake. I stand outside the changing rooms to *ooh* and *aah* when they emerge for the three-way mirror check. Only after a careful inspection do I reassure them that their thighs, legs, waist or bottom do not look too big in that outfit; otherwise, it would be taken as insincere.

It takes all I have not to roll my eyes when they hand me a piece of clothing and plead, "Can you see if this comes in a smaller size?" Give me a break. Where should I look? The children's department?

I really did screw up, though. Being a self-appointed good sport, I tried out for the volleyball team with my friends. Here's the bad part: I made it.

It seems I have a killer serve. I use it for self-defense. The harder I ram the ball, the less likely it will be returned and force me to clod around the court keeping it in play.

To make matters worse, we keep winning. This is the first winning season of any girl's sport in our school's history. Volleyball fever took over, and attendance soared. Just my luck. And those pep rallies. There's a thrill. Jumping around high-fiving while my name echoes over the PA system.

In our small town, making it to State Finals is newsworthy. Our team was pictured sitting in the bleachers in a "V for Victory" formation. I was the connecting bottom of the "V," front and center in all my glory.

"Loni Leads the Charge to State!" read the headline. Not

bad. I didn't even pretend to protest when Mom bought copies for the relatives. I was pleased when the team framed the picture and hung it in the tunnel between our locker room and the arena. It soon became our team gesture to blow kisses at our picture every time we passed it.

It was the night of the final game, and we had home-court advantage. The series was tied two games to two. I led the team's run for our triumphant entrance. Cheers stormed down the tunnel to meet us. We glanced at the banners posted along the walls, taking energy from the words.

YOU GO, GIRLS! YES YOU CAN! WE'RE #1!

We were ready to blow kisses at our picture when shock froze me. Two words were written in red on the glass. Two words that totally changed the headline.

"Loni THE BULL leads the charge to State!"

The horns drawn on my head completed the insult.

I felt myself emptying until I wasn't me anymore. I was nobody. The team bunched behind me.

"Who did this?"

"Who would be so mean?"

Their questions had no answers. They thought they were as upset as I was, but they were wrong. I wasn't upset at all. I was in shock.

So this is the truth, I thought. *This is who I am.*

And all the words around me didn't heal the hurt because nobody said the three words I needed to hear most: "That's not true."

The team moved me down the tunnel. There was no time to sort myself. What was real seemed like a dream, and I couldn't shake myself awake. The chants of "Loni! Loni!" sounded hollow. I let the cheers of the many be muted by the jeers of the few.

We won the coin toss and took to the court for my first serve. Around me the team was pumped and ready to go.

I rolled the volleyball in my palms to get its feel and mechanically went into my serving stance. All I could see were the words . . . THE BULL. THE BULL. THE BULL.

I tossed the ball up, but before my fist made contact the shout "OLE!" hit me. I stutter-stepped and missed the ball. I told myself not to look, but my eyes were drawn anyway. I couldn't pick out who it was. The team tried to buck me up with back slaps and "that's okays." But it didn't help.

I went through the rotations until I was at the net. My concentration scurried between the game and the bleachers. When the ball skimmed the air above my head, a loud snorting sound came from the front row.

"That's taking the bull by the horns!" someone yelled. The player behind me made the save and set up the ball for me to spike. But I wasn't looking at the ball. I was staring into the faces of the five high-school guys who were mocking me. My humiliation only fueled their taunts.

"Give me a B, give me a U, give me a double L, too. What's that smell? LONI! LONI! LONI!"

Why didn't someone shut them up?

The coach called a time-out. "Loni, can you get your head in the game?"

I shrugged.

"Why are you letting a few people who don't even know you decide for you who you are?"

I shrugged again.

"Loni, you're valuable as a person and to your team. Unkind words don't change who you are unless you decide they change you," she said.

Sounds good in theory, I thought, *but this is the real world.*

"I'm keeping you in, but if you can't work through this I'll pull you."

I nodded.

I walked past the boys to take my place in the game.

With each step I took, they stomped their feet to shake the floor. I got the point. Very funny.

I also had to walk past my teammates, and in spite of my weak showing, they were still rooting for me. "You can do it." "You're the best."

Something in me gave way. The quote on a magnet on my grandma's refrigerator popped into my thoughts: "God don't make no junk."

I knew what I knew, and I knew myself—I wasn't junk. I felt my value to the very depths of my soul. Who was I anyway? What did some immature boys know about me? There were so many people who loved and supported me, and it was time to do my best for them and for myself.

And just like that, I was free of them. Oh, they continued to stomp their feet with each of my steps. I didn't like it, but it didn't matter. They were powerless over my life.

The game was close, and we played hard. The winning serve fell to me. It was my moment, and I took it. The ball went up, my fist came forward and hit it right on. It was a perfect power serve unreturnable by the other team. The crowd went wild. The pep band started beating out our school song. The team huddled around me.

Shouts of "Loni! Loni!" vibrated the arena. The funny thing is, the cheers didn't feed me like they used to. They were great, but the joy I felt, the freedom I felt, the sense of myself I had filled me more than any cheers.

There was more than one victory that day, and the game was not the most important one.

Loni Taylor
As told to Cynthia Hamond

Again

If when you wake up in the morning,
And the hurting is so great,
You don't want to get out of bed
And face a world of hate.

If everything in life goes wrong
And nothing you do seems right,
You just try a little harder
And soon you'll see the light.

For every person who has put you down
And filled your life with pain,
You must strive to achieve greatness
And show them you can win.

For every disappointment,
For the times you are let down,
There will be a better moment
And your life will turn around.

Because everyone feels heartache
And everyone feels pain,
But only those who have true courage
Can get up and try again.

Teal Henderson

Why I Have to Take U.S. History Again

I think of myself as an intelligent, sensitive human being with the soul of a clown, which always forces me to blow it at the most important moments.

Jim Morrison

What was I thinking? Why couldn't I have left well enough alone? Stupid, stupid Valentine's Day. I had to write that dumb poem, and I had to go and put it in Lisa's locker. Why do they have those vents on lockers anyway? What needs to breathe in your locker? I don't keep puppies in my locker, and I don't know anyone who does. And my textbooks are just as stale as ever, with or without air. But they have to put those vents on, just big enough to stick a stupid valentine with a stupid poem inside.

It all started at the beginning of last year in U.S. History class. I was walking into class with my friend Dave, minding my own business, talking about some play in some game that we both watched the night before, when I saw something bright out of the corner of my eye. I looked over. Actually, it wasn't a bright spot at all, but a head of brilliant blonde hair. Beneath that hair were two amazing, beautiful blue eyes. I didn't know it then, but that moment was the beginning of the end for my chance of a good grade in U.S. History.

I spent the next twelve weeks staring at that beautiful head (or at least the back of it). Seating was alphabetical, but I was fortunate enough to be three rows back and four seats over from Lisa so that if I stretched my neck in just the right way, I could see that head. When the bell rang, I would try to get up at just the right time so that I could bump into her or catch her glance as she left the room. I'm sure Mr. Houston, our teacher, must have given his lecture every day, but all I can remember is something-something Appamatox and something-something Battle of the Bulge (although that last one might have been from *Saving Private Ryan*).

We broke for the holidays, and all I could think about was Lisa. I would go play video games or hang out at the mall and hope to see her. Surely Lisa shopped at the Gap. Maybe I'd see here there. I think I once heard her say she liked movies. Maybe I'd catch her at the movie theater. I saw a girl at the mall that I thought I once saw talking to Lisa at school so I followed her around for about twenty minutes, but it turned out she was with her mom and she looked at me like I was a little creepy, so I gave that up.

So anyway, the next semester started. Lisa never made her move, and so I somehow decided it was a good idea to write a stupid poem and put it in Lisa's locker, through those evil vents. I knew when Lisa's next class got out, and I somehow got a hall pass so I could sneak out of my class early and position myself at the wall around the corner from her locker before she did. My plan worked, and I was there in time to see Lisa open her locker. The bright red envelope came flying out and nearly poked her in the eye. It hit the ground, and Tyler Coleman picked it up.

"What's this?" he asked. "Did someone send you a valentine? Who's your *boyfriend?*" Lisa's friends suddenly gathered around. Tyler opened the envelope and began to read my poem.

Dear Lisa:

You may not know much about me
So I'm sending you this little plea
Today is Valentine's Day
And I have something to say

I have admired you from afar
I wish I had a car
So I could take you out on a date
To the movies or maybe to rollerskate

Because I think you are cool
The best in our dumb school
So please hear what I have to say
It's really important, okay?

The words resonated in my head, each one striking me with the force of a sledge hammer. And there was my name at the bottom of the page—for all the world to see! *What was I thinking?* Everyone laughed. The force of their laughter caused me to move, ever so slightly, and someone noticed me. I had nowhere to run and had to walk past them all on my way to my next class: U.S. History. They saw me.

"Look, Lisa, it's your *boyfriend.*" "Why don't you give him a big kiss?" "Hey, superdweeb, come over here and give your girlfriend a big old kiss."

Tyler grabbed my arm and tried to shove me toward Lisa. She turned away with a look as though someone had just shoved dog poop in her face. I think I turned a new color of red that's not even available in the Crayola 64 box of crayons. All I could hear was the laughing. Other kids started coming around to see what was so funny, and Tyler handed over the card so they could pass it around. I tried to move, but Tyler had a firm grip on my arm. How could this possibly get any worse?

I looked to Lisa for some support, some sign that she wasn't part of this ugly mob. But her expression had changed from a look of disgust to laughter, too. She had joined in with the rest. This was clearly the single worst event of my entire life.

If I was distracted in U.S. History before, now multiply that by ten. I couldn't even look at the back of Lisa's head because everyone was looking at me to see if I was looking at the back of Lisa's head. I could only wallow in self-pity. The whole rest of the year I was either Lisa's *boyfriend* or superdweeb. Everyone forgot my name.

That day, I went home and tried to hide under the covers of my bed. My mother came in and asked me what was wrong. I couldn't possibly tell her. But I had to tell someone.

She eventually managed to get the story out of me. I told her everything—about Lisa, the blonde hair, the blue eyes, the attempts to accidentally bump into her, the staring contest and, finally, the evil locker slots and how they forced me to put that card with the poem inside.

She just looked at me and smiled. She smiled. She didn't laugh; she didn't cry. She didn't pat me on the head and tell me everything was going to be okay. She didn't try to turn the whole experience into some kind of lesson. She didn't scold me, and she didn't compliment me. She just smiled.

At first I thought maybe she was possessed, or maybe she had been cooking with wine again. But then she took my hand and asked me a question: "If you could go back and do it again, what would you have done differently?"

I thought about it. I could have not stared at Lisa's big, blonde head. I could have not tried to bump into her. I could have not put that card in her locker. Sure, I could have avoided the whole ugly mess, and people would still remember my first name.

"And so then where would you be?" my mom asked. *I'd be a happy, anonymous ninth grader.* "Is that how you think of yourself?" she asked. *How did I think of myself?* Right then, I didn't think much of myself. I felt like a big loser. She must have known.

"You aren't a loser. How do you think any boy ever got to meet any girl? By hiding in the corner? By letting boys like Tyler decide who you can like and who you can't? In my opinion, this is Lisa's big loss. I think your poem is sweet."

She said all that because that's what mothers are supposed to say. I knew that. And I still felt bad, but I started to see things from her point of view. How could I have not taken the chance? In that moment when I put the card in Lisa's locker, I had felt brave and adventurous and strong. How dare they laugh at me? I had dared to take my shot.

That moment didn't last very long because the next day I got my report card, and it turned out I failed U.S. History. So now I have to go to summer school. But it's okay, because there's this new girl, Carolyn, who just transferred in and she has to go to summer school, too, and you should see the back of her head. . . .

Tal Vigderson

Good-Bye My Angel Dear

My days draw long and weary
When you're no longer near.
Confidence is filled with questions
Strength replaced with fear.

The assuredness that I awake with each day
Is nowhere to be found,
As though my dreams and aspirations
Were buried underground.

I hear your voice being carried by wind
Like your fingers through my hair.
I close my eyes and remember your kiss
And wish that you were there.

So with nothing left but one thing to say
To resolve my heartbreak here,
Good-bye my darling and my love
Good-bye my angel dear.

Tyler Phillips

Applying Myself

Those who dream by day are cognizant of many things which those who dream only by night may miss.

Edgar Allen Poe

At thirteen years old, I was like any other kid my age. I liked computer and Nintendo games. I complained about too much homework, and I hated when my little brother ate the last Fruit Roll-Up in the box. I guess I looked like any other kid my age, too. I wore baggy pants and over-size T-shirts—you know, the typical middle-school prison garb. However, inside I harbored a secret that made me feel different and weird.

You see, I was diagnosed with ADD. This is the hip term for attention deficit disorder. I couldn't even get the cool-kid type where you're hyper. I had to get the dreamier, "space-cadet" type. I can look straight into your eyes and not hear a word you're saying. It's sort of like in the Charlie Brown TV specials. All the adults' voices in the cartoon sound like endless droning. "Mwop, mwop, mwop, mwop." I appear to be listening while all the while my mind is somewhere miles away.

After extensive and boring tests, the doctor explained to my mom that I was what they called "dual exceptional." It sounds pretty cool, doesn't it? No, it doesn't mean that I have any special dueling abilities like the swordsmen in *The Three Musketeers*. It also doesn't mean that I have a major psychiatric disorder like multiple personalities. That might be kind of cool in a weird sort of way. What "dual exceptional" means is that I am what they call "gifted." This means I'm pretty bright, and yet I'm also learning disabled. This makes school challenging for me.

Yes, you can be gifted and learning disabled at the same time. The two words are not a contradiction in terms. I once heard a comedian refer to the words "jumbo shrimp" as one of these conflicted phrases.

I've learned to accept the fact that I'm an enigma to some. Still, it is a bummer to be misunderstood. The whole syndrome can sometimes make me feel like I am on the outside looking in. Everyone else seems to be getting it, and I'm not.

What really burns me up, though, is when teachers don't get it. In middle school, I took Language Arts with Mrs. Smith. She had piercing brown eyes that made you feel like you had done something wrong. Her no-nonsense, rigid posture made her look as though she'd forgotten to take the wire coat hanger out of her dress. Her face was angular, stiff and white, like a freshly starched and laundered hanky. A smile rarely creased her well-powdered complexion. I could imagine only an intermittent smirk grazing those thin red lips as she X'd her way through someone's failing test paper with her glorious red marker.

I was enrolled in Mrs. Smith's gifted section. That first day, she not only set down the rules of her cellblock, but she handed out copies of them for us to memorize and be tested on the following day. I knew right away that I had better "advocate" for myself. This is just some big, fancy-shmancy term that means to stand up for yourself. In my case, trying to explain, for the umpteenth time, about my learning disabilities. Basically, I have lousy reading comprehension and my handwriting is the pits. So I told her that I have ADD and that I might need to take home some reading assignments because my concentration is better when I am in a quiet setting. I went on to explain to her about my "fine motor skill" problems, which make my handwriting look like chicken scratch. I asked her if I might be able to use my word processor at home to do written assignments.

As I explained all this to Mrs. Smith, she gave me a squinty-eyed look down her bespectacled nose and said, "You are no different from anyone else, young man. If I do for you, I have to do for all the others." She snorted once and then added, "I will not give you an unfair advantage over your peers!" And with that, the bell rang and a herd of students swept me away to my next period.

The comprehension packets were rough. You had to read them, digest them and write an essay on them, all within the forty-five-minute allotted time. Not only couldn't I finish the reading, I couldn't write my essay fast enough or neatly enough to be legible. The result was that each paper came back decorated by Mrs. Smith's flaming red pen. She was like the mad Zorro of red X's.

One day, after she had handed me back my fifth X'd-out paper of the term, I approached her desk for the second time.

"Would you mind very much if I completed the next packet at home, Mrs. Smith? I think I might do better where there is less distraction." Then I backed away from her desk as though I were within firing range of her loaded mouth.

Mrs. Smith bit her thin red lips as her trademark smirk spread across them. "It's against school policy, young man. No unfair advantages. I have treated all students the same in the thirty years I have taught here." Then she flared her nose, clicked her heels and turned away from me, in more ways than one.

So I did what any other kid would do in my situation: I smuggled the packet out of the classroom. I felt like I was doing something illegal, and yet my motives were pure. I had to prove to her, or rather prove to myself, that I could do the work under the right conditions.

I secretly unfolded the contraband on my bed that night. The story, which had seemed so confusing in class, became quite clear to me in the still of my room. I not only got it, I could even relate to it. It was the true story of Louis Braille. He lived in the 1800s and was blinded by a childhood accident. During this time, society shut off the blind from having much of an education. Many were left with the bleak future of becoming homeless beggars. Despite much misunderstanding of his disability, Louis Braille "advocated" for himself. He developed a reading system of raised dots for the blind, which enabled him to read on a par with his peers. A world of books and knowledge opened up to him that he and others like him were literally blind to before. I was like Louis in my classroom setting. I was being made to learn like the other students who were sighted in a way I wasn't.

That night I sat down at my word processor. My thoughts spilled out so fast that my fingers danced across the keyboard, straining to keep up. I explained myself in terms of Louis, in hopes that Mrs. Smith would finally understand me. Funny thing is, somewhere along the line I began to understand myself in a way I never had before.

I cited many other famous people who were in some way different in their learning styles and abilities throughout history. Hans Christian Andersen was said to have been learning disabled, and yet he wrote some of the best fairy tales of our time. I summed it all up by asking, "If I were a student with a vision impairment, would I be seated in the back of the room?" I questioned, "Would I have my glasses taken away from me so that I would not have an unfair advantage over other, glassless students?"

Mrs. Smith never looked at me as she handed my paper back facedown on my desk that day. She never even commented that my work was done on the word processor. As my eyes focused in on the white page, I found an A decorating the margin instead of her customary X. Underneath were her neatly red-penned words: "See what you can do when you apply yourself?"

I took the paper, tucked it away in my folder and shook my head. I guess some people will never get it!

C. S. Dweck

2

DRUGS & ALCOHOL

Resolve to be thyself; and know that he who finds himself loses his misery.

Matthew Arnold

The Last Song for Christy

Matt never did drugs. He spent his afternoons and nights riding his skateboard through backstreets of the small town that raised him. His friends would experiment with the usual substances, but not Matt.

Christy was his sister; six years older. She and Matt were close. They both liked tattoos and metal guitar riffs. Christy would paint incredible portraits and abstract images, and Matt would jam on his guitar. They shared stories, and they always said "I love you" before bed.

When Matt and I started dating, the first family member I was introduced to was his sister, Christy.

"See this tattoo on my wrist. Christy has it, too. We got them together." He lit up whenever he talked about her.

Matt was at the peak of his skateboarding career, and Christy was still painting. She was beautiful. They looked a lot alike—black hair, blue eyes. Christy was petite—her makeup dark and interesting—her lips, red and passionate. She looked the part she played—the artist, the once-rebel who survived hell and was now back, living life while revisiting the shadows of her past with each stroke of her paintbrush.

When Matt was in junior high, the police took Christy away. His parents wouldn't tell him why, but he found out on his own. Heroin. She had been doing heroin, and they caught her. She was only eighteen. She spent the next several months in rehab while Matt waited, guitar riffs, skate tricks—waited.

When she finally did come home, things were different. Christy seemed distant and Matt didn't know what to say. A few months later, they came again—the police. Matt was sleeping, and they knocked down the door. His sister was screaming as they dragged her away, this time to prison.

I asked Matt what it was like, how that affected him. I tried to imagine hearing her scream. I wondered how it was possible for Matt to sleep when he knew his sister was cold and alone in her cell somewhere.

"I couldn't," he said. "I couldn't sleep."

"Did you visit her?" I asked.

Matt was silent.

"Did you ever talk to her about it, tell her how much it hurt you, tell her that you couldn't sleep, tell her that you were afraid?"

There was a long silence. "She's okay now. She's been clean for eight years. She's great. It's over. The drugs, it's all over." Matt spoke to the wind when he spoke of Christy's past. His voice would fade out into oblivion and then he'd change the subject.

When Christy was finally released from jail and then rehab, Matt's family decided to move. They moved south, away from Christy's reputation and the backstreets where Matt had conquered curbsides and half-pipes in the small town by the sea. Christy was clean and never again did Matt wake up to his sister's arrests, or a cold sweat after the nightmares that plagued him while she was away. She had been clean for six months, and then two years, and then four. Matt went to high school and Christy moved back up north to go to school.

"Were you afraid?" I asked.

"Nope. She was going back to school. I was glad. She was going to pursue her art. She was so talented, you know," Matt whispered.

I knew. I had seen her artwork. It hung in Matt's room, in his kitchen and bathroom. She had even painted straight on the walls. Matt let her paint all over them.

Matt and I dated during my senior year. He was my first serious relationship. Christy came down to visit Matt and the family pretty often, and whenever she came down, Matt would rush to be with her. She was the woman in his life, more than I ever was. Christy and Matt were best friends. They were like nothing I had ever seen. Matt would light up when Christy entered a room. He was so proud of her. She was his angel, his big sister, and everything she said was amusing, brilliant or just cool.

I got the call a few months ago. Even though Matt and I had broken up over a year before, we were still close friends. The call wasn't from him, though. It was from another friend.

"Becca, look . . . I thought I should tell you. Christy died. She overdosed. Heroin. I'm sorry."

The air went numb, and the murmur of the TV in the other room muted. I dropped the phone and stared at the wall for what seemed like hours.

"But she was clean. Ten years now! She was clean . . ." I mumbled softly, my voice tainting the wind that blew on that rainy afternoon. I called Matt. He was with his family up north, where it happened.

Matt told me, "She wasn't supposed to die. She was going to be married in a couple of months. They had the date and everything. We found this picture of her. She was wearing wings. You should see it; she looks like an angel."

He wasn't crying. I searched the blues of his eyes for a tear, but he was hypnotized. The shock. The impossibility of his earth angel lost somewhere in the universe. It was too much.

"The last time I saw her, she was so happy. I had my guitar and I was playing for her, and she was laughing. She was so beautiful and so happy. She was going to be a makeup artist. She would have been the best." Matt was smiling, and I took his hand.

She didn't have to die. She was clean for ten years, and then one day she started up again. Her body couldn't take it. She passed out, and they couldn't revive her. They couldn't make her come back.

Matt spoke during the funeral. His words were soft and eloquent, and he looked out at Christy's friends and family and told them how much he loved her, how much he will always love her. He showed his tattoo, the one that he and his sister got together. Some laughed. Some cried.

The picture that Matt had mentioned to me was perched behind the podium, between lilies and roses. Matt was right. She did look like an angel—red lips and blue eyes, wearing white and angel wings.

That night, after the funeral, Matt and I went down to the cove where he and Christy used to laugh. "How could she do this? Why? Why did she have to do this?" he asked.

He cried. I cried, too.

I talked to Matt the other day. I asked him how he was doing.

"I'm okay," he said. "Most of the time. Sometimes I can't sleep. I'm waiting for Christy to come home or for her to call. Sometimes I have these nightmares. I play the guitar a lot, even more than I used to. I have to practice. I'm in a band now, and we play gigs and stuff. The last song of the set is always the best. That's the song I practice over and over again until it's perfect. It has to be just perfect because I play it for Christy. The last song is always for Christy."

Rebecca Woolf

The Final Act

Screeching tires, shattering glass,
Twisting metal, fiberglass.
The scene is set, it all goes black,
The curtain raised, the final act.
Sirens raging in the night,
Sounds of horror, gasps of fright.
Intense pain, the smell of blood,
Tearing eyes begin to flood.

They pull out bodies one by one.
What's going on? We were only having fun!
My friend is missing. What did I do?
Her belongings everywhere,
In the road there lies her shoe.

A man is leaning over me and looks into my eyes,
"What were you thinking, son?
Did you really think that you could drive?"
He pulls up the sheet, still looking at me,
"If you'd only called your mom or dad, you'd still be
    alive."

I start to scream, I start to yell
But no one can hear me, no one can tell.
They put me in an ambulance, they take me away.
The doctor at the hospital exclaims, "DOA!"

My father's in shock, my mother in tears,
She collapses in grief, overcome by the fear.
They take me to this house and place me in this box.
I keep asking what is happening,
But I can't make it stop.

Everyone is crying, my family is so sad.
I wish someone would answer me,
I'm starting to get mad.
My mother leans over and kisses me good-bye,
My father pulls her away, while she is screaming,
  "WHY?"

They lower my body into a dirt grave,
It feels so cold, I yell to be saved.
Then I see an angel, I begin to cry.
Can you tell me what is happening?
And she tells me that I died.

I can't be dead, I'm still so young!
I want to do so many things
Like sing and dance and run.
What about college or graduation day?
What about a wedding? Please—I want to stay.

The angel looks upon me, and with a saddened voice,
"It didn't have to end like this, you knew you had a choice.
I'm sorry, it's too late now, time I can't turn back.
Your life is finished—that, my son, is fact."

Why did this happen? I didn't want to die!
The angel embraces me and with her words she sighs,
"Son, this is the consequence you paid to drink and drive.
I wish you made a better choice, if you did you'd be alive.
It doesn't matter if you beg me, or plead on bended knee,
There is nothing I can do, you have to come with me."

Looking at my family, I say my last good-bye.
"I'm sorry I disappointed you, Dad.
Mommy, please don't cry.
I didn't mean to hurt you, or cause you any pain.
I'm sorry all you're left with is a grave that bears my name.
I'm sorry all your dreams for me have all been ripped away,
The plans for my future now buried in a grave.

"It was a stupid thing to do,
I wish I could take it back.
But the curtain is being lowered now.
So ends my final act."

Lisa Teller

A Sobering Experience

When most of my classmates were starting their sophomore year of high school in 1998, I was just coming out of a coma. I'd missed the entire summer, and when I woke up, I was a fifteen-year-old with the mind of an eight-year-old.

A few months earlier, on June 12, we had just finished our last day of classes before exam week. To celebrate, I made plans to go to a party with my friend Dean. I knew my dad wouldn't approve of me partying with Dean since he was a junior and I was a freshman, so I said we were going to a hamburger place in town. My dad agreed to let me go, but said I had to be home by 11:00 P.M.

I don't remember most of what happened that night— a lot of what I know is pieced together from things I've been told. I do know that after Dean picked me up, we met up with some guys at a lake near my house. A few of them, including Dean, were smoking pot. I knew I shouldn't drive with someone who had been doing drugs, but when it came time to get in the car with Dean, I guess I figured that if he thought he was okay to drive, he probably was. So we went to the party. My brother was there and has since told me that I spent most of the night sitting in a chair in the garage, watching what was going on. I was only fifteen, and I was surrounded by all these eighteen-, nineteen- and twenty-year-olds. I don't remember having anything to drink, but I do remember seeing Dean drinking beer.

When it was almost 11:00, I told Dean I had to get home, and he said he'd take me. He invited a couple of friends to come with us, and we headed for the car. Again, I didn't really think about not driving with this guy, even though he'd been drinking and getting high. You learn about all this stuff in school, but when you're caught up in the moment, for some reason it doesn't really click. I guess I never thought anything bad could happen to me. But on the ride home, Dean was driving really fast—maybe close to 100 mph. We were on dirt roads and he was making the car fishtail, playing it all cool like it was so fun. That's when I realized I'd made a horrible mistake. I screamed at Dean from the passenger seat to slow down, but he didn't. We got to the top of a steep hill, and Dean was going so fast that the car flew into the air. We landed in the wrong lane and, as Dean swerved to try to get back on the right side, he overcorrected and my side of the car crashed into four trees. My head smacked into those trees one after the other.

The guy sitting behind me in the car broke his leg, but Dean and the guy behind him were fine. For a month after the accident, it was uncertain if I would live. I was in a coma until September, and I don't remember much until October. I had no broken bones, scratches or cuts, just one giant bruise down my chest from the seat belt. I would have gone through the windshield and died without that seat belt.

My parents lived the worst nightmare, constantly by my side, fearing I would die at any moment. When I came out of the coma, I recognized my family, but I was not the same person who got into Dean's car before the accident. My brain had bounced around against my skull, and I suffered a traumatic brain injury. Basically, the side of my brain that sends messages to my body to tell it how to move was severely damaged. I don't know how long it will take me to regain my motor skills entirely, or if I ever will.

Even after going through a lengthy rehabilitation in the hospital, I still walked so badly that people on the street stared and wondered what was wrong with me. It's a miracle that I can walk at all, let alone play sports. When I was a freshman, I dreamed of playing basketball for the WNBA, but that dream died the night of the accident. Now, I'm so glad because I am playing again, and I've worked on getting my stride back. But I'll never get back to the level where I used to be. My knee jerks back awkwardly when I run, and my coordination will never be the same.

The effects of the brain injury have not been just physical. When I first got back to school, I was put into a special resource room to do communication, speech, occupational and physical therapy. Eventually, I started taking regular classes again—and I will graduate on time—but the accident has messed up my memory and my ability to concentrate, and studying is really hard. I have to write myself notes to remember things, and even after a couple of years of handwriting therapy, my writing is still not very fast or clear. My speech has improved, but it's not great. Most people don't realize it, but all of these little things pretty much make up who you are, and when they're gone, a piece of you is changed forever.

Then again, in some ways I've changed for the better since the accident. I used to think that life was all a big joke. Now I know it's much more precious, and I think Dean knows that, too. He and I weren't allowed to see each other when I returned to school. He never went to jail, but he had to pay a fine. My parents will always be angry with Dean, and I get angry sometimes, too. But I don't necessarily blame him. He once said to me, "I wish I had died in that accident; I wish I hadn't hurt you. But I did and I'm sorry." I know I can't change what happened, but neither can he, so we just have to let go of the things that make us sad or angry and live each day in gratitude.

Sarah Jackson
As told to Jennifer Braunschweiger

Hitting Bottom

"People don't change that much. . . ."
"Yes, they do. They grow up and they accept
responsibilities, and they realize that 'die young,
stay pretty' isn't exactly all it's cracked up to be."
Drue and Jen, *Dawson's Creek*

It began when I was eleven. My family and I had just
moved to a new town. Making new friends was never difficult for me before, but I was going through an awkward
stage, and I was feeling self-conscious about my appearance. I was having a hard time reaching out to meet new
people. So when I saw some kids smoking, I figured if I
could join them for a cigarette I could meet some potential "friends." We hung out and smoked and continued
this ritual pretty much every day. Before long I was introduced to other kids, and eventually I started drinking and
getting high right along with them—it seemed the natural, easy thing to do. Soon, drugs and alcohol became my
friends, too. A few years later, I was using cocaine and
running away from home.

The first time I ran away I was thirteen. I had come home late one evening, and my mom was still up. She saw me sitting in a friend's car in front of our house. She was pretty strict about me being in my friends' cars. I was so stoned I knew at that point I couldn't go into my house, so I left with my friend.

After that night, over the next year and a half, I ran away twenty-three times. I managed to get caught every time, but within twenty-four hours I'd leave again. I was so hooked on drugs that I was afraid if I stayed at home, I wouldn't be able to get the drugs I wanted and needed so much.

I would stay at friends' houses until their parents figured out what was going on. Instead of returning home, I chose to live on the streets with friends or by myself. In colder weather, basements of apartment complexes became my source for shelter.

My mom didn't know why I was running away. I didn't communicate with her. She obviously knew something was wrong, but she just couldn't figure out what it was that was causing me to leave home. She tried putting me in treatment centers. Eventually, I ended up in one. During that first treatment center visit, I told her what was going on.

When I returned home from treatment I was off drugs, but after a few weeks I started using again. I continued this pattern for a while, having relapse after relapse. Finally, my mom quit her job to dedicate all of her time to helping me.

I went through three more short-term treatment programs, each one lasting only eleven to fourteen days. Each time, I was sincere about wanting to quit drugs, but I didn't know how. I felt like I didn't have enough time in those brief programs to learn how to live my life without drugs. By then, my self-esteem was so low that I was battling an eating disorder as well.

When I turned fourteen, I was receiving intensive counseling, and my mom decided I needed long-term treatment. In my state, at fourteen you're allowed to legally deny medical treatment. So when my mom wanted to put me into a six- to nine-month treatment program, I refused. I was at the lowest of lows in my life at that point. I had already overdosed on peyote and, not knowing how to turn my life around, I looked at suicide as my only way out. I just didn't see how another treatment center was going to help me.

My mom and I took our battle to court. She told the judge about my past, my drug use and that I was an addict. The next day he placed me in a treatment center. I haven't gotten high since that day, five and a half years ago.

The treatment center was like a big family. We would go to school for half the day and then receive intensive counseling. Prior to my admittance to the center, I had been using cocaine heavily, so I went through withdrawals.

The real turning point in my recovery happened when I met someone my own age who really wanted to quit. She kept telling me, "Help me, and I'll help you." That moved me so much, and it still moves me when I think about it. Having a peer say, "Hey, you can do it," made me want to do it this time.

I also met a woman in a Narcotics Anonymous meeting who had a major impact on me. She stood up and started talking about what was going on in her life. I remember watching her and thinking that she glowed. It's hard to describe, but for some reason she just glowed. Everything about her life was okay now, even the parts she was not happy with. I remember looking at her and thinking, *I just want to be a little bit shiny. I don't need to glow, but just shine a little.* That day I decided I was going to do everything in my power to live a healthy life.

Wanting something and following through with it were

two completely different things for me then. After I finished treatment, we moved again. I was turning fifteen, and I knew that before long everyone at my school would find out about my past. I was going to be in the same position I was in when I was eleven, with no friends, only this time I couldn't use drugs to help me make them.

I was so determined to stay on track that I sought help from my guidance counselor right away. I told her that I didn't trust myself not to slip back into my old lifestyle. She surprised me by asking me to tell my story to fifth and sixth graders. I told her I had never spoken in front of people before, but she assured me that I would do just fine.

I was really scared about sharing my past with a bunch of strangers, so I asked my mom if she would join me. We sat down that evening and planned the presentation. We had our first heart-to-heart since I was ten years old.

We did two presentations at an elementary school, and it made the front page of all the local newspapers. Suddenly, schools were calling us. I was in awe. I couldn't believe people wanted me to come to their schools and talk, that they considered me to be somebody who could help other kids.

I realized that doing these presentations helped boost my self-esteem and confirmed for me that I never wanted to do drugs again. It hit me that I might be helping to save someone's life or preventing another kid from getting involved with drugs.

My mom and I still speak at schools and treatment centers together. Kids call me at home sometimes after our talks. Some thank me. Some share their own stories. Some even tell me that I shine—and that is the best part of all.

Jenny Hungerford
As told to Susan K. Perry

That Warm Night

I was invited to a party,
  a few roads across town.
I thought I'd meet my friends there,
  but they were not around.

So I hopped into my beat-up car,
  ready for adventure.
My mom came racing to my door,
  I was ready for my lecture.

Instead she told me softly,
  to be careful that warm night.
I promised her that I'd drive safe,
  that everything would be all right.

I arrived at the location,
  and accepted a small drink.
I didn't really want it,
  but I didn't stop to think.

Soon I was gulping cocktails,
  feeling lighter with each sip.
And I felt so free, invincible,
  as I swallowed the last drip.

The room was spinning freely,
  as I danced across the floor.
And I wondered why I hadn't ever
  drank this much before.

Then, despite my happiness and fun,
  my head began to ache.
I found my car keys in my purse,
  'cause my brain was going to break.

I stumbled across the gardens,
  unlocked my beat-up car.
Started up the engine,
  headed across town once more.

But something tragic happened,
  I didn't see the light.
I didn't see the people, either,
  crossing that warm night.

As I slid across the pavement,
  I knew my time had come.
My head just kept on spinning,
  all this for just some fun.

The next moments were quite hazy,
  as I lay mangled in the car.
Pain shooting through my body,
  never thought it'd go this far.

Heard sirens in the background,
  rushing to my aid.
But as I closed my tired eyes,
  I knew it was too late.

As I saw the world below me,
   my heart just filled with dread.
I saw the people that I hit,
   and knew that they were dead.

I cried so hard on that warm night,
   as I floated through the sky.
Knowing that it was my fault,
   and I never said good-bye.

Now I'm floating up to heaven,
   where I really don't belong.
Brought so much pain to others,
   did something really wrong.

I killed six happy people,
   four kids, a man and wife.
And I'm lying in a coffin,
   because I lost my precious life.

I see my mother's upset face,
   her eyes so filled with tears.
"This wasn't supposed to happen,
   this is exactly what I feared."

I was just a normal teen,
   who had too much to drink.
I had a boyfriend, did well in school,
   but that night I didn't think.

So the next time you're invited
   to a party with your friends,
Please remember this could be
   the night when it could end.

I learned all this the hard way,
   and made a terrible mistake.
So please don't do what I did,
   and drink as much as you can take.

I had so much before me,
    a great future straight ahead.
I wanted to be an actress,
    but I can't because I'm dead.

It happened all so quickly,
    didn't even get to fight.
Didn't know how fast my life could end,
    I'll always remember that warm night.

Sarah Woo

What She Doesn't Know

My friend has a problem, and sometimes I feel like I'm the only one who notices her when she's lost and she's tormented and she's alone in the world. And when she's high, she comes to me and she tells me what she's done, whether it's speed or cocaine or something bigger and faster, something harder and louder, something else that takes the person I laugh with and depend on away.

She is ripping herself away from her truth, and the only way I can reach her is to let her know that I care about her. All I can do is listen to her babble when she's high, and weep when she's coming down, because I can't fix her. All I can be is a friend to her until she realizes she has a problem, until she stops running from her daytime self to the lure of things that make her worries rest. I can't make her stop. So it's been hard, to have her pass out and the line go dead. To have her come to my house running on speed not to be with me, but so that she doesn't get caught.

It is my right to help her. And to point out to her how strong she is, how real and breathing and clear she is to me, and to everyone. She is calling for help but doesn't know it yet. She is yelling and swallowing her tears, because somewhere she knows that she can't keep packing herself away. Some time this anger or fury or sadness will find her, and she needs to stand in its torrential downpour and get filled by it, because somewhere inside her she is empty. I can't be her mother, and I can't be with her all the time, telling her what she can put in her body and what she can't. So she has gotten lost somewhere in the deep end, and I can't pull her out, but I can show her how she can do it herself.

I am watching her, and I am hugging her and trying to remind her of the countless reasons why I am so much better from knowing her. I can listen to her when she needs me, and when she doesn't. I can let her know that, no matter what she does, she is my friend, and nothing will change that. I can take a step back and see what's taking parts of her away. I can encourage her to answer honestly when I ask how she is. I can remind her about moderation. I can point out the people who love her. I can show her how much she needs to stop for herself. I can be a positive influence on her. I can listen to her when her voice hints of this thing that she is missing and can't find. She needs to see for herself that her daytime self is alive and beating and multicolored. I can help her remember what her life was like before the dealers and the midnight fixes. I can help her stand tall and strong, on feet and legs and ankles she trusts. I can help her see that life is not about three-hour solutions that make her wake up feeling dead. I can be someone safe to her. I can care about her so much that I point her to the exit and hold her hand as she gets there.

My friend has a problem, and I am helping her. I am listening, and I am talking, and I am working with her, and I am learning how to be the best to her. I have unshakable confidence in her, and I know that she can stand where she is and she can stop. I can be the person she turns to, because she can't see right now that she can turn to herself. She can't see it yet, but soon.

Kate Reder

[EDITORS' NOTE: *If you have a friend who has a drug or drinking problem (or any problem that is causing himself or herself harm), it is absolutely necessary to speak with an adult about getting professional help for your friend. We have listed some hotline numbers and Web sites below that you can call, but it is important to speak to an adult you trust as soon as possible.*]

Al-Anon/Alateen: 800-344-2666
For friends and family of people with drinking problems.

Center for Substance Abuse Treatment: 800-662-HELP

Alcoholics Anonymous: *www.alcoholics-anonymous.org*

Narcotics Anonymous: *www.na.org*

The Man My Father Was

My parents divorced when I was seven years old. This came as no surprise to everyone around them. My father had been an alcoholic for many years, and it was only a matter of time before it took its toll on their marriage. After the divorce, my mom remarried and my dad moved to a town about thirty minutes away. By the time I was twelve, I felt stable and even happy. I liked having two families.

It was around this time that my dad was fired from his job of nearly ten years. We all knew that it was because of the drinking. We also knew that it would be hard for a nearly fifty-year-old man to find a new job. For a year and a half he remained unemployed, and his situation seemed more and more desperate. He continued to be a big part of my life, though. No longer stuck at work, he attended all of my basketball games and kept our relationship as strong as it ever was.

Finally, he got a job—in the next state. In a few months, my father was settled in his new home and job, while I was left to try and adjust to life without him. He managed to turn his financial situation around, but I was worried about him. He didn't make any new friends and, when he wasn't with me, he was in his apartment alone. He seemed lonely.

When it was my dad's weekend to pick me up, he would drive three hours to get me and we would stay in a hotel. I loved those weekends together, but as time went on my dad seemed to cancel his time with me more and more frequently. He always seemed to get a "stomach flu," and when we did spend the weekend together, he was often in the bathroom vomiting. We all noticed how emaciated he had become; his legs were even thinner than mine. But although he was physically deteriorating, my dad was determined to maintain his relationship with his family. He called his daughter every day.

One night my dad didn't call. I was worried, but my mom calmed me down. We reasoned that he was probably out too late to call and didn't want to wake me. But when he didn't call the next night either, I was really worried.

The next morning, my mom and I decided that we should look into the situation. She told me she would call his office and tried to reassure me on the way to school. I felt strange that day laughing with my friends, like I shouldn't be so happy. I had this weird feeling that something bad had happened.

When I got home, I immediately asked her what his office had told her. As it turned out, they, too, had not heard from him. They got suspicious and went to his apartment to see what was going on. My father never answered the door, so they got someone to break in. They found my dad lying on the bathroom floor in a pool of blood. The police later said that he had died two days before he was found.

After hearing the news, I was in bad shape. I felt like there was no point to life. I took a few days off school and spent them looking at photo albums and going through my dad's old stuff. My father was not a perfect man—

sometimes he was insensitive, sometimes unfair, some-times unforgiving or hurtful or unreliable. My father dis-appointed me a lot. But when I look back at the man my father was, I am not disappointed. My father was only human. He did teach me how to throw a ball, to wash a car, to appreciate music, to play golf, to love to read, to argue intelligently, to do crossword puzzles, to play the guitar and to be proud of myself. Some children never even get to meet their fathers; I was fortunate enough to know mine for fourteen years.

My father's death is now a part of me, embedded deep within me. I am growing stronger every day. My mother has taught me, rather than forget about my father's prob-lems and struggles, to learn from them. My mother is there whenever I need her; her support has been the anchor that has kept me from drifting away.

As I place the flowers next to my father's ashes, I say a silent prayer and wait there for just a moment. I recall everything about my dad—the good and the bad alike—and I remember the man my father was.

Kristine Flaherty

A Sobering Place

Learn from the mistakes of others—you can never live long enough to make them all yourself.

John Luther

"What will you have?" the waiter asks.

"A Shirley Temple," I shoot back. When I go out I always order the same drink. The sparkling Sprite with grenadine and a maraschino cherry allows me to pretend, to fit in with my friends somehow, to cast aside the hurt of my childhood.

I don't drink and I've never been drunk, but now and then I do wonder what it would feel like. I'm afraid, though, that one sip might lead to many more, and that one day I might become an alcoholic.

That's what my mother is.

The sweet Shirley Temple hides a bitter past and a picture etched in my memory: Mom is sitting on the couch, legs crossed, drinking malt liquor. I tend to forget that I was the one who grabbed it from the refrigerator for her. I tapped the top, even tilted it to the glass and poured it for her. At five years old, I was my mother's bartender.

When I was a little girl, I had long hair, and I thought that made me pretty.

"More hair," Mom would say, as she braided the last of four ponytails.

"Grow longer," I'd answer, while she wrapped yellow ribbons around my braids.

But we didn't have our little ritual on weekends. On weekends Mom got drunk. She was a mean drunk and didn't clean the house or comb my hair. She broke lamps, cursed Dad and even threw things at him. The arguments always ended the same way: She'd leave, dressed to the nines in high heels and a sleek dress that showed off her long legs. I cried when she left. She would be gone for one, sometimes two days at a time, partying. I would wonder if she was ever coming back.

She always did. Groggy, tired. I didn't care. I was just glad Mom was back. I hated her drinking, but I didn't hate her. I loved her then, and I love her now. I separated my mom from the alcohol, decided the liquor was the monster.

When I grow up, I vowed to myself, *I won't curse out my husband or act mean with my children. I won't drink.*

The message never rang so loud in my head as it did when I was sixteen. When most kids were circling the local McDonald's on Friday and Saturday nights, I was out cruising the city streets with my dad, looking for Mom's car. Dad, a career military man, searched for hours, fearful she would drive home drunk, get a DUI or have an accident. But when he found her in a club, she would refuse to leave. So I'd slide over into his seat and put the car in gear. He'd slip into the parking lot and drive out in her car. I would follow him home, pull into the driveway behind him and slam the door, thinking about Mom out there stranded in some nightclub. It didn't make sense:

Mom would get drunk; Dad and I would leave her. I didn't think that either of them was right.

My mother had been raised poor in the Deep South. She had been shuttled from house to house until she was a teenager, and she had no idea who her father was—these were her demons, and she was unable to drink them away. So she tried again and again to rehabilitate herself. Once I even spent a week with her in rehab, telling my side of the story, trying to help. The scene always played out the same way: She would enter an angry woman and leave as my mother, the woman who had tied yellow ribbons in my hair. But soon the demons would find a home in her again, pushing her down those twelve steps she had so painstakingly climbed.

They say alcoholics have to hit rock bottom before they can change. Mom didn't land there until after she divorced my father. My father left, taking my little brother and me with him to South Carolina. Alcohol had won, and she had lost everything—her marriage, her children, her home. My brother and I had never truly bonded with our father, whose work took him to Korea and later to Operation Desert Storm in the Middle East, but we decided to live with him anyway.

After losing her marriage and her children, my mother continued to drink for another seven years. Mom doesn't drink anymore. "I just got tired, Boo," she said recently. "Getting up drunk, going to bed drunk, I got tired of living that life."

Nearly three decades after she sipped her first rum and Coke at a military dance, she stopped. No more malt liquor, no more brandy, no more whiskey sours. She's a devoted participant in a Twelve-Step program and hasn't had a drink in nearly five years.

Meanwhile, I kept my promise. I didn't drink, either. I stepped outside my mother's footsteps and walked in another direction. It took me, literally and figuratively, to a sobering place. Occasionally, I get an urge to leave there. When I do, I grab something sweet—a Shirley Temple.

Monique Fields

3

FAMILY
MATTERS

The family is one of nature's masterpieces.

George Santayana

What Siblings Know

When I was twelve and my brother David was seventeen, we were home one Halloween night watching a horror movie we'd rented. It was an entertaining but silly movie about a woman who becomes a witch. The woman who played the witch was young and looked like a model. Every time she cast a spell, her long red hair whipped around her face and her eyes got bright green. Once when this happened, my brother said, "Wow, she looks really hot."

I stared at him. I was astonished at what he'd said. I hadn't noticed it before, but until that night I'd never, ever heard my brother voice an attraction to women, even though he was a teenager and supposedly in the prime of his life.

This is what I remember when people ask me when I first knew my brother was gay. I didn't realize he was different until I heard him saying something that most guys his age would say without a second thought.

My brother tried to like girls. The thought of him trying—even by saying something as trivial as "She looks hot" about an actress on a television screen—breaks my heart. All that time he was trying, through middle school and high school and into college, he couldn't tell me or my parents how hard it was for him. He was all alone.

When I was twelve, David went out of state for college. He came home for holidays and a few weeks in the summer, and he called every week, but every year he seemed to pull farther away from me and my parents. When he was home, he was quiet and distant, and on the phone he was polite but tense, the way people get when they are hiding really big secrets.

My parents were slow, but they weren't stupid. A couple of years after David left for college, when they still hadn't heard mention of any girlfriends or even dates, they became suspicious. My mother started asking me questions, thinking that I must know something she didn't know, because siblings tell each other things they don't tell their parents. But David hadn't told me anything. He never had, not even before he left for college. I always knew he loved me, but he was more independent than the rest of us, and I never felt he needed me.

The next time David came home, I did a terrible thing. I wanted to borrow his leather backpack and I knew he wouldn't let me if I asked him, so I just took it. But before I filled it with my things, I had to take out his things to make room. There were some schoolbooks and a fancy notebook bound with a rubber band. I was curious. I pulled off the rubber band and started reading.

Immediately, I found myself immersed in a world of suppressed anger, self-loathing and tentative romances. I learned more about my brother in those pages than I ever could from him, at least back then. I learned that he'd known he was gay his entire life, but that not until he escaped to college did he admit it to another human being. That human being was his roommate, Rob. I remembered him mentioning how Rob had transferred dorm rooms in the middle of the semester, and when I read my brother's journal I learned that Rob changed rooms because he didn't want to live with someone who was gay.

It was a little while—a few pages into the journal—before my brother told anyone else. He joined a campus group and made some gay friends, and slowly his life forked into two lives. There was the life my parents and I saw—a life with lies and friends who didn't know him, and no one to love—and there was a second life, a life with friends and crushes and dates. A life where he was happy.

I put the backpack—and the little notebook—back in my brother's room, and I never told him what I'd learned. But my parents continued to badger me about David and his lack of love life—they knew he was gay, I'm sure, but denied it even to themselves—and eventually I called him up. "David," I said, "you have to tell them."

He didn't ask me how I knew, and I didn't tell him. But looking back, I understand that reading my brother's journal—a horrible crime I would never commit again—only filled in some of the details. Somehow, I already knew the story. Maybe it is true that siblings know each other better than their parents know them. I like to think so.

The next Thanksgiving, after a pretty typical family meal, my brother suggested we all take a walk. We walked past the end of our street and onto the grounds of the high school, then onto the track. Then my brother stopped. "I have something to tell you," he said. I felt my parents' hearts skip a beat—they wanted so badly, back then, for it not to be true. "I wanted to tell you that I'm gay."

My parents were pretty rational, considering. They told David that he was just experimenting, that eventually he'd find a woman he wanted to marry. He listened to them, then politely but firmly said that this was something that wasn't going to change. They argued but never raised their voices, and eventually we went home and took naps in separate rooms. The following days were very quiet. Then David went back to school, to his happy life.

It was five years before my parents came to truly accept my brother. My brother was fortunate to be out of the house during that time, but I was not so lucky. My parents fought more than ever, my father drank a lot, and I spent time out of the house. But slowly—*very* slowly—my parents got used to the idea. After a year, my mother told one of her friends about David, then my father told one of his. They received love and support—David was a great kid, said my parents' friends. That hadn't changed. Secretly, I'm sure they were relieved that it wasn't their kid who was gay. After my parents learned not to hide it, there was still the matter of being proud of David, of not only tolerating hearing about his romantic life, but wanting to hear about it.

About a week before Christmas one year, my brother called home to ask my parents if he could bring a friend home for the holiday. A boyfriend. My parents told David they'd think about it, then called him back and said absolutely not. My brother felt hurt and rejected, and when he came home, relations between him and my parents were strained. Then he and my father got into a fight on Christmas Eve, and David took an early flight back to school. Christmas Day was sadder and lonelier than it had ever been.

I called David a few days later. "You can't rush them," I said, feeling guilty for defending them.

"It's been three years," said David. He was frustrated, which I understood. So was I. I didn't understand why my parents couldn't just get over it. It seemed simple. Every time my mother asked me how a date had gone or said she liked a boy I'd introduced to her, I thought, *What's so different between me and David? Don't you want him to be happy, too?*

But David's patience paid off. My mother joined a support group for parents of gays and lesbians, and soon she was succeeding in dragging my father with her to the meetings. She was even asked to speak at a conference for high-school teachers about being unbiased toward homosexuality in the classroom. Time passed. My parents eased into not only accepting the fact that David wasn't ever going to be straight, but also that it wasn't a bad thing at all. That for David, it was a very good thing.

Then they did the craziest and most wonderful thing. I still laugh when I think about it. They made a list of all the people they hadn't told about David, including old friends, siblings and their own parents, and they planned a three-week road trip across the country. They had news to deliver, and they wanted to deliver it in person and do some sightseeing in the meantime. They'd gotten this idea in their heads that it wasn't enough for David to come out of the closet. He would never feel they'd truly accepted him until they came out of the closet, too, as the loving parents of a gay son.

David's apartment was the last stop on their journey, and I took an airplane up to meet them when they arrived. We took another family walk, and David told us about his new boyfriend and I told them about mine. Finally, after so much pain and hard work, my brother's two lives started to merge.

Danielle Collier

How to Scare a Big Sister

When we were little, my brother and I had a special kind of relationship. I scared him, and he would cry. I don't remember why I thought scaring him was so funny. It was probably the fact that when I ran out and yelled "boo," especially if I hid well and got him as he wandered past, lost in his three-year-old thoughts, he would leap into the air like a shocked frog.

This method provided years of youthful mirth, but over time I found it increasingly harder to scare my little brother. He was just getting too old to be startled by my simple scare. Afraid that the balance of sibling power was threatened by this development, I frantically switched tactics. More sophisticated scares. Rubber snakes under his pillows, ghost stories about a mean old lady haunting his clothing chest, randomly ducking his head underwater as we played in the pool. I wasn't above any trick. He was getting bigger, sure, but not so big that I couldn't make him scream with terror. It was my duty and my passion.

Sadly, all good things must end. All of a sudden, little Daniel was almost as tall as his antagonist sister (and gaining fast). I could hardly get a shudder out of him with the best of my schemes. Even a professional mistress of fear like myself knows when to give up a hopeless cause. I declared peace and made amends with my little brother—he took it very well, demanding no reparations.

I should have realized that I wouldn't get away with my crimes so easily. Destiny was about to get me back.

I came home from school one day and found an empty house. It didn't faze me—it was normal in my family. Mom and Dad often worked late, and my little brother and sister stayed at a friend's house in the afternoons. My older brother usually showed up by dinnertime. I liked having the quiet house all to myself. It meant I could watch TV and listen to my music as loud as I wanted. On that day, however, the noise felt empty and false—it felt like I was trying to cover up the silence. I could feel the absence of sound hiding behind corners like a big kid waiting to jump out at me. I couldn't understand why I felt so uneasy.

After a while, I realized that it was getting late—*really* late. My family was usually home by five-thirty, and it was already close to seven. It was my little sister's baby-sitter, finally bringing her home, who filled me in on the situation. Everyone was at the hospital. In the emergency room.

"Daniel had a bike accident."

I immediately felt better—my little brother was always breaking toes and skinning knees. The explanation had restored a sense of normalcy to my world. The baby-sitter was still speaking.

"He borrowed a neighbor's old bike. The handlebars fell off in his hands."

I stopped listening. My crazy brother! I could just see him zipping down the street, slapstick-style, with a sheepish look on his face and handlebars in his hands, steering into thin air. I only heard bits and pieces of what the baby-sitter was trying to tell me—

"... With the towel soaked in blood ..."

I was going to tease him when he got home with his stitches—

"... Couldn't find the tooth ..."

My mind was chattering to itself, to block out a feeling I wasn't quite familiar with. I was afraid. It wasn't funny anymore, and yet I heard a surge of hysterical laughter coming from my mouth—

"... Surgery ... we don't know ..."

I sat down to let it sink in. And to calm myself. Daniel didn't come home that night. My big brother finally wandered in—he had been crying, though he would never admit it now. He gave me the story, as he knew it.

My little brother had been racing down a steep hill on a borrowed bike. All of a sudden, a screw fell off and the handlebars of his bike were no longer attached to the rest of the bike. He had no helmet on. If a car had been coming, it would have hit him. Luckily, Daniel skidded sideways into the gravel on the shoulder of the road. Face first.

If he had hit at a slightly sharper angle, he would have broken his neck.

My little brother lay bleeding by a ditch while his friends turned their bikes around and rode back up the hill. Somehow, the two other little boys managed to get him to the nearest parent.

Daniel lost his tooth completely. His skin was horribly scarred. My little brother had to endure a series of oral surgeries. I felt sick at heart—his face was a swollen mess, black and blue and bright red. I almost cried every time he smiled, his gash of a mouth opening to reveal a horribly jagged line of teeth and gums. But he didn't smile much because it hurt. My poor baby brother.

If you look at him now, you would never guess that Daniel had ever had an accident. His porcelain tooth is perfect. His skin, miraculously, healed without even the hint of a scar. When he smiles, it doesn't hurt.

And now we're pretty much even. It takes a lot to scare a big sister.

Natalie Atkins

Sixty-Second Flashback

I sit in my Honda Civic stopped at a red light, staring straight ahead, when I catch a glimpse of a white Subaru. Out of habit, I turn my head to see if it is someone I know, someone I love deeply but haven't seen in three months—to see if it is Zach, my older brother, my other half. The man driving the Subaru reminds me an awful lot of Zach, but it's not Zach.

Suddenly, I drift off into my memories and remember all the things about my brother I love and miss so much. I think of how his dishwater blond hair would curl, and how he would try so hard to straighten it by wearing a baseball hat until his hair was dry, or by plastering it with gel, only to make it curl even more. I think of how he would get angry with me for trying to wear his baggy pants and shirts so I could look like him. He wanted to be his own person. I remember how, whenever I was down, he would hug me and tell me how beautiful I was and then cheer me up even more by cracking some off-the-wall joke. He had a sense of humor that, no matter how upset somebody was, could always make that person laugh.

I recalled a conversation he and I had when I was

fourteen and he was eighteen. We were both going through a tough time with our parents, though our situations were different. We were driving in his Subaru, practically brand-new then, and for the first time he opened up to me. I felt like he looked at me as his equal instead of his little sister. He began talking to me about how much he loved music and how music was his outlet for stress when things got too rough for him to handle. He looked me in the eyes, which he rarely did because he usually avoided direct eye contact, and he told me that I also possessed something deep down that would allow me to create when I felt I had nowhere to turn. He told me I just needed to search my soul, and I would find it. At that moment, I looked at him and wished so much that I could play the guitar like him or draw like him. He seemed to possess so many talents that I envied, and to hear him say that he saw creativity inside of me made me want to hug him. I didn't, though.

I remember him always being holed up in his room whenever he was home, which wasn't very often. He preferred going out partying with his friends. He was messing around with different kinds of drugs, which made him moody and difficult to tolerate. When he was around the house, there was a constant tension because he didn't want any of us telling him what to do; he didn't want to hear a thing we had to say. I guess that's why I was so surprised when he took me with him that day in the car and spoke to me with such sincerity.

My eyes begin to well up with tears as I remember the time, not too long ago, when his dog of ten years got cancer and had to be put to sleep. He slept in the garage with her for the last week of her life, and we were all together when she died. The look of loss in his eyes and the river of tears that flooded his cheeks told more about his love for his dog than any words he could have spoken. As he

READER/CUSTOMER CARE SURVEY

We care about your opinions! Please take a moment to fill out our online Reader Survey at **http://survey.hcibooks.com**.
As a **"THANK YOU"** you will receive a **VALUABLE INSTANT COUPON** towards future book purchases as well as a **SPECIAL GIFT** available
only online! Or, you may mail this card back to us and we will send you a copy of our exciting catalog with your valuable coupon inside.
(PLEASE PRINT IN ALL CAPS)

First Name _____ MI. _____ Last Name _____

Address _____ City _____

State _____ Zip _____ Email: _____

1. Gender
❑ Female   ❑ Male

2. Age
❑ 8 or younger
❑ 9-12   ❑ 13-16
❑ 17-20   ❑ 21-30
❑ 31+

3. Did you receive this book as a gift?
❑ Yes   ❑ No

4. How did you find out about the book
❑ Online
❑ Store Display
❑ Teen Magazine
❑ Interview/Review
❑ Book Club/Mail Order
❑ Price Club (Sam's Club, Costco's, etc.)
❑ Retail Store (Target, Wal-Mart, etc.)

5. Where do you usually buy books
(please choose one)
❑ Online
❑ Bookstore
❑ Online
❑ Book Club/Mail Order
❑ Price Club (Sam's Club, Costco's, etc.)
❑ Retail Store (Target, Wal-Mart, etc.)

6. What magazines do you like to read *(please choose one)*
❑ Teen People
❑ Seventeen
❑ YM
❑ Cosmo Girl
❑ Rolling Stone
❑ Teen Ink
❑ Christian Magazines
❑ Series Books (Chicken Soup, Fearless, etc.)

7. What books do you like to read *(please choose one)*
❑ Fiction
❑ Self-help
❑ Reality Stories/Memoirs
❑ Sports

8. What attracts you most to a book
(please choose one)
❑ Title
❑ Cover Design
❑ Author
❑ Content

TAPE IN MIDDLE; DO NOT STAPLE

BUSINESS REPLY MAIL
FIRST-CLASS MAIL PERMIT NO 45 DEERFIELD BEACH, FL

POSTAGE WILL BE PAID BY ADDRESSEE

Chicken Soup for the Soul® (Teens)
Health Communications, Inc.
3201 SW 15th Street
Deerfield Beach FL 33442-9875

FOLD HERE

Books for Life

Do you have your own Chicken Soup story
that you would like to send us?
Please submit at: **www.chickensoup.com**

Comments

bent over and held her limp, lifeless body in his arms, his own body began to shake, and I realized how attached to her he was. As he stood up, I put my arms around him, hoping he would realize I was there for him, but he was distant and in his own world.

Later that day, he came walking through the garage door with sunglasses on, even though it was a rainy day, so that we couldn't see his red, puffy eyes. He always wore choker necklaces, but he had another necklace on that hadn't been there earlier. He pulled the necklace out from under his shirt and showed us that he was wearing his dog, Annie's, name tag.

I cry even more as I begin thinking about why we haven't spoken for three months. I had to set boundaries. I vividly recall the night when I awoke to hear him calling someone a bitch and a whore. I stood in the hallway and heard my brother calling his girlfriend names, thrashing all around the kitchen like a mad rabbit. He was incredibly drunk. The hurtful words that spewed out of his mouth were ones I would only expect a deranged lunatic to say. They were not words that should be spoken to a loved one.

The next day I decided we needed to discuss the previous night. He stood in the family room with a vacant, yet defiant, look in his eyes as I began pouring open my soul about how much I worried about his alcohol consumption. It seemed the more I said, the further away he went. Finally, he looked at me, told me I was overreacting and that he was perfectly fine. I stood and listened to him deny my concerns, knowing that his denial was just a way to convince himself there was no problem. I gathered all the courage I had and proceeded to tell him that until he quit drinking and got help, there could be no brother-sister relationship between us. The look he gave me said more than words could ever express. I knew he thought I

was overreacting and that I wouldn't follow through—
after all, I never had before.

He moved out two weeks later when my parents and I
gave him the ultimatum of living at home sober or moving
out. He chose the latter of the two. He was furious with us
for making him choose. He has stayed away for three
months now.

The light turns green, and I begin to cross the intersec-
tion while looking into the windows of the white Subaru.
The man driving the car is built just like Zach. I realize
how much I want to see him and wonder if I made the
right decision. Then I think to myself what my dad told
me the day Zach left: "Tiani, he may not realize it now, but
he will thank you one day for loving him so much, that
you put your foot down to him and let him know how
things were going to be. Your mom and I love you and
respect you for being so strong and caring that you would
risk not talking to him to make him face the facts and get
better." At that moment I knew I made the correct decision, and I said a little prayer that I would see my brother
again soon.

Tiani Crocker

[EDITORS' NOTE: *We received the following update from Tiani:
"Zach's drinking is no longer a problem; it has stopped controlling
his life as well as our relationship. He has since moved back to
Washington, is attending massage school, and is focusing on his
health and fitness. He has grown in amazing ways—he has a
stronger, healthier connection with the entire family, and we are all
proud of him. I feel blessed to have our relationship back stronger
than before, but even more blessed to have him as a male role model
for my son."*]

Change

There will be a time when you believe every-thing is finished. That will be the beginning.

Louis L'Amour

If change is a scary thing, then I can honestly say that I was nearly scared to death at the age of sixteen. We had to leave the only home and friends I had ever known and move. "We'll all make a new start, Carrie," my parents kept saying. Just because my parents had decided to work on their marriage and "start over," I didn't see why I had to give up everything.

I pouted and protested until they sold the house, boxed up our lives and moved. Then I just shut up; I had no choice. But I didn't give up. Purposely, I let my grades slip, didn't join in any social activities, and, above all, I never admitted that anything was as nice here as it had been in our old hometown.

That strategy didn't last long. Not because I had tons of new friends or was won over by this new town they called home. It was because my parents began fighting, and they were fighting about *me*. "Discussing" is what

they called it, but fighting is what it was. Loud disagree-
ments followed by tension-filled silences were becoming
the norm.

Believe me, my parents needed to work on their marriage. They had separated and come back together so
many times that I classified my birthday pictures as "they
were separated that year," or "that's the year they were
trying to work it out again."

I guess I was just tired of trying to guess if a slammed
door meant my father was out of our lives again or just
going for a walk to let off steam. Or if my mother's smile
was a happy one or the forced one she used to reassure
me that "we'll be just fine without your father."

It was bad enough that they kept splitting up. But I
couldn't handle being the reason for this dreaded occur-
rence. So I cleaned myself up, worked hard in my classes
and began to meet friends. Things at home mellowed out,
but I was afraid to think or feel anything that might cause
so much as a ripple. It was my turn to be the keeper of the
peace.

Things seemed to be getting back to "fine," until one
night the front door slammed and my mother's morning
smile was the "we'll-be-just-fine-without-him" one. I had
been the best I could be, and it hadn't been enough.

At night, I crawled into bed exhausted with nothing to
fill me, nothing to renew me for the next day. The hollow
me crumbled in on itself.

Then I met the little girl next door.

I was alone on the front porch steps, trying to work up
the energy just to go inside. The rhythm of her jump rope
clacking on the sidewalk as she counted out her skips had
a calming effect on me. Her hair was fanned out behind
her and shining in the setting sun.

"Forty-eight, forty-nine, fifty," she counted, half out of
breath. How simple she made it all seem.

"Sixty-three, sixty-four . . . oh, no!" She looked over at me, distressed. "Look, the handle came off! Can I call a do-over? I was skipping my best ever. The miss shouldn't count. It wasn't my fault it broke."

I knew exactly how she felt. I was doing my best when my parents' marriage broke.

She plopped herself on the step next to me. "So, what do you think? Do I get a do-over?"

She was so serious. I wanted her to know that I understood the weight of her question, but I just couldn't hold back the smile that had welled up from within me. She looked up, waiting for my answer.

"Well, I know you didn't step on the rope and make the handle pull out because I was watching you." She gave a serious nod. "And it isn't as if your shoe came off because you didn't tie it tightly enough." She studied her shoes and nodded again.

"So, given all the circumstances, I do believe that you're entitled to a do-over."

"Me, too," she said, dropping the handle and rope into my lap. "You fix the handle, and I'll let you keep count for me. I stopped at sixty-four, and I bet I can skip over a hundred and that's my highest good counting number."

So I fixed her rope and counted her do-over up to one hundred and twelve.

"One hundred and twelve!" She gave me a high-five. "That's higher than Amy at school, and she's a grade ahead of me!"

That is when the miracle happened. It was a little thing, heartfelt and easily given. Then she hugged me! The warmth of her hug made my heart smile and, just like the sun coming out from behind the clouds, I understood.

"Meet me tomorrow," she said, completely unaware of all she had just given me.

My parents did get a divorce, and it was very painful.

But it wasn't me who caused it, and there was nothing I could have done to prevent it. With my new understanding that came from the innocence of a little girl, I too had earned a do-over.

Carrie Hill
As told to Cynthia Hamond

Table for Three

I'm awakened by the sound of voices arguing in the garage. Rolling over, I squint my eyes at the alarm clock, realizing it's only five in the morning. I recognize the two voices as my mom and dad's. I hear my father's voice rising as my mom's darts around in hysteria. I'm familiar with this sickening duet, only just not at this early hour.

I recall a conversation I had with my dad and realize its implications are just now taking effect. Last week over fries at McDonald's, he shared a secret with me that would forever change my life. He began by asking if I was happy with the way things were at home. I knew he was referring to the tension that existed between him and my mom. It's not that I was happy with the way things were, but I was frightened by the thought of divorce. It's sort of like hanging on to an iceberg.

Divorce is rampant among my friends' parents, and although I knew that it was inevitable that we three would soon join the group, this was one club I did not want to be a member of.

Then out of nowhere, he was sharing this loaded "secret" with me—a secret I never wanted to hear. He was telling me that he'd be leaving my mother next week, all the while assuring me that he'd always be there for me. I found myself nodding my head as if I understood, when all along I really didn't. He told me they hadn't been happy for a very long time, and I'm thinking, *If you're both not happy, why the big secret? Why isn't Mom here sharing this awful moment?*

He hugged me in an awkward kind of bear hug, and I got all stiff to his touch. Scratching his nose, he informed me that he wasn't ready to tell my mom he was leaving just yet. I asked him *when* he was going to tell her, and he closed his eyes while sighing, "When the moment's right."

So for two weeks now, I have stared into my mom's eyes, while never revealing the secret. I am betraying her just like my dad is. I try to convince myself that the conversation at McDonald's never really happened at all.

Now, as I lie in bed listening to my mom's muffled cries, I realize that the moment has arrived. Although my mom and I have not always seen eye-to-eye on a lot of things, such as dating, driving, school, friends, life . . . right now my stomach is aching for her. Each of her sobs shoots through me like a dart piercing my chest. The agony is so great that I finally understand what a broken heart must feel like.

I shuffle out of bed and quietly make my way down the long hallway towards the garage from where the voices seem to be coming. Slowly, I open the door wide enough to see but not be seen.

The scene being played out by my parents makes me want to vomit. My mom is holding on to the bottom of my dad's leather jacket. She is straining to hold him back, so that he won't leave her. This is not the proud woman who once refused to accept my grandmother's financial help back when my dad first lost his job. Her face is red, awash in tears, and her nose runs while she howls in pain. She has no pride; he is taking it with him.

He grabs his coat from her and pushes her back with one hand. He tells her it's over. ". . . It's been over for a very long time, and we both know it."

She howls again, and through her wailing I hear her moaning, "No, no, no, no," like some strange hypnotic chant. And then suddenly her tone changes to one of anger as she screams, *"You were just going to sneak out in the night . . . weren't you? . . . You're a child. . . . You have no backbone, you coward. . . . I hate you, you pig!"* She's still not letting go of her grip on his jacket.

He pulls away from her, and she's left holding only his jacket in her hands. He kneels down, tossing his packed valise into the open door of our family van. Then he gets behind the wheel and, without another word, he backs up out of the driveway and out of our lives forever.

Now all that's left is the echo of her tortured cries. I'm not worried about the neighbors hearing what went on. They're used to the sound of my parents' war; each gave up their dignity a long time ago. We don't know what shame feels like anymore.

As my mom leans against the wall wailing in spasms of anguish, all I can think of is what I might have done to cause this. Was it because I talked back to my mother that time, when we were out having a nice family dinner? She got so angry with me, and I remember my dad told her not to lose her cool and that I was right. Her frozen glance across the table suggested that she did not at all like this friendly alliance my dad and I had formed. There was screaming and yelling and people were staring, but my parents didn't seem to care. Next thing I knew, my dad stormed out of the restaurant for the refuge of the car.

That was always the pattern: a knockdown fight followed by my dad retreating to some remote corner. My mother turned to me that night as we sat alone at our table for three and said, "Please don't destroy my marriage. I don't think I can live without him."

I felt sorry for her now and wondered whether I was the driving wedge between my parents. I was always Daddy's little girl, and she was my rival for his affection. My mom described our relationship as black and white. If she said up, I said down; if she said fat, I said thin. It was not something I could stop myself from doing.

I pulled the door to the garage closed and headed back to my room. Once inside, I pressed my forehead against the cool windowpane, hoping his car would be coming back. Maybe it was all a bad dream and soon I'd wake up.

Then I felt her hand touch my shoulder. My rival, my sparring partner, took my head in her hands and turned it towards her. She wasn't crying anymore as she pressed my cheek to hers, yet I could still feel the wetness of her tears. There were no words spoken between us that morning. For once, we both felt the same thing. We were in agreement in our grief. And now we were left with one chair painfully empty at our table for three.

Isabel Philley
As told to C. S. Dweck

A Most Precious Gift

Divorce. The word alone sends chills down some people's backs, but not mine. It may sound unusual, but my parents' divorce was, in a way, the best thing that ever happened to our family. You see, I can hardly recollect what it was like for my parents to be married. It all seems like a very distant memory, like a story from another lifetime.

It was the New Year's Eve right after my sixth birthday when my father moved out. All I remember was being in my family room and receiving a good-bye hug from him. My brother, who was four, consoled my mom and me. My dad left us all crying miserably. I thought I was never going to see my beloved daddy again. But the following Monday night, there he was. And our weekly dinner ritual was born.

He came to pick my brother and me up for dinner every Monday and Thursday night. And every other weekend he would take us to his new apartment where we would spend the night. For some reason, I learned to love my new life. I knew that every week I couldn't make other plans on our dinner nights; it was our precious time to spend with our dad. I learned how to pack a bag for the weekend trips to the apartment, trying hard not to miss a thing. Over the years our dinner ritual had to work around dance, basketball, tennis, art classes and golf leagues. But it always came first.

Three years after my parents got divorced, when I was nine, my mother got remarried to Marty. He's wonderful and has been making me giggle ever since with his brilliant sense of humor. Adding another man to his children's lives may have angered some fathers, but not mine. My dad took our new stepfather out and befriended him.

With our new stepfather came an older stepbrother and an enormous extended family. Three years later, my dad finally found the love of his life, and my brother and I were blessed with a not-at-all-wicked stepmother, Suzi. Suzi's son and daughter quickly became part of the family as well.

Now that my mom and Marty have been married for over nine years and my dad and Suzi for six, it has become impossible for me to even imagine my parents married to each other. Over the years, when people have been introduced to all of my parents and observe their relationships with each other, they tell me that my family is a prime example of how life should be after a divorce.

When I meet new people and they find out that my parents are divorced, they always apologize and sympathize. But to me, my parents' divorce is not something to be sorry about. A divorce in itself is sad, an ending, but the outcome in our case has been great for all of us. For our birthdays we all go out to dinner, the six of us. My parents have remained friends, and my mom and Suzi have even golfed together.

I wouldn't change anything about my life. I have eight grandparents, four parents, four siblings, too many aunts and uncles to count, and an endless amount of cousins. Love and support surround me no matter what or whose house I happen to be at. With the help of my family I have learned to cope during the hard times. But above all, I have learned that love is immeasurable and, when shared, the most precious gift of all.

Jessica Colman

,   # Memories of My Mother

*I still miss those I loved who are no longer with
me but I find I am grateful for having loved
them. The gratitude has finally conquered the
loss.*

Rita Mae Brown

In January of 1998, I got the kind of call all actresses
hope for: I had won the role of Julie Emrick on a new TV
drama called *Felicity*. It should have been one of the most
exciting moments of my life, but three months earlier
something had happened that would forever put things
in perspective. In October 1997, my mom, Christine
Johnson, was diagnosed with cancer. Ten months later,
she died at age fifty-three, and my life would never be the
same.

My mom was my best friend. She taught me to appreciate every day. I think that is the key to life. I try to keep
remembering that, to kind of make it a habit. And when I
get all caught up in everything, I just stop and think
about her.

I was like her sidekick growing up in Cape Cod,

Massachusetts. My brother, Greig Jr., now thirty-three, and my sister, Julie, now thirty-two, were both older than me (I'm twenty-nine), so when they started school, it was just me and my mom together all day, running errands or just hanging out.

We even remained close through my rebellious period. In high school, I was staying out too late, doing the normal teenage stuff, so my parents sent me to a private boarding school in New Hampshire. I got kicked out after eight months for getting caught in the boys' dorm. Oops! My punishment was having to go to a small local church school. When I did something wrong, if I tried to deny it or hide it, my mom would get angry. But if I admitted and apologized, she'd be totally cool. She was really fair.

She was also super-supportive. Ever since I was a kid, I knew I wanted to perform. She was always my biggest fan. She wasn't a pushy stage mom at all, but she was definitely in my corner. She was really into personal growth (a longtime clothing store manager, she opened a self-help bookstore at one point) and encouraged the people around her to follow their dreams.

When I decided to move to New York City at nineteen to pursue an acting career, my mom and my dad, Greig Johnson, a car salesman, never said, "That's risky," or, "Don't do that." Two years later, in 1993, I moved to Los Angeles and got my first TV role as Kimberly, the Pink Power Ranger on *Mighty Morphin Power Rangers.*

Everything was going smoothly until the fall of 1997, when my life came to a screeching halt. My mom's doctors thought she had cysts on her uterus that had grown and needed to be removed. But what should have been a simple hysterectomy turned into something far worse. Mom already kind of suspected. A couple of days before her surgery, she called me up really frightened and said, "Amy Jo, what if I have cancer?" and I was like, "Mom, you

can't say that. No. No. No." So she went in for the operation. They didn't expect to find cancer, but it was everywhere. A rare type of cancer, it had started in her appendix,
and by the time the doctors found it, it had spread all over
her body.

I'll never forget the moment when my dad called and
told me the news. It was Halloween. In shock, I flew back
East to be with my family. I remember sitting up one
night with my dad, probably two days after we found out.
He told me he knew she was going to die, he just knew it.
I was like, "No, we've got to have hope."

My mom handled the news—and her terminal prognosis
—with incredible bravery. That Christmas, which she
knew would probably be her last, she bought us all tickets
to see *The Lion King* on Broadway in New York. It was really
emotional because the story is about the circle of life and
dying and coming back again. I looked over at my mom
during the scene where Simba sees his father's ghost. She
had tears in her eyes. But she never broke down in front of
any of us kids or her friends. I think my dad's the only one
who saw how frightened she must have been.

In the beginning, we had several disappointments. My
mom tried different chemotherapies. She also went to a
hospital in Washington, D.C., for a surgery the doctors
hoped might give her more time. My sister and I slept on
little cots in her hospital room. It was like a slumber party.

But the surgery was a letdown. They opened her up
again and said there was nothing they could do. The cancer had spread too much. Everyone was trying to help,
recommending holistic medicines and special diets. We
searched on the Internet for anything that might cure
cancer. There are just a million things out there that
people are trying to sell and tell you. Finally, my mom
said, "Stop! I don't want to try anything else. Don't bring
me any more crazy teas!"

That winter and spring, I traveled back and forth constantly between L.A. and Cape Cod. The people at *Felicity* were incredible. A couple of times, they stopped production or rearranged the schedule so I could go home. And the producers would send my mom hats and T-shirts and letters saying, "We love your daughter." I think it was a comfort for her to know that I would be taken care of when she was gone.

My mom didn't want to die in a hospital, so hospice workers came to our home in July of 1998. They were great because they helped my mom accept the fact that she was going to die. That allowed her to say good-bye to everybody. One day, she gathered her favorite jewelry and possessions and had each person she loved come upstairs, and she gave everything away. She gave some people back gifts that she remembered they had given to her, like, twenty years ago.

She kept her sense of humor until she died. Four days after the doctors had predicted she'd pass away, she was sitting in bed and started singing! She looked at my sister and me and jokingly said, "What am I going to do? A woman can't live without her jewels."

She wanted me to go back to work, where they were rearranging production for me, but I told her I was staying with her. Finally, she insisted: "This could go on for a month. You have to go." I said good-bye so many times. I'd hug her, kiss her, run downstairs, get in the car and then run back up. I did that, like, seven times. Finally, she said, "Amy Jo, this is getting ridiculous. Just go." It was the hardest good-bye I've said or will ever have to. Three days after that, on August 19, 1998, she died.

My sister called and told me the news. I cried all over my house. Then, I went to my living room and just sat there, and suddenly, I got the most incredible feeling I've ever had. It was like my mom was in the room with me. It was like she came over and gave me peace, and it made me feel ready to go home for the funeral and be strong for my dad and the rest of the family.

Amy Jo Johnson
As told to Linda Friedman

The Last Months

I was happy to be home that night all bundled up in my fleece blanket, so soft, so warm. It was January first of the new millennium, and it was cool and breezy outside. My dad was looking at our Christmas tree, still decorated with a lifetime of memories. Dad had insisted on having the perfect tree, so we did. It was lushly green, and the smell of pine had permeated throughout the entire house since the day it arrived. It was huge—ten feet tall and five feet wide. And now my dad was just staring at it.

Suddenly, I noticed that tears were rolling down his dark cheeks. I didn't understand this uncharacteristic show of emotion. It confused me, so I decided to leave him alone. I peered out from the kitchen to see what he was doing, but tried not to make it obvious that I was watching him. He touched each ornament and held it tightly. It looked as if he were trying to staunch the flow of dark and consuming thoughts.

That was the month I started to see my dad become weak and frail. Not knowing what was wrong, my mom took him to see the doctor. After undergoing X rays and blood work, they returned home to anxiously await the results. Finally, the doctor called. My dad was in serious danger of having another heart attack, and he had to be checked into the hospital immediately.

I cannot remember a time when my dad was really well. He had already suffered a series of heart attacks, as well as complications from bypass surgery. This time, Dad was in the hospital for two long weeks. He was hooked up to so many I.V. tubes and monitors that it made it hard for him to communicate with us. Eventually, he progressed enough to be able to come home.

Every couple of days, a nurse would come to the house and help my dad with his rehabilitation. One day, as we waited for her to arrive, I noticed something unusual. My dad wasn't breathing. My mom ran over to him and shook him.

"What? What's wrong?" he asked.

"You weren't breathing," I told him.

He answered with a simple, "Oh," then fell back into an uneasy sleep. A few minutes later, I looked over at him.

"Mom . . ." I gasped and pointed at him. She woke him up again.

"Why don't we keep you up until the nurse gets here?" she asked him, her voice cracking. He slightly nodded his gray head in agreement. I didn't know what to say, so I didn't say a word.

The nurse finally arrived. She looked him over and said, "We have to get you to the emergency room."

My father frowned. He reminded me of a child not wanting to do what he is told. With a forlorn look on his face, he asked, "Do I have to?" The nurse nodded.

There were so many things to say, but no one was sure how to say them. When my dad was about to leave, I gave him a lingering hug and held him tight. I didn't want to let him go. As he got into the car, I told him I loved him.

He turned and smiled at me and nodded in acknowl-
edgment. I watched as they pulled out of the driveway
and down the street. I watched until the car vanished
behind a big tree that stood on the side of the road. That
was the last time I saw my dad.

Things have changed in my life over the past eight
months. There is not as much laughter, and there are
times I feel angry and depressed. Going places is not as
enjoyable without my dad. When I see a family with their
father, I feel envious. Sometimes when I come home, I forget that he is gone and go into his room to talk to him. I
always feel empty when I realize he's not there.

My river of tears for him still floods every so often. I
know this river will go on forever and never dry out, just
as my love and memories of my dad will never dry up
either. They will last forever, just like his spirit.

My time has come,
And so I'm gone.
To a better place,
Far beyond.

I love you all
As you can see.
But it's better now,
Because I'm free . . .

Traci Kornhauser

Our Song

What is there to do when people die—people so dear and rare—but bring them back by remembering?

May Sarton

You asked me to sing to you. I complained, "Aw, Mom, I'll wake people up." Once again, I let my ever-present stage fright come before you. Looking back, it's hard to believe I was so selfish. But you persisted, and eventually I caved.

I sang our favorites—Barbra Streisand, Linda Ronstadt and Bette Midler. My voice was quiet and hushed, commensurate with the dim light in the room. I made sure the sound didn't penetrate the walls. You listened with your eyes closed, then thanked me and told me how lovely and peaceful it was.

When we brought you home that last week in January, I would sit with you in the evenings. I read to you from *The Tragedy of Richard the Third,* knowing it was your favorite. Of course, I made sarcastic comments along the way. "Lady Anne was the biggest idiot in the world." My eyes searched yours for a response, hoping they would open and smile at my glib attempts.

I read you poetry from Robbie Burns and Walt Whitman, and rubbed lotion on your hands. Finally, I worked up the courage to sing to you again. You weren't able to ask me this time. Grandma peeked through the door and gave us a tearful smile. I stopped. "Keep singing to your mother," she said. When I finished Dad asked me, "Would you sing at the memorial service?" You were lying right beside me, and suddenly it seemed so perverse to have this conversation in front of you. "I don't know if I can. I'll try." We didn't speak of it again.

That Saturday, after you were gone, I went home and practiced. I needed you to hear me one last time, beautiful and unblemished.

And then there I was, standing at the podium. I didn't tell anyone what was planned in case I chickened out. While the minister told me when to come up during the service, Shirley, who was giving the eulogy, asked, "But what if someone stands up before Jennifer?" I shot back, "Well, now—they'll just have to wait, won't they?" She laughed, "You are just like your mother." I smiled and thanked her for the compliment.

My hands shook as I faced the microphone. I spoke a few words to gather my courage and compose myself. Then, very quietly, I sang "Somewhere over the Rainbow."

I thought back to when I was a little girl. You would call me on the phone during one of your trips to watch *The Wizard of Oz* with me on TV. Miles apart and racking up the long distance charges, we would both squeal during the tornado scene. We sang duets, and trios when Ashlea rode in the car with us. It was our song.

I finished the last line, "If happy little bluebirds fly, beyond the rainbow, why oh why can't I?" Then I whispered, "Mom, you have beautiful wings now. May they take you wherever you want to go. . . ."

At least a hundred people witnessed the most difficult moment of my life, but only one person mattered. Of course I will sing for you, Mom. Feel free to ask me anytime.

Jennifer Dalrymple-Mozisek

It's Been a While

It's been a while since I've heard your voice,
That warm comforting voice,
Always uttering helpful words of wisdom.
You always knew so much more about life than I,
Teaching me day by day.

You watched me grow into a woman,
Always supporting me no matter what.
You were proud of what I was becoming,
Loving me endlessly without question, never judging.
While you were watching me mature into the person I am
     today,
I was watching you struggle to stay alive.

You said over and over that everything would end up all
     right in the end.
You always knew just what to say to make the world seem
     like it was on our side.
You were wrong this time, Mom—
The world wasn't on our side.

It took you away from me,
Leaving me alone, longing for your love, motherless.
Without someone to tell me I was beautiful,
To wipe my tears away as they rolled down my cheek,
Without someone to share my fears, my joys and my
    triumphs.

I heard your voice again last night.
I've missed it every day since you've been gone.
I saw your smile again last night,
I've been wishing for it every hour since you've been away.

In my dream you said
You'd always be near
And now that I think of it,
You said the same thing
The day you died.

You always did know just what to say
To make the world seem like it
Was on our side.

                                    Catherine Starr

Reaching Mom

It wasn't always just my mom and me. There was a time when my dad was in the picture, but that was such a long time ago. It may as well have been in another life-time. I don't remember much about him. When I try to form a picture of him in my mind, all I get is a hazy image of a tall man with dark hair. And though it's hard to tell, I think he's smiling. We don't talk about him, though. Anything about my dad is taboo. I don't know how I know that. I just know it. It's this unspoken rule that my mother made and I've just always obeyed. But I have a feeling he was a good man. Just conjuring up that picture of him makes me feel a bit safer. She never spoke of him. Not since it happened. I think she blames herself.

The details are difficult. I remember all the wrong parts. I was so young. Was I about four when it happened? That sounds right for some reason. I had just turned four. My birthday was a few days before it happened. I think that's why my mom always seems sad around the time of my birthday. But she hides it. Says it's the time of year; says that her eyes are watery because of all the pollen in the air. That's what she always said. But I can hear her sometimes in the middle of the night. Tiny, suppressed sobs coming from her room.

It was springtime. A cool day, I remember, because my mom struggled to get me to zip up my jacket. I hated how the zipper cut into my neck. It was morning. I remember the smell of the dew as we walked from the house to the car. I remember the long gulps of air I took, as if to drink it in. To this day, I find myself holding my breath sometimes, on spring mornings, waiting for the bus at the end of my driveway.

I don't remember where we were going, but I knew that wherever it was, we were going to meet daddy there. And that made me happy. A light drizzle started as we got on the road. I would watch the little droplets of rain as they landed at the top of the window and follow them as they became tinier and tinier and finally disappeared as they reached the bottom. It was a game I used to play, and still find myself playing when my mind wanders off on long car rides.

The droplets got bigger and bigger until it became a full-fledged storm, cascading down on the car until finally my eyes became all confused. That's when my mother started getting this strange look on her face. A determined look, eyes squinting into the fog. Trying desperately to see around each drop of rain. And her knuckles were white as she gripped the steering wheel. I remember balling up my own little fists to see if they would do the same thing. Turn white. Just as I was studying the way little mountains of bone formed and disappeared as I clenched and unclenched my fists, there was a shrieking sound. The car braked and I was pushed forward, just about hitting my head on the dash. My mom threw open the car door and ran outside screaming.

The next thing I remember was sitting on the sofa at my Aunt Rosa's house. Aunt Rosa was by my side explaining something to me, but I couldn't understand the words. They didn't mean anything. They were just a jumble of sounds put together, and I started laughing at how funny she sounded. She held her head in her hands and her whole body shook. I tried to explain to her what was so funny. But she just cried. So I shut my mouth.

And once more it becomes hazy.

It's funny how I can remember the events leading up to the accident with such amazing clarity, but I don't remember much about the time after it happened at all. I mean, I can remember pieces: feelings, colors, images. But nothing that tells a story.

There was a lot of black. I can see people crying and my mother sitting on the couch surrounded by people I knew to be her friends. The woman sitting next to her was her best friend Carmen. She sat holding Mom's hand. A helpless look upon her face. I remember wanting more than anything to see my dad, but I kept telling myself that he was away on business and would come back soon, like he always did.

Soon the colors started getting brighter. People weren't always crying. And we started doing the things we normally did. But it wasn't like before. Mom always looked like she was far away. I'd sing to her, dance for her, play with her hair—anything to try and get her to smile at me the way she used to. Anything to get more than just a pat on the head and that faraway smile. I just couldn't reach her.

It's been that way ever since.

Since then I've gleaned bits of conversations and can sort of piece together what happened. I mean, I knew my dad died in a car accident. But I also knew that there was more to it than that. We had been on our way to pick him up at the airport. He was away on business. He went away a lot, I remember. But we were running late because of the rain traffic. We got there just in time to see the accident.

My dad leaning out into the street, hailing a cab. Waving for a taxi. And as the taxi tried to stop for him, it skidded and ran up onto the sidewalk. Hitting him. Killing my father on impact, they said. And my mom saw the whole thing happen.

He must've thought we forgot about him, since we were pretty late. And so he would have to find his own way home.

Just then we pulled up.

It was raining too hard. The street was too wet. The taxi's brakes were in need of a tune-up. So many factors figured into his death. But my mom blamed only herself.

So really my whole life has been tinged with this unspoken sadness.

My mom's still distant. Years and years have passed. I'm about to go off to college. And still, she's in her own prison to which only she holds the key. It's been just her and me for so long, you'd have thought that maybe we'd have formed some sort of bond. Just the two of us. Facing the world together. But no. She's in her corner and I'm in mine. There've been times when I've tried to reach out, like I did when I was little. Times when I'd try and get her to open up to me by opening up to her. But there's just no doing.

That's not to say she's been a bad mother. She's always provided me with what I needed, working long hours just so I could have the luxuries a kid with two parents has. She's been a good mom.

And now it's time for me to go.

We're on our way upstate to school. Most of my belongings are packed in the back of our van. Mom's driving and I'm listening to the newest Counting Crows album. It's raining, and I'm watching the droplets of water race to the bottom of the window. I feel like it's my last chance. It's now or never. And so I say it.

"Dad would've been proud of me, don'tcha think? Going off to college? All grown up?"

Except it comes out more like, "Dadwould'vebeenproud ofmedon'tchathink?goingofftocollege?allgrownup?"

School's pretty far upstate. At this point, we're almost there. Driving along what seems like an endless stretch of deserted road. So when the car jerks to a stop, we're in no danger of an accident.

My mother turns to me slowly, with tears running down her face. But she's smiling. At first she just stares into my eyes and I'm amazed at how "present" she is. She takes my hand in hers and says, "Yes, honey. Daddy would've been so proud." And suddenly I realized that I'd never had time to grieve over the loss of my father. I'd spent my whole life grieving over the loss of my mom. Somehow losing her was worse than losing my father, because she was still with me. But an empty shell of a person. She's here now. She's with me. That's what matters. And she exudes this warmth. This warmth that I've felt before, but not for a very long time. And suddenly I'm crying, too. Not because I miss my dad and wish he were here with me, but because, finally, after all this time, she's ready to come back to life.

Analise Antone

[EDITORS' NOTE: *This story is not entirely factual. Some aspects have been fictionalized.*]

4

SUICIDE

Often the test of courage is not to die but to live.

Vittorio Alfieri

I Never Knew

The difference between holding on to a hurt or releasing it with forgiveness is like the difference between laying your head down at night on a pillow filled with thorns or a pillow filled with rose petals.

Loren Fischer

She was my best friend, and I loved her. She was the coolest girl in junior high and everyone wanted to be like her . . . and she chose me to be her best friend. Her name was Cindy. She was beautiful with her black hair and tall, thin body. While the rest of us in eighth and ninth grade were still looking amorphous, trying to take shape, Cindy was already beautifully poised in her adult body.

Her mother had died when she was a little girl. She was an only child, and she lived alone with her father. By the time we would get home from school every day, he would already be at work. He wouldn't come home until two or three in the morning, so we had free reign of the house. No parental supervision was the greatest thing we could ask for as teenagers. Her house was a big, two-story that was concealed by a large grove of orange trees. You couldn't see the house from the street, and we liked it that way. It added to the mystique and allure that we were always trying to create.

At school she was pretty much the center of attention. One whole corner of the quad was dedicated to Cindy and her "followers." If there was new music, clothes, hairstyles or even new ways to take notes or study, you could be fairly sure that it came out of that corner of the quad. Even the school faculty caught on to the power this girl held and convinced her to run for class president. Cindy and I were voted in as class president and vice president by a landslide.

By day, we were the acting liaison between students and faculty; by night, we hosted social activities at Cindy's house. If we weren't having a party, people would come just to hang out. Kids would be there for all kinds of reasons—to talk about relationships, their parents, to do their homework, or just because they knew someone they liked would be showing up.

After everyone left, I would usually spend the night. My mom wouldn't like it very much if it was a school night. Sometimes Cindy would come back to my house to spend the night, but my mom didn't like that much either because we would stay up all night laughing and talking. Cindy didn't like to be home alone.

That following summer, after I came home from vacation with my family, things were starting to change. Cindy looked thinner than usual with dark circles under her eyes, and she had started to smoke. The strikingly beautiful girl looked pale and gaunt. She said she missed me a lot. While it was a boost to my ego, I couldn't believe it could be entirely true. After all, there were always people trying to be close to her and get into her circle of friends.

My solution: two weeks at the beach. Our parents pitched in to rent a beach house for two weeks. My mom would be the only supervision. In Cindy's inimitable style, we collected a group of beach friends within a couple of days. We'd all hang out at this local café during the day, when we were not in the water or on the sand, and at night we'd hang out around this fire pit on the beach.

Cindy started to look like her old self, but better. She was tan. She looked great in a bikini, and all the guys on the beach wanted to be around her. But she was still smoking. She told me it calmed her nerves.

One night, Cindy came back to the beach house very late. She was all disoriented and noticeably excited. She told me she and this one guy had been drinking and smoking marijuana, and they had gotten together. She said that I had to try marijuana because it made everything better, clearer, in fact. She said she really liked this guy and wanted to run away with him. I knew she was just high, and she'd feel differently in the morning.

When school started that next year, things weren't the same, and I missed the old routine. Cindy wanted to get into different things than I wanted, and she started hanging around guys more and more. We would still hang out from time to time, but it wasn't as fun as it used to be. Cindy would get really serious and tell me that I just didn't understand how things were. I just thought that she was maturing faster emotionally than the rest of us, like she had physically.

One morning when I arrived at school, there were police cars all around and a lot of nervous activity in the halls. When I proceeded toward my locker, my counselor and another woman stopped me. I was asked to follow them to the office. My heart was pounding so fast and hard that I could hardly catch my breath. My head was racing with the different scenarios that might have caused this odd behavior.

When we all sat down in my counselor's office, the principal came in and took a seat. Was I in some kind of trouble? The principal began by talking about life and maturity and circumstances. Now my head was really spinning. What was he trying to say? And then my world froze in time with the words, ". . . and Cindy took her own life last night using her father's gun." I couldn't talk; I couldn't move. Tears started streaming from my eyes before my heart could even comprehend the pain. She was only fifteen years old.

As the suicide note explained, her father had repeatedly sexually abused her and she knew no other way out. Months after he was arrested, he finally confessed. The note also said something else. It said that the only family she ever knew and cared about was me. She left me a ring that her mother had left to her.

I cried for weeks. How is it that I never knew? We were closer than anyone and talked about everything; how come she never told me that? I was certain that I could have helped her, and I began to blame myself.

After weeks of grief counseling, I came to understand that the burden of Cindy's sexual abuse was too much for her to bear, especially when she started to become intimate with boys. The counselor explained to me that her shame was too great to talk about, even to her best friend. It dawned on me how alone she must have felt, and it suddenly became clear to me why she never wanted to spend the night alone in her own house.

My own suffering—weeks of pain and confusion—was eased greatly with all the help and support I received. Teachers, counselors, friends and family members all nurtured me. It was clear to everyone that this situation was going to change my life forever, but because I let help in, it subsequently added to my life an aspect of wisdom and compassion. I wish that Cindy could have known the relief that comes from letting others help you with your pain.

Cindy's suicide note also requested that she be cremated. The note said that I should spread her ashes wherever I wanted to. I chose the ocean off the beach where we had spent two weeks that summer.

On the day of the memorial, we rented a boat to take us out to sea. The boat was packed with friends and teachers, even though it was a rainy, overcast day. We stood on the bow and took turns sharing our experiences and love for our friend. When it came time for me to free her ashes, I hesitated. I didn't want to turn them loose in a sea that looked dark and menacing. I thought she had had enough of that in her own life.

My hesitancy gained attention, and both my mother and my counselor stepped up on the platform and put their arms around me. With their support I opened the lid and set my friend free. As some of the ashes hit the surface of the water, the sun broke through for a moment and sent beautiful rays of light that sparkled on the surface of the water. The clouds parted some more and soon the whole boat was bathed in warm sunlight. At that moment, I felt calmer than I had in weeks. Somehow I knew that the angels had come for my friend and that she would be all right—and so would I.

Rosanne Martorella

[EDITORS' NOTE: *Some of the critical signs to watch for if you think someone you know may be suicidal are:*
• *A sudden change in behavior (especially calmness after a period of anxiety or a lift in mood after a period of deep depression,*

which would indicate that the person now has the energy to act on suicidal thoughts).
- *Preoccupation with death.*
- *Giving away belongings.*
- *Direct or indirect threats to commit suicide. (It is particularly important to pay attention and take seriously any talk of suicide even if it seems like the person is "joking.")*

If you or someone you know is feeling suicidal or is showing any of the critical warning signs above, reach out to a professional you can trust (such as a school counselor) or call one of the hotlines listed below.]

800-SUICIDE: 800-784-2433

Yellow Ribbon Project: 303-429-3530, 3531, 3532
www.yellowribbon.org
Helps prevent teen suicide.

Youth Crisis Line: 800-843-5200, *twenty-four hours*
www.befrienders.org
Can refer you to a crisis hotline in your area.

I Am

I am a poet writing of my pain.
I am a person living a life of shame.
I am your daughter hiding my depression.
I am your sister making a good impression.
I am your friend acting like I'm fine.
I am a wisher wishing this life weren't mine.
I am a girl who thinks of suicide.
I am a teenager pushing her tears aside.
I am a student who doesn't have a clue.
I am the girl sitting next to you.
I am the one asking you to care.
I am your best friend hoping you'll be there.

Krysteen Hernandez

Beyond Surviving:
Suggestions for Survivors

Hundreds of books have been written about loss and grief. Few have addressed the aftermath of suicide for survivors. Here again, there are no answers; only suggestions from those who have lived through and beyond the event.

1. Know you can survive. You may not think so, but you can.
2. Struggle with "why" it happened until you no longer need to know "why" or until you are satisfied with partial answers.
3. Know you may feel overwhelmed by the intensity of your feelings, but all your feelings are normal.
4. Anger, guilt, confusion and forgetfulness are common responses. You are not crazy; you are in mourning.
5. Be aware you may feel appropriate anger at the person, at the world, at God or at yourself. It's okay to express it.
6. You may feel guilty for what you think you did or did not do. Guilt can turn into regret, through forgiving.
7. Having suicidal thoughts is common. It does not

mean that you will act on those thoughts.

8. Remember to take one moment or one day at a time.
9. Find a good listener with whom to share. Call someone if you need to talk.
10. Don't be afraid to cry. Tears are healing.
11. Give yourself time to heal.
12. Remember, the choice was not yours. No one is the
    sole influence of another's life.
13. Expect setbacks. If emotions return like a tidal wave,
    you may only be experiencing a remnant of grief, an
    unfinished piece.
14. Try to put off major decisions.
15. Give yourself permission to get professional help.
16. Be aware of the pain of your family and friends.
17. Be patient with yourself and with others who may
    not understand.
18. Set your own limits and learn to say no.
19. Steer clear of people who want to tell you what or
    how to feel.
20. Know that there are support groups that can be
    helpful, such as Compassionate Friends or Survivors
    of Suicide groups. If not, ask a professional to help
    start one.
21. Call on your personal faith to help you through.
22. It is common to experience physical reactions to your
    grief, e.g., headaches, loss of appetite, inability to sleep.
23. The willingness to laugh with others and at yourself
    is healing.
24. Wear out your questions, anger, guilt or other feel-
    ings until you can let them go. Letting go doesn't
    mean forgetting.
25. Know that you will never be the same again, but
    you can survive and even go beyond just surviving.

Iris M. Bolton

Learning from My Past

As the days pass slowly
And the weeks creep by
I find myself obsessing
About ways that I could die.

I lay awake at night
Thinking of my pain.
There's no way it can get better;
I have nothing left to gain.

Suddenly thoughts of death
Are controlling my every move,
And every battle with my mind
I always seem to lose.

I no longer want to be around
The people that I love.
All that I can think about
Is what's waiting up above.

I cut my arms with razor blades
To dull the pain inside,
But that can only last so long;
I don't want to be alive.

I manage to keep my composure
When people are around.
They wouldn't understand me
So I don't make a sound.

I smile when I have to.
I break down when I don't.
I know I should be strong,
But I also know I won't.

So I make a plan to take some pills.
It shouldn't take too long.
I write out notes to all my friends
To read when I am gone.

I ask my mom to understand
That life is just too hard.
My mind can't fight it anymore;
My heart is far too scarred.

I plan it out so perfectly
I even set the date.
I'm pretty sure I'm ready;
I know this is my fate.

My bed is made up neatly
As I take them one by one.
I start to feel a little scared;
I know I'm almost done.

All that I can think about
Is how I'm letting go,
And how much I love my family.
I really hope they know.

My eyes are getting heavy.
My body feels so weak.
Everything inside is numb.
That's the way it has to be.

I'm glad that Mom's not here right now
To watch me slowly die,
But still I wish that I could say,
"I love you and good-bye."

I give in to the darkness.
I slowly slip away.
I hope I go to heaven
Where dark night turns to day.

I wake up in confusion,
I don't know where I am.
Is this heaven, or is it hell,
The land of the eternally damned?

There are people all around
Although I can barely see,
I can hear the soothing voices
Of people dear to me.

My family and friends are here
Comforting one another.
I can hardly make out any words
Until I hear my mother.

Each tear she cries feels like a knife
Stabbing at my soul.
I let my pain and suffering
Blind me from my goal.

At one point I was determined
To make it through this test,
To lead a life of fulfillment
And to do my very best.

But I somehow lost all sight of that.
I hope she can forgive.
I promise not to waste
My second chance to live.

I sit up in my hospital bed
Tears streaming down my cheeks.
My mother rushes over crying
Like she hasn't seen me in weeks.

I tell her that I'm sorry
For causing her so much strife.
I tell her that I will succeed
In leading a better life.

Together we figured out a way
For me to get some help.
I know now that I can go to her
Instead of doing it by myself.

I know that it's not over yet;
It's a long road up ahead,
But I appreciate the little things
Because I could be dead.

I've learned to live each passing day
As if it were my last.
I look forward to the future
And I'm learning from my past.

Rachael Bennett

Another Statistic

I don't want to be another statistic
Some suicidal teen
Who makes a choice to kill herself
When the world just seems too mean.
She can't go on with life
Or so to her it seems
Reality has fallen short
And so have her many dreams.

I don't want to be another statistic
Some pregnant little girl
Who met this great guy
And then gave sex a whirl.
She was only fifteen
But it felt so right
She thought they'd be together
For more than just a night.

I don't want to be another statistic
Some kid strung out on crack
Who started at a party
And now he can't turn back.

First cigarettes and alcohol
Now meth, crack and cocaine
He's been smoking it so long
That now he's gone insane.

I don't want to be another statistic
Some girl left in the rain
Who was walking home from school
Then raped and left in pain.
She can't tell her parents
And it hurts to tell her friends
She doesn't know what she'll do
To make this nightmare end.

I don't want to be another statistic
Some kid out of school
Who dropped out really early
And was acting like a fool.
He thought that it was boring
He thought that it was dumb
He doesn't have an education
But lives on the streets like a bum.

I don't want to be another statistic
Some stereotypical teen
I'm gonna make a difference
I'll finish with my dream.
I won't end up pregnant
On drugs or even dead
I won't drop out of school
Because I'll use my head.

I don't want to be another statistic
To fit into some mold
Of what society thinks of kids today
Because it's getting kind of old.
Not all of us are bad
In fact most of us are good
When will the world see us
And give us credit like they should?

Amanda Parmenter

5

TRAGEDY

I'm convinced that tragedy wants to harden us and that our mission is to never let it.

Sally Reardon, Felicity

An Unbreakable Bond

Becca and I met in the first grade. She was a new student registering at our school and I, well, I was in trouble
for daring Kenny Boucher to stick raisins up his nose. We
spent the entire afternoon in the principal's office
together and came away from the experience completely
inseparable. At a parent-teacher conference, my first-
grade teacher told my mother that elementary friendships never last, that within two months everyone has a
new best friend. She was wrong. Through elementary
when best friends change every week, middle school
when no one is ever "cool" enough and junior high when
everyone reevaluates everything about themselves, we
remained steadfast. And together, with excitement and
apprehension, we entered high school.

It's truly amazing how your entire priority system
changes when you enter those intimidating double doors.
Instead of sleepovers and birthday parties, it becomes dating and dances. The first dance was homecoming. I didn't
really think about it; I had better things to do such as football games, seeing movies or going out to eat. Besides, I
wasn't allowed to date. I didn't want to be another
freshman dork at a dance without a guy. My reasons were

good enough for me, but they didn't satisfy Becca.

The Friday morning of the game, she appeared at my locker, where I pretended to be furiously looking for my biology book.

"I didn't know you weren't going to the dance," she accused me.

I shrugged, still burrowing.

"Come on," she pleaded. "Please go with me."

I dug still, wishing I'd never heard of homecoming.

"Why won't you go?"

Silence from my end.

"Is this because you don't have a date?"

I stopped furrowing through my stuff. "Maybe."

She sighed in frustration and turned away. I sighed in relief, although I knew she wasn't going to forget the conversation even if she had to find me a date.

The second confrontation occurred at the actual game.

"I don't have a date either," she announced to me.

"Becca, you told me you had a date. You've had a date for several weeks." I was starting to get slightly annoyed. Slightly. "Would you just leave me alone already?" I looked up at her. That was really the wrong move to make. Becca had that "wounded puppy" look in her eyes. I hated that look.

"Please . . ."

"Will you leave me alone if I give you an answer?"

She grinned a characteristic Becca grin. "Yes," was her quick reply.

"Call me tomorrow, okay?"

At promptly two o'clock on the day of the dance, I received the dreaded call.

"What have you decided?" she asked, trying to sound like she really didn't care.

"I guess . . ." I moaned, desperately searching for the

I'm-sorry-but-I-can't-make-it speech I had been rehearsing all day.

"Yes! Thank you. Thank you! You have no idea how happy I am! We'll pick you up at seven, 'kay?"

"You don't need to pick me up . . ." I began.

"Don't worry about it. It's on our way. Love ya, bye."

"Bye." I didn't want to admit it, but her excitement was catching. Maybe that night wouldn't be so bad after all.

Okay, I'll say it, the dance was fun. Becca and I had the time of our lives, dancing like maniacs. It seemed like eleven came way too fast. One second we were dancing to "Time of Your Life" and the next the lights were coming back on in the gym. Becca threw her arm around my shoulder.

"So, what do you think? Glad you came?"

I grinned at her. "Thanks for talking me into it."

"No problem, babe. Come on, let's go home."

Arm in arm, we left the building, totally wrapped up in life. It seemed that we were heading into the happiest time of our lives, and the next three years were looking really good.

"This is weird," Matt commented, turning on his windshield wipers. I cast a nervous glance out the back window. It was beginning to hail with a ferocity that you usually don't see in the middle of October.

"Are we almost home?" Becca asked, with just a twinge of anxiety in her voice.

"Yeah, a few more miles."

Squinting out the front window, I watched the tree limbs laying in the bed of the truck in front of us wave in the strong wind.

"I don't think I like being behind this truck," Matt said nervously. "I'm going to get in the other lane."

Just as he turned his blinker on, I caught sight of the truck again. "Matt!" I screamed in terror. The next few seconds seemed to last forever, yet they went by faster than my mind could process what was happening. The huge truck spun out of control, landing on its side. Tree limbs, leaves and everything else imaginable came flying towards Matt's car in a tangled mess. With a sickening crash, we came to a rest on the side of the road.

I pried open my eyes. Broken branches and twigs were piled on my lap. The speed and force of the twigs hitting me had etched a pattern of bleeding scratches into my arms, face, and generally every other exposed area of skin. I couldn't even see anyone in the front seat.

"Becca? Matt?"

No reply. Flying out of the car at warp speed, I ran around and pulled on Matt's door. He was lost in a tangled mess.

"Hold on. Hold on. I can get out." He emerged, and I could hardly believe he was still alive. It didn't even look like he had actual skin remaining on his face. But he was conscious, and at that moment, that was all I cared about.

I ran around to the other side and flung open Becca's door. Small tree branches were so densely packed into the front of the car that I couldn't even see her. In a mix of fear and frenzy, I broke them away until I finally uncovered her.

"Sara?"

"Um-hmm. Are you all right?"

"Yeah, I'm fine. I think . . . You look awful. Are you okay?"

I think at that point my heart started beating again. "Yeah, fine. I'm glad you are. That was way too close. Can you get out?"

"No."

"I'm going to find someone who can call for help," Matt announced, sprinting back in the direction we had come from. I prayed that someone would drive by; however, I knew that in the current weather condition, it was highly unlikely.

"Okay, we'll wait for somebody to get here." I knelt by the door to keep her company.

"I'm really glad you came to the dance with me," she told me with a smile.

"I'm glad I came, too."

Her smile turned to a grimace, and I followed her glance. Suddenly, I thought I was going to be sick. A large tree limb, at least as big around as my arm, protruded from her chest. Her entire left side was covered in blood and more was added to it with each pulse of her heart.

"You'll be okay," I told her, feeling the phlegm in my throat. Taking her hand, I held on to it for dear life. My heart was smashed into a pulp as I watched her. With every breath I took, I could feel tiny, razor-sharp daggers stabbing every square inch of my body.

She smiled again at me. Again, my heart took a beating. "You're so sweet, thanks."

My face was wet, and I wasn't sure whether it was with blood, rain or tears. It was probably all three. Soon, Becca's hand grew cold and the blood that pulsed from her chest became significantly less with each beat.

"Hey, Sara?" she whispered.

"Hmm?" I managed, barely a sound at all.

"Girl, I love you so much. Don't let them keep us apart, okay?"

Not really sure what she meant, I was willing to agree with anything. "Yeah, I'll ride to the hospital with you."

She shook her head. "That's not what I meant, and you know it. Promise?"

I searched for my voice for what seemed like priceless years. "I promise." Becca smiled in her characteristically sweet way at me. Nodding, her eyes shut peacefully. The grip on my hand loosened.

In a panicked choke, I thrust my head into the car, mere

centimeters from hers. "Becca! Becca! Stay awake! Becca, no! Come on, girl! Bec—"

Running out of voice, I stared in disbelief at the blood-covered, cold body of the person who had been closer to me than anyone else for eight years. Eight long years that had ended in a single unbelievable moment. I laid my head on her lap and sobbed her name until every last ounce of strength in me was gone. Dissolving into body-wracking tears, I fell onto the cold ground and grasped her hand again. The cold hail pounded my back, and I was all alone.

Walking through those double doors again for the first time in two weeks, I braced myself as yet another wave of grief and loss blasted me in the face. It took complete concentration to make the interminable walk to my locker. I was aware that people were actually stopping to watch me go by. Finally I got there, and all I could do was stand there and stare at the cold, gray metal door.

Looking to the ceiling for some kind of help, some kind of comfort, I prepared myself for the inevitable. There would be no little card taped to the top shelf, no recent sign of someone else's presence besides my own there. Bracing myself against every emotion that beat against my body, I slowly spun my combination lock. Twenty-one . . . thirty-nine . . . twenty-two . . . click. I painfully swallowed the hard lump in my throat, removed the lock and slowly swung the door open.

A new card was taped to the shelf, the handwriting on the envelope so unmistakably familiar. And yet . . . it just couldn't be. Using every bit of control I had left, I peeled the envelope from the shelf. The well-known scent it carried actually knocked me over. Sitting hard on the floor, new tears came running down my cheeks in a rushing torrent. There was nothing left to do. I had to open it.

Opening the card, I could barely read the lines through my blurred vision.

Sara,

Hey, I know you didn't really want to come to the dance tonight, but I'm glad you agreed to it. Girl, I love you, and I hope I didn't drive you nuts trying to convince you to do this. We've always stuck together, and it'll never change, right? Hope you have fun. I'll see you soon.
Becca

I let my eyes wander to the inside of the locker door and found exactly the picture I didn't want to see. It had always been one of my favorites, dating back only about two months to band camp. We had our arms around each other, saluting with our instruments. The picture showed us laughing about something or other. We were always laughing about something. . . .

I didn't know how I was going to keep my promise to Becca. It seemed that fate had done a pretty good job of separating us. Already, I couldn't vividly recall her smile, her laugh, her voice, her expressions.

The bell rang, but as everyone drifted to class, I slipped outside. I lifted my face to the sky and let the sunlight dry my tears. New resolve filled my being. I grasped every memory, insignificant as some seemed, of my best friend and locked them into the big, empty space in my heart. They came nowhere near filling the gap, but I would never let them go, and for the first time I understood what Becca had meant in her final breaths. There was nothing that could ever keep us apart; time had proven that was impossible. Turning back to the school building I had entered for the first time not long ago, I knew that this time I had the strength to go back inside.

After all, this time I wasn't alone. I carried the spirit of my best friend, and she and I would never truly be apart. She lives on in every smile I give away.

Sara Preston

[EDITORS' NOTE: *This story is not entirely factual. Some aspects have been fictionalized.*]

Losing the Best

My childhood was easy. You might even say I was spoiled, mostly by my mother. She was always in the mood to spoil me. If there was something I wanted, I knew to go to my mother. She was an angelically beautiful woman. She had this heavenly smell, kind of like ripe strawberries. And her hands felt like velvet, like a newborn baby's fat and tender cheeks.

On the other hand, for as long as I've known him, my father has been an overweight, balding man with thick bifocals. According to my mom, he used to be "a real catch," whatever that's supposed to mean. All I know is he has worked hard all his life to make sure my life is full of all the opportunity it can be. He has been saving money for my college education since I was five. I don't think I have ever told him I appreciate him.

My best friend Donny was two and I was three the summer his family moved across the street from ours. One of the first conscious memories I have is of the two of us. It was the Fourth of July. The neighborhood families had a small fireworks show in the street in front of my house. The only part of the evening I remember is when I was lying on my mom's shoulder. I remember looking over and seeing Donny lying on his mother's shoulder, looking at me and smiling.

Later, when we were in school, Donny and I would spend the night at each other's houses on the weekend. This is when we would talk. We had anything-goes, no-holds-barred conversations. We talked about what we thought about life and what we wanted to be when we grew up. Donny wanted to be a billionaire, and I wanted to be everything from a teacher to an architect. For me, it changed almost as often as my underwear.

For my sixteenth birthday, my mother wanted to get me a new car. My father said, "Joyce, let him get a job and buy his own car. He will appreciate it more." He has always been an advocate for working hard and earning the things you want. During one of our father-son talks, he told me, "Life has this peculiar way of leveling out. What I mean is, if you work hard in life, like I have, you will get a break. In my case, the break has been our financial stability and our wonderful family. If you take it easy, you will get knocked down later."

I was young, dumb and didn't listen. I rarely did my homework, and I scraped by on the tests. I didn't cheat, lie or steal, not too much anyway. I just took it easy and put forth as little effort as possible to get by.

My mother wouldn't give in on the new car, so my father finally did. Mom bought me this cool black Toyota 4x4, with an earsplitting CD player and blinding KC lights. I felt invincible. The first thing I did that day was buy a radar detector. It became my "lookout man." I never got pulled over for speeding. With my truck, I found a new freedom. With the radar detector, I acquired a new sense of rebellion.

My seventeenth birthday was the year my father's advice caught up to me. All day I had pleaded with my mom to lift my barely existing curfew for one night. Since

I knew exactly what levers to pull and buttons to push, I got my way.

That night, Donny and I went camping with a couple of friends of ours. We took my truck and John's truck over Cook Mountain and down into the Lake Abundance campground. John and Rick made a stop in Cook City, while Donny and I drove on to the campsite. We had been to the site at least a hundred times with our Boy Scout troop, and knew the forty-five-minute drive like the back of our hands.

Donny and I started setting up camp. About a half-hour after we arrived, John and Rick pulled up. They unpacked John's truck and helped us finish setting up. Then we all relaxed around the huge fire Rick built. That is when John revealed the surprise he and Rick picked up in Cook City. They had found a bum standing at the edge of town with a sign that read, "Why Lie? Need Beer." They made him an offer and he accepted. They paid him the change from what was spent out of fifteen dollars for a twelve-pack of Bud Light. He made somewhere around six bucks. I'm sure the whole thing was John's idea because he was always doing the kind of crazy stuff he could get into a lot of trouble over.

None of us had ever had more than a sip of our father's beer before, and I was kind of hesitant. My dad had lectured me on the responsibilities and dangers of drinking alcohol many times.

"Don't worry, it won't hurt ya," Rick said, after he was halfway through his first.

That has got to be the weakest argument that has ever come out of anybody's mouth, but it was enough to convince me. I thought to myself, *Three beers, what is that going to do to me? At the worst, I'll get sick and puke.*

After we had guzzled, chugged and ripped apart three cans each, Rick spouted out, "I'm not feeling anything. We need some more." It was time for a beer run.

Donny and I were voted to go, so we jumped into my truck and went tearing off towards Cook City. We were both kind of excited by this little campsite rebellion. It was the first time we had ever done anything we knew our parents wouldn't approve of—unless you count the time we snuck out of my house and got caught, but that shouldn't count, because we didn't do anything.

I was probably driving a little too fast, but I am not sure because things were a little blurry—not to the point where I don't remember anything, just to the point where things like speed and seatbelts don't seem to matter. Donny suggested we take the shortcut. It would cut at least ten minutes off the trip, so we cut across Rattlesnake Field.

It was mostly grass, the waist-high kind, perfect for lying on your back and watching the clouds roll by or a good game of hide-and-seek. The field was a whole lot steeper than the access road we had come in on. My truck would have made it on any given day, but it was night and we couldn't see very well.

The truck came to a quick stop with a loud thud. We had hit something and were hung up. I looked out my window. "I don't see anything; you got anything over on your side?" I asked Donny.

"Yeah, you hit a tree," he said. "There is a rather large tree just behind your right front wheel." It wasn't really a tree; I wasn't that drunk. It was a log that had been hidden by the tall grass.

At this point, I wasn't exactly sure what to do so I did what any young driver would have done: I floored the gas. The tires were ripping and spinning, and I was rooting for my truck. The log slipped out of place and threw my truck off balance. The truck started to roll. As I felt the truck start to fall off balance, I remember that feeling of panic you get when you know something bad is inevitable. I was almost immediately thrown from my door. Donny went through his window. I was thrown up the hill and out of the path of the truck; Donny was thrown downhill, under the truck and crushed as the truck rolled over him and on down. I remember hearing Donny yelp as the truck rolled over him.

I started to run for help, but I heard his voice pleading, "Don't leave me! Please, Drew, don't leave me!" I immediately turned back.

I slid down and crawled over to where he was. It was worse than I thought it would be. There was blood, a lot of blood. I think I even saw some bone. I wanted to run and get help, but I stayed there with him. I braced myself against the hill and set his head in my lap. He had a grass stain on his forehead and some blood-soaked dirt in the corners of his mouth. As I listened to him wheeze for air, I caressed his hair, the same haircut he had had since third grade. His broken ribs shifted with pain to the slow and inconsistent rhythm of every breath. I was crying as I held him. I felt like a first-grader who had been punched in the stomach by the school bully. An angry, sad, ashamed pit of emotions raged inside of me, like a pot of boiling oil. I wanted to scream, but I was crying too hard. I tried to apologize for doing this to him, but I was crying too hard. Then I noticed Donny's breaths were getting fewer and farther between. With one final sigh and quickening tightness of pain, they stopped.

I set his head down and started running. I didn't stop until I had reached the campsite. I am not sure why I went there first. That is just where my legs took me. Rick and John were asleep by the fire. I splashed them with water, explained what happened and started running towards Cook City. John and Rick just laid there stunned into half-soberness and scared into solemn remorse.

I made it to Cook City in about thirty minutes. I went

straight to the twenty-four-hour convenience store where Rick and John had bought the beer. I asked the clerk to call 911.

I led the police to the accident. Donny's body was still lying there limp and cold, like an old doll nobody wants, tossed into the closet. The police questioned me all night, and then there were more questions the next day. "How did this happen? What did you do then? Why did you do this instead of this?" I was sick of all the questions.

I hate that night. I wish I could forget it ever happened. I don't think I ever talked to Rick or John again. I saw them in the halls at school, but none of us made eye contact.

When Donny died, so did a part of myself. I was a junior in high school, and I nearly didn't finish that year. I could feel the other kids staring. I could hear them in the halls. I cried myself to sleep every night asking Donny to forgive me. The guilt was overwhelming. I dropped out of school my senior year. I just couldn't concentrate, and I couldn't take all the kids asking me if I was all right all the time.

It has taken me a long time, but I have progressed. I don't cry myself to sleep anymore, although sometimes I wake up, in the middle of the night, in a cold sweat crying out for Donny. My fiancée, Jennifer, has gotten used to it. At first, it scared her even more than it did me, but now she calms my nerves and sings me back to sleep. Tomorrow is our big day. I am going to marry her and begin a new chapter of my life. I only wish Donny was going to be my best man.

Garrett Drew

[EDITORS' NOTE: *This story is not entirely factual. Some aspects have been fictionalized.*]

Turn It Upside Down

I spent a little over a year working with Kris at the Creamery, an ice-cream shop in our city. He was a year younger than me, about sixteen. We didn't attend the same high school and didn't have a lot in common—we simply worked together for an entire summer and school year. Outside of work I didn't know a lot about Kris. He was close to his family, talked about his friends and his girlfriend a lot and was active in his church. But at work, I knew him well.

Kris was probably one of the most uplifting people whom I have known. He loved to joke around, often blockading one of us into the huge walk-in freezer where all the ice cream was kept. He was a tall guy with smiling brown eyes and sideburns that he grew really long. He had so much energy and was always the first to do the jobs the rest of us hated, such as cleaning out the bath-rooms or taking out the huge bags of sticky trash. I loved nights that I got to work with him. They went by fast and were fun. Plus, he was the only boy working at the Creamery, so I felt safe when I walked out the door, some-times around midnight, to go home.

I remember one night in particular. I came in at 5:00 P.M.

that night to work the closing shift with Kris and Melanie. It was a hot summer day, and I was in a terrible mood, not at all looking forward to the night ahead. Kris could tell right away I was in a bad mood and tried to cheer me up, but it was pretty much to no avail. I had decided that it was just going to be a rotten day, and there was nothing anyone could do to change that. We finished up early, took out the trash and were walking to our cars after saying goodnight. Suddenly, I heard someone chasing after me. Before I could turn around to see who it was, Kris had picked me up and successfully turned me over so that he was holding me in the air upside down. I screamed until he finally let go, and I yelled at him, asking what in the heck he was doing. His reply was that he had to get me to smile at least once that night.

"Well," I told him, "it didn't work. I didn't smile."

"Yes, you did," he said. "You just had to be upside down to see it." He was basically implicating that my frown had been turned upside down. He flashed me a smile and said goodnight, and I smiled all the way home.

After a year and a half at the Creamery, I decided I wanted to move on, so I wasn't there the night it happened. On July 15, 1999, they had just finished closing and Kris was the only one behind the store when he got into his car around 11:00 P.M. He never made it out of the parking lot.

I was eating breakfast and watching the news the following morning. I listened with absolute terror as the reporter recounted the story. "A seventeen-year-old boy was the victim of a random act of violence last night. Two fifteen-year-old boys and a seventeen-year-old boy are in custody for what was appears to have been an attempted carjacking in Old Colorado City." My heart stopped, my whole body went numb, and I knew even before his picture flashed on the screen and she said his name. "Kristopher Lohrmeyer died instantly from a single gunshot wound to the head."

Something changed for me the night Kris died. I realized that nothing in our future is certain. The only thing I am ever going to have control over is my own attitude. And the most important thing I can do is to open my heart to everyone, just as Kris did to all of us. And it is because of him that I now know how to turn my own frowns upside down.

Jessie Williams

Sorrowful Lesson

The mall was overcrowded, shoppers rushed from store
   to store;
Nobody paid attention, as she crouched there on the
   floor.
She didn't look in trouble, and she didn't seem afraid;
Apparently, she stopped to rest, she did not need my aid.

A little girl of eight or nine, and cute as she could be,
I wondered, should I stop and ask, if she needs help from
   me?
I wondered if her mother had just left her there alone,
I thought, as I walked by her, in my haste to get back
   home.

As I left the mall, I could not get her off my mind.
Did that little girl need help? Was I just acting blind?
It bothered me so much, I had to go back in the mall;
I had to get this settled in my mind once and for all.

The mall began to close, I heard some chain doors coming
   down,
But, as I looked, the little girl was nowhere to be found.

Is it my imagination, that again is running wild?
Thinking I had lost my chance to help this poor lost child.

I guess she must be fine or she would still be sitting here,
I get way too emotional at Christmastime each year.
I had to leave and get back home, where it is safe and
    warm,
The weather forecast for that night, a chilling winter storm.

Late that night it happened, as the weather station said,
Frigid cold and heavy snow while I was snug in bed.
In the morning, I awoke to winter's nasty caper,
The only place I'd go that day was out to get the paper.

Cozy in my kitchen, with my news and cup of tea,
But as I saw the front page, it just devastated me.
On the front page down below, a little headline read,
"At the local shopping mall, a little girl found dead."

It was 4 A.M. this morning when police received the call,
The caller said a little girl was dead behind the mall.
It was the chilling elements that brought her close to death,
As she lay down, she fell asleep and breathed her final
    breath.

I could not read the rest of it, as I began to weep,
While I slept safe, a little girl had frozen in her sleep.
Many years have passed me now, but it still haunts my
    dreams;
Was the little girl they found the same one I had seen?

I can't forget that little girl, no matter how I try,
But now when someone seems in need, I never pass
   them by.
The lesson I have learned from this was difficult but true,
The last chance that someone may have could very well
   be you.

James Kisner

Someone to Watch over Me

To feel the love of people whom we love is a fire that feeds our life.

Pablo Neruda

"I'm off!" eighteen-year-old Charissa Harris sang. "I'm going to find something gorgeous to wear for graduation!"

Sandy Beard smiled at her daughter. *She's got her whole future ahead of her,* Sandy thought. But that future would soon be in jeopardy—and fate would deliver the Garland, Texas, girl into the hands of an angel. . . .

The setting sun hung red in the sky as Charissa drove home. Suddenly, she felt a jolt from behind. "No!" she cried, as her car crashed into a tree—and her world went dark.

Riding up on his motorcycle, fifty-four-year-old Jack Hadlock saw a commotion. Several drivers had stopped when they saw the accident—but only Jack had taken first-aid classes for his job at Southwestern Bell. Now he thought, *Maybe this is what they were for.* He parked his bike and rushed toward the wreck.

When he got to the car, what he saw made him pale. A

girl about the age of his twin sons was pinned between the car's bucket seats, her neck pinched into her chest at a grotesque angle.

Quickly, Jack found her pulse. Then he put his ear to her mouth. She wasn't breathing. *I've got to clear her airway!* he thought. Heart pounding, he gently straightened her neck. Suddenly, the girl coughed and began breathing.

"You're going to be okay," he whispered.

Fading in and out of consciousness, Charissa saw only a glimmer of light from her rescuer's glasses. *Who are you?* she tried to say. *Are you an angel?*

Moments later, the paramedics arrived, and Jack helped them lift the girl into the ambulance.

At the hospital, doctors told Sandy that her daughter's heart had stopped twice, her skull was fractured and her pelvis was broken. Now she lay in a coma. "If it weren't for a man on the scene who cleared her airway, she would have died before she got here," they added.

Why did this happen? Sandy wept. *Why my baby?*

The day after Charissa arrived at the hospital, a man was brought in to the bed across from hers. He'd been on a motorcycle, Sandy heard nurses say, when a car had swerved in front of him, forcing him into the barrier. They'd operated on his eye and knee.

"The strange thing is," he told a nurse, "just yesterday I stopped to help a girl who'd been in a car accident. I wonder where that little girl is now. . . ."

The nurse's hand flew to her mouth. "Mr. Hadlock," she said, "there's your little girl!"

Trembling, Sandy rose to her feet. So *this* was the man who had saved her daughter's life.

"This is Jack Hadlock," the nurse said. "He's . . ."

"My hero!" Sandy cried.

Jack blushed. "I would have done the same for anybody," he said.

"But you didn't do it for anybody," she cried. "You did it for my little girl!"

Eight days after his accident, Jack was released. But he couldn't stop thinking about Charissa and called regularly to check on her.

Then one morning, Charissa awoke—she felt her mother's hand and heard her father's voice, but looking up, she made out only shadows . . . and glimmers of light. "The angel . . . ," she murmured.

"Rest," Sandy soothed. But as Charissa grew stronger, a doctor explained to her that she'd need therapy to walk.

"And my eyesight . . . ?"

A long silence. "I'm sorry," the doctor finally said. "You may see light and colors, but . . ."

As Charissa burst into tears, her mother took her in her arms. "All that matters is that you're alive!" Sandy cried. Then she told Charissa about Jack. "He's been watching over you," she said. "You're not alone."

Mom's right, Charissa thought. *I have so much to be grateful for.*

Anxiously, she awaited Jack's visit. *What will I say?* she fretted. But as Jack sat down by her bed, a familiar light danced off his gold-rimmed glasses. His gentle voice made her feel at ease—like she'd known him forever.

"Thank you for saving my life," she choked.

Squeezing her hand, his eyes welled with emotion. "Get better, okay?" he said gruffly.

Charissa struggled to do just that. *Mom was right,* she thought. *I'm not alone!* And as the months went by, Jack comforted her and cheered her progress. He beamed when she managed to brush her hair or cut her steak herself. And when Charissa took her first steps in three months, he applauded.

"You said I'd do it!" she exulted.

Soon after, Charissa went home. Jack and his wife visited often, and one day, Charissa had a favor to ask. Her high school was holding a special graduation ceremony to replace the one she'd missed. "Jack, will you come with me?"

"Wouldn't miss it," he smiled.

And as the principal announced her name, Jack guided Charissa to the stage. The audience rose to its feet.

"Everyone loves you!" Jack reminded her.

Today, Charissa attends a combined college and rehab program in Austin. Once a week her phone rings, and a voice she'll never forget asks, "How are things going, little girl?"

"Just fine, Jack," she says. *He's still watching over me,* she smiles. *My angel.*

Eva Unga
Excerpted from Woman's World. *©1998 Eva Unga.*

A House Is Not a Home

My first year of high school felt awkward. After leaving junior high at the head of my class with all the seniority the upper grade levels could afford me, it felt strange starting over as a freshman. The school was twice as big as my old school, and to make matters worse, my closest friends were sent to a different high school. I felt very isolated.

I missed my old teachers so much that I would go back and visit them. They would encourage me to get involved in school activities so that I could meet new people. They told me that in time I would adjust and probably end up loving my new school more than I had my old one. They made me promise that when that happened I would still come by and visit them from time to time. I understand the psychology in what they were saying, but I took some comfort in it nonetheless.

One Sunday afternoon not long after I had started high school, I was sitting at home at our dining-room table doing homework. It was a cold and windy fall day, and we had a fire going in our fireplace. As usual, my red tabby cat was lying on top of all my papers, purring loudly and occasionally swatting at my pen for entertainment's sake.

She was never far from me. I had rescued her when she was a kitten, and somehow she knew that I was the one responsible for giving her "the good life."

My mother kept stoking the fire to keep the house nice and warm. Suddenly, I smelled something strange, and then I noticed it . . . smoke pouring in through the seams of the ceiling. The smoke began to fill the room so quickly that we could barely see. Groping our way to the front door, we all ran out into the front yard. By the time we made our way outside, the whole roof was engulfed in flames and it was spreading quickly. I ran to the neighbors to call the fire department, while I watched my mother run back into the house.

My mother then ran out of the house carrying a small metal box full of important documents. She dropped the case on the lawn and, in a crazed state, ran back into the house. I knew what she was after. My father had died when I was young, and I was certain that she was not going to let his pictures and letters go up in flames. They were the only things that she had to remember him by. Still I screamed at her, "Mom! No!"

I was about to run in after her when I felt a large hand hold me back. It was a fireman. I hadn't even noticed that the street had already filled with fire trucks. I was trying to free myself from his grasp, yelling, "You don't understand, my mother's in there!"

He held on to me while other firefighters ran into the house. He knew that I wasn't acting very coherently and that if he were to let go, I'd run. He was right.

"It's all right, they'll get her," he said.

He wrapped a blanket around me and sat me down in our car. Soon after that, a fireman emerged from our house with my mom in tow. He quickly took her over to the truck and put an oxygen mask on her. I ran over and hugged her. All the times I ever argued with her and hated her vanished at the thought of losing her.

"She's going to be okay," said the fireman. "She just inhaled a little smoke." And then he ran back to fight the fire while my mother and I sat there dazed. I remember watching my house burn down and thinking that there was nothing I could do about it.

Five hours later, the fire was finally out. Our house was almost completely burned down. But then it struck me . . . I hadn't seen my cat. Where was my cat? Much to my horror, I realized that she was nowhere to be found. Then all at once it hit me—the new school, the fire, my cat—I broke down in tears and cried and cried. I was suffering loss, big time.

The firemen wouldn't let us go back into the house that night. It was still too dangerous. Dead or alive, I couldn't imagine leaving without knowing about my cat. Regardless, I had to go. We piled into the car with just the clothes on our backs and a few of the firemen's blankets, and made our way to my grandparents' house to spend the night.

The next day, Monday, I went to school. When the fire broke out, I was still wearing the dress I had worn to church that morning, but I had no shoes! I had kicked them off when I was doing my homework. They became yet another casualty of the fire. So I had to borrow some tennis shoes from my aunt. Why couldn't I just stay home from school? My mother wouldn't hear of it, but I was totally embarrassed by everything. The clothes I was wearing looked weird, I had no books or homework, and my backpack was gone. I had my life in that backpack! The more I tried to fit in, the worse it got. Was I destined to be an outcast and a geek all my life? That's what it felt like. I didn't want to grow up, change or have to handle life if it was going to be this way. I just wanted to curl up and die.

I walked around school like a zombie. Everything felt surreal, and I wasn't sure what was going to happen. All the security I had known, from my old school, my friends, my house and my cat had all been ripped away.

When I walked through what used to be my house after school that day, I was shocked to see how much damage there was—whatever hadn't burned was destroyed by the water and chemicals they had used to put out the fire. The only material things not destroyed were the photo albums, documents and some other personal items that my mother had managed to heroically rescue. But my cat was gone and my heart ached for her.

There was no time to grieve. My mother rushed me out of the house. We would have to find a place to live, and I would have to go buy some clothes for school. We had to borrow money from my grandparents because there were no credit cards, cash or even any identification to be able to withdraw money from the bank. Everything had gone up in smoke.

That week the rubble that used to be our house was being cleared off the lot. Even though we had rented an apartment nearby, I would go over to watch them clear away debris, hoping that my cat was somewhere to be found. She was gone. I kept thinking about her as that vulnerable little kitten. In the early morning when I would disturb her and get out of bed, she would tag along after me, climb up my robe and crawl into my pocket to fall asleep. I was missing her terribly.

It always seems that bad news spreads quickly, and in my case it was no different. Everyone in high school, including the teachers, was aware of my plight. I was embarrassed as if somehow I were responsible. What a way to start off at a new school! This was not the kind of attention I was looking for.

The next day at school, people were acting even more

strange than usual. I was getting ready for gym class at my locker. People were milling around me, asking me to hurry up. I thought it strange, but in light of the past few weeks, nothing would surprise me. It almost seemed that they were trying to shove me into the gym—then I saw why. There was a big table set up with all kinds of "stuff" on it, just for me. They had taken up a collection and bought me school supplies, notebooks, all kinds of different clothes—jeans, tops, sweatsuits. It was like Christmas. I was overcome by emotion. People who had never spoken to me before were coming up to me to introduce themselves. I got all kinds of invitations to their houses. Their genuine outpouring of concern really touched me. In that instant, I finally breathed a sigh of relief and thought for the first time that things were going to be okay. I made friends that day.

A month later, I was at my house watching them rebuild it. But this time it was different—I wasn't alone. I was with two of my new friends from school. It took a fire for me to stop focusing on my feelings of insecurity and open up to all the wonderful people around me. Now I was sitting there watching my house being rebuilt when I realized my life was doing the same thing.

While we sat there on the curb, planning my new bedroom, I heard someone walk up to me from behind and say, "Does this belong to you?" When I turned around to see who it was, I couldn't believe my eyes. A woman was standing there holding my cat! I leapt up and grabbed her out of the woman's arms. I held her close to me and cried into that beautiful orange fur. She purred happily. My friends were hugging me, hugging the cat and jumping around.

Apparently, my cat had been so freaked by the fire that she ran over a mile away. Her collar had our phone number on it, but our phones had been destroyed and disconnected. This wonderful woman took her in and worked hard to find out whose cat it was. Somehow, she knew this cat was loved and sorely missed.

As I sat there with my friends and my cat curled up in my lap, all the overwhelming feelings of loss and tragedy seemed to diminish. I felt gratitude for my life, my new friends, the kindness of a stranger and the loud purr of my beloved cat. My cat was back and so was I.

Zan Gaudioso

Building Bridges

*When written in Chinese, the word "crisis"
is composed of two characters. One represents
danger and the other represents opportunity.*
John F. Kennedy

The day started out just like most other Tuesdays. I'm in a show choir called "Unclaimed Freight" at Columbine High School; we rehearse in the mornings before school. I got to school at 6:50 A.M., saw friends and said hello on my way in.

We went through the day normally until fifth period, which for me is Concert Choir. We were starting our warm-ups when a student in the choir came into the room and said there was a guy downstairs with a gun.

This student was known to be a jokester. But he had a pretty serious look on his face, and I saw kids running by when I looked out the window. The choir director told us all to chill out. He didn't want us to panic—there were 114 choir members. He was walking toward the door near the stairwell when two girls opened the door, and we heard two shotgun bursts. Half the choir hit the ground.

My first instinct was to run. I went out the opposite door that the two girls had come in, into a corridor that leads to the auditorium.

I saw a stampede of people running down the hallways. I heard screams. I decided I wasn't going to try and join the mob, so I ran into the auditorium. I stood at the back of the auditorium, wondering what refuge kids were finding behind plastic chairs. Then I heard the semi-automatic fire. At some point, somebody pulled the fire alarm down, so lots of kids in the east end of the school got out without a notion of what was happening.

I headed out the north door. I saw the fire doors at the north hallway—the main hallway—were closed, so I turned and ran for the front door. As I got closer I saw there were already bullet holes in the glass.

Seeing the bullet holes made me run even faster. I reached the front door and pushed it open. The bullets had weakened the glass, and shattered glass came showering out of the door all over me. I just kept running. I didn't even notice the blood all over me until much later. I later went to the hospital for stitches.

About fifteen kids followed me and got out the front door. I learned later that we barely made it out. Seconds later one of the shooters, Dylan, came into the main office and started spraying bullets.

I saw a friend, and we ran to her house. From her house we could see the front of the school. We watched the police, the firefighters, the paramedics, the SWAT teams from Denver and other areas, and the National Guard as they showed up. State patrolmen and sheriffs pulled up and got out of their cars with their guns. They stood behind trees and told kids to run.

The next few hours seemed to last forever. At first I thought a kid was in the school with a gun and that he may have shot a few kids, maybe injuring somebody, but

I hoped he hadn't caused much harm. As I watched the different teams of police show up and heard on the radio there were two gunmen, possibly three, I started to realize how big this really was.

A group of police drove a fire truck close to the building. They jumped out and ran inside. I found out later that lots of those guys weren't trained to be in the positions they were leading. They went in and risked their lives—they didn't even think about it, they just did it to save lives.

It scared me to death when later reports on the radio said that twenty-five kids were killed. I hadn't seen my best friend, Dustin, come out. I prayed he was all right. I didn't find out he was safe until much later. He had hidden in a bathroom in the kitchen and was evacuated with other kids who hid nearby.

It was a living nightmare. It was a bad day multiplied by the biggest number you can think of. The day seemed to go on for years—hours were days; everything was wrong.

The night of the shootings a lot of us went to a service at St. Francis Cabrini Catholic Church. It was really emotional for all of us because we knew our friends who should be there were gone forever. I couldn't even imagine that friends of mine—Cory, Rachel, Isaiah, Cassie—wouldn't be back at school. How could their lives end so violently? How could Eric's and Dylan's minds get so messed up?

For the longest time I didn't know what day it was, the day of the week, the date—it all just kind of ran together. I didn't eat anything for three days—I had a sick feeling inside. I kept crying. Every emotion ran through my head. I was sad, mad, confused, helpless and lost.

I spent a little time with my parents. I hugged them a lot and told them I loved them. But I needed to be with my friends, the people who had experienced this with me. People can say, "I know how you feel," but it's not true if you weren't there.

There were lots of counselors around. Media were everywhere. People showed up trying to get kids to come to their church. What touched me most were the people who came just to be available for us. They were there if we needed someone to talk to. They didn't force themselves on us at all.

We had lots of get-togethers on private property where the media couldn't get to us. We would just go and be together—the first week that's all we did. We didn't have to speak to each other—it was enough to share the silence with each other.

The first place that the faculty and students got back together was at a community church. The student body was sitting together waiting for the faculty. The choir decided we wanted to sing because before the tragedy we were practicing some very spiritual, very touching songs that had a high level of difficulty. We got up together and went up on the stage. The faculty still hadn't made it in, so I was "volunteered" to conduct.

We started singing "Ave Maria." I had chills and the hair on the back of my neck was standing up. We hadn't warmed up and the song has some very high notes for females. But they were just ripping them out—the sound was unbelievable.

As we sang "The Lord's Prayer," the faculty came into the sanctuary and started singing with us. Then the whole student body joined in. Here we were, together for the first time after a living nightmare, singing "The Lord's Prayer." As I conducted and heard the most beautiful sounds ever, I felt the love in that room. At that moment I knew we would be all right.

Charlie Simmons

$\overline{6}$
ABUSE

*The untold truths
Of wisdom lie
Solely in the beating
Of the heart of an
Ill-treated child
Whose wounds will
Heal and heart will seal, but
Memory will never die.*

Savannah Marion

Losing Myself

Remember that the road to healing winds through pain, anguish, sickness and many tears.

Amanda Ford

I was like any other average ninth-grader. I was active in sports, had my circle of friends and got good grades. Until the day I was introduced to *him*. There was something in his eyes that attracted me. Somehow I thought that he needed me, just as much as I needed to be loved. After flirting for months, we finally became a couple. We were together every single moment from that day on. Slowly, day-by-day, my family and friends saw me changing. I was in love.

After about two months, however, he started to try to control me and even raise his voice to me. I told myself it was okay because he really did love me. Or so I thought. The first time he ever hurt me, we were skiing with friends and had lost each other on the slopes. When he found me, he said it was my fault. He proceeded to push me and call me nasty names, while people just stared at us. I ran into the bathroom with my best friend and cried my eyes out. The next thing I knew, he was in the bathroom hugging me, overflowing with kisses and saying how sorry he was. So I forgave him and put that day in the back of my mind.

Things did not go back to normal, though. He became possessive and jealous. He made rules stating I could no longer wear my hair down, wear shorts in the summertime or have any sign of another boy in my room. If another boy even glanced at me in school, he would yell at me. My grades dropped, I lost my ambition for sports, I started losing my friends, and my family became my worst enemy. I didn't want to listen to what they thought about my relationship or how much I had changed. I cried every single night because of the way I was beginning to feel about myself. He would yell at me or blame me for everything. A couple of times, I tried hurting myself because I felt I wasn't good enough for him and that there wasn't any other reason to be alive. I tried to justify his actions by believing they showed how much he cared about me. As a ninth-grader, it made me feel important to be in love and have a steady boyfriend.

My parents tried taking me to counseling and talked to all my teachers about my relationship. I started skipping school. The violence escalated. He tried to choke me on several occasions, and once he tried to break my arm because his brother looked at me in my swimsuit. I felt hopeless and depressed. He had so much control over my mind that I could not accept anyone else's opinion of him. I told myself that they just didn't understand how much he loved me. He only did what he did because he cared.

The physical abuse continued to get worse. He forced me to do sexual things with him. He also hit, choked and pushed me around. He tried drowning me once. Fortunately, I fell on some rocks before he had the chance to get me under the water. He also cut *my* wrists because *his* life was in the dumps. This went on for nine months.

Finally, my parents took me on a trip for a week. While I was on vacation, he cheated on me, and I built up enough courage to break up with him. One night I lay in bed and thought of everything he had done to me. It was clear what I had to do.

I spent the last two weeks of summer break trying to get my old friends back before returning to school. When I went back to school, he was in my gym class. I was nice to him because I still feared him. When I got up the nerve to tell him that it was over for good, he went psycho, pushed me to the ground and kicked me several times. Nobody came to help me. The next day, I discovered an eight-inch bruise on my leg.

It took me three days to show the bruise to my parents. To my surprise, after everything I had put them through, they helped me. They took me straight to the police station to file charges. I wanted to just let it go, but I was also determined that this should not and would not happen to anyone he "loved" in the future. At home, I continued to receive threatening phone calls from him saying that he was going to kill me. He told my parents that he would hurt me if he got the chance.

My court experience took over a year and was horribly painful. I found out that he had a violent past and that it wasn't the first time that he had abuse charges brought against him. I was never notified about the final court hearing, so it happened without me and, to my knowledge, nothing severe happened to him. The justice system let me down, but I chose to go on with my life.

I am very lucky to be where I am today. I am nineteen years old, and I have grown and healed a lot. It took me over three years to tell my parents everything that he did to me. My parents and I are very close now. The healing process may continue for years to come, but I deal with my pain by sharing my story with other young teens, hoping to help prevent this from happening to anybody else. I do not wake up every day hating him. I feel bad for him, and I know he needs help, wherever he is. I have learned instead to focus on living my life to the fullest and cherishing the people I truly love.

Jenny Deyo

Help Me

I hear your loud screaming
As I scramble down under my duvet.
Your angry, hateful obscenities are getting louder.
I try to cover my ears.

Your footsteps stop outside my door.
Suddenly, the door opens up.
I shake in terror in the dark
As you shove me violently down to the floor.

You start to yell at me,
Verbally abuse me.
Learning a long time ago not to talk back
I only listen, intimidated and terrified.

A sudden blow on my cheek interrupts my silent prayers
Another blow on my back
My tiny legs, my head, my neck.
Stop bashing me up!

I cry out, hurt and traumatized
In agony I howl.

The only thing I get in return is
Another strike for being too loud.

Help me, Mama.
Don't lie about my injuries.
Help me, Mama.
Take me away from this nightmare I'm in.

Mama is nowhere in sight
While her little girl is being slammed
Against the wall.
Where are you? Why aren't you helping me?

All I can hear is the sound of my own bone breaking.
I can taste blood in my mouth.
Daddy yanks me by my hair,
Dragging me down the stairs.

Help me, Mama,
Help me.

Under the light I can see my scars
My legs twisted
My black-and-blue arms
My ears ringing.

I look around, whimpering
As Daddy cries out, "Shut up,
You bad girl! Neighbors will hear!"
I cut short, scared to death.

As I lie here on the cold floor
Who is to rescue me?
No more Mama's comforting hugs.
Oh, Mama, has he killed you already?

The thought of living without you terrifies me.
I start to cry loudly.
Knowing I have got to stop
I bite my lips.

Too late,
Daddy comes back.
He is hurting me again,
He twists my little arm behind my back.

Mama.
Help me!

I slowly drift away
Everything seems so blurry and distant.
Maybe I am dying,
Maybe that will be better.

I wake up the next morning,
The sun shining on my face.
Doctor's face clouds with concern.
I nod as he asks if I'm okay.

But I'm not okay,
Daddy's there!
Instead of the angry face I saw last night,
He puts on a mask of happiness.

"I'm so glad you're awake!
Let's celebrate!"
The doctor pats me on the head
Walking away.

I try to call him, to ask him to come back
Desperately I try to say,

"Don't leave me alone with him."
But my lips are too sore and I cannot speak.

A short while later I am better . . .
Healthy enough to go home.
I plead the nurse with my begging eyes,
I am too scared to tell them what's going on.

I have no choice but to follow Daddy,
As he grabs my hand tightly, leading me away.
No, I want to stay!
Leave me alone!

I turn back, but nobody notices me,
My hurt and battered tiny body.
Returning back to where I was harmed
Back I go.

Help me, Mama.

Hawon Lee

Nightmares

A new dawn emerges
with its layers and layers
of pinks and yellows.

As the sun swallows up my
bedroom with satin rays of sunlight
I wake . . .
sweaty and screaming
foolish and alone.
And so I continue on . . .
living each day
feeling his sweat . . .
and hearing his heavy breath
in the back of my mind
every time silence creeps up on me.

Later I watch the sun, so naive
crawl under the horizon . . .
and I get restless as dusk approaches
for I know that when my head hits
that pillow . . .
the fight begins . . .

and he always wins
in the end.

Carrying my innocence off
holding it up to the moonlight
kicking and screaming until
. . . finally . . .
he leaves it and walks away
while it is raw and naked
shaking on the cold ground.

. . . until a new dawn emerges
with its layers and layers
of pinks and yellows . . .
Good morning.

Kara MacDonald

[EDITORS' NOTE: *If you or someone you know is or has been abused or molested, the following resources will prove helpful for both information and support. If you or someone you know is hurt or in danger, try to get help as soon as possible from a friend or parent.* **Call 911 or the police** *as soon as you safely can.*]

Child Help USA: 800-422-4453
Twenty-four-hour child abuse hotline. Telephone counseling and referrals.

Covenant House Nineline: 800-999-9999
Crisis line for youth and parents. Referrals throughout the U.S.

National Child Abuse Hotline: 800-422-4453
Twenty-four hours. Crisis intervention, information and referrals.

RAINN (Rape Abuse & Incest National Network):
www.rainn.org

The National Sexual Assault Hotline: 800-656-HOPE
Free. Confidential. 24/7.

Victims of Crime Resource Center: 800-842-8467
Monday Through Friday; 8:00 A.M.–6:00 P.M.

Youth Crisis Hotline: 800-448-4663

7

ON COURAGE

One of the most courageous things you can do is identify yourself, know who you are, what you believe in and where you want to go.

Shiela Murray Bethel

The Birth of an Adult

The ultimate measure of a man is not where he stands in moments of comfort and convenience, but where he stands at times of challenge and controversy.

Martin Luther King, Jr.

The doctors started to rush into the room. The delivery was going smoothly, but to me it felt like hysteria. The walls were a chalky gray like the wall of a jail cell. It wasn't the best setting for Jamie's labor, but it would have to do. Jamie was only a seventeen-year-old junior in high school. And now she was giving birth. She lay back in pain. Her only movements consisted of shaking her head from side to side, in an effort to escape the pain.

I took Jamie's hand, comforting her and trying to soothe her agony. Her eyes opened, and she looked at me. Our eyes met, and suddenly I felt every emotion I have ever known. I always knew Jamie would challenge me to better myself; however, I didn't think it would entail being her sidekick during her pregnancy.

All this began on the afternoon of New Year's Eve, 1997.

I sat in Jamie's basement awaiting the urgent news she had to tell me. She collapsed onto the couch and told me how she had broken up with her boyfriend, Eric, who had left the country to study abroad. This came as something of a relief, although I did my best not to show it. I didn't think Eric, or any other guy she had dated, was good enough for her. Okay, I'll admit it, I was—how should I put it—a little jealous. But I'd convinced myself we were better off as friends, anyway. And now she needed one.

Then the real news came: She was six weeks pregnant. Tears rolled down her face as she told me. I sat in shock and disbelief. The words were not registering in my head. She reached out and gave me a hug, which must have lasted only a few seconds but seemed like hours. My arms were still at my sides. We talked for a little while, and then I left her house and drove around in my car. I was in shock. I was upset about her lack of birth control because this whole ordeal could have been prevented. I was too young to deal with her pregnancy. Being a seventeen-year-old and a junior in high school was confusing enough without dealing with my own real-life afterschool special.

That evening I arrived at a party to drink my worries away. The air was filled with smoke and the partygoers reeked of alcohol. I could not take the atmosphere for long, so I left. I went to Jamie's house and stood on her front porch staring at the front door. *What should I do?* I asked myself. My foot started to turn from the door, but my hand reached out and pushed the doorbell. I wanted to run and go back to the party. I wanted to have fun this New Year's Eve. Suddenly, the door opened and Jamie stood in the doorway with her head down. "You can't spend New Year's Eve by yourself," I blurted out. She smiled, and we hugged in the doorway. This symbolized the beginning of the new journey that lay ahead for us. That night, we sat and laughed like usual while watching

Dick Clark ring in the New Year. After that night, my life would change. I wouldn't be a crazy teenager anymore. I would become a young adult.

Weeks passed, and Jamie told her parents about the pregnancy. She and her parents made the decision to go through with the pregnancy, but to give the baby up for adoption. My parents talked with her parents and offered their support, almost like they were discussing our marriage; Jamie and I were growing and maturing together.

During her first trimester, I found myself at Jamie's house every day after school giving her a foot massage while she relaxed and watched her soap opera. She wasn't able to walk very much. I made snacks for her and enough food runs to Taco Bell to last us both a lifetime. My friends were not considerate about what I was going through. While I was busy helping a friend, they were busy making fun of me. They would call Jamie's house wondering what I was doing. They already knew, but they just wanted to poke fun. At school, the jokes surfaced like, "Gonna be a good daddy?" and "What are you doing this weekend . . . Lamaze class?" I shrugged them off and ignored them. I went on with my daily chores and focused on Jamie. I tried to make her life as easy as possible.

Later, one Saturday afternoon as I was catching up on sleep, Jamie called.

"Did you want to do something today?" she asked.

"What did you have in mind?" I replied.

"I want you to help me choose the baby's family," she said.

My ears turned hot, and I felt uneasy. But I told her I would pick her up. As I drove to her house, I thought about how much I had changed. I was more responsible, but I still considered myself a child. I felt I had no business choosing a path for an unborn baby. I groaned and doubted myself. I arrived at her house and helped her into the car.

As we were driving to the adoption agency, Jamie pointed out to me, "You're not speeding."

It occurred to me that I was no longer a crazy driver, thinking about how quickly I could get from one place to the other. I was now responsible for making sure we got there safely.

"I'm driving for three people now," I told her.

We arrived at the agency and were seated in a conference room. Fifty manila folders lay on the table, each containing a couple. One of these folders would be the lucky one. One of these couples would be the parents of Jamie's baby. The counselor and Jamie and I went through each folder discussing their spiritual, psychological, financial, genealogical and emotional backgrounds. I began browsing through one folder, which read "Jennifer and Ben." The folder was more like a booklet chronicling their life with pictures of where they'd been, who they are and who they wanted to become. Their explanation of why they wanted a baby caught my attention. This couple intrigued me. We kept narrowing down the couples, until we were down to two couples: Jennifer and Ben and Jamie's pick. We discussed both couples, finally agreeing on Jennifer and Ben.

As we were getting ready to leave, I took a picture of Jennifer and Ben out of the folder and slipped it into my jacket pocket without Jamie noticing. I wanted to have a record of them before their life was to be changed forever. I put on my jacket, and we left the agency.

It was a miserably cold spring day. After helping Jamie into the car, I walked around the car and a warm breeze struck me. I stood by the trunk of my car feeling the summer draft. I couldn't understand it. It was a cold day, but the wind was warmer than an August breeze. It felt like a sign, an anonymous thank you. We drove away and I thought about the decision we made. I thought about the families we didn't pick. How much longer would it take for them to receive the gift of a child?

A few weeks later we met Jennifer and Ben for the first time. They impressed me. They were a close couple, and I knew they would apply the love they had for each other to their child. Jamie told them that I urged her to pick them, which made this meeting even more overwhelming for me. I tried not to show it, though, as we bonded almost immediately. They urged Jamie to take a childbirth class so she would be ready for all of the upcoming events. She needed a partner for the class, so I agreed. She signed up for a class, and every Tuesday night Jamie and I attended together.

The first class was awkward. I had never felt so out of place in my entire life. Jamie and I sat down together, trying to ignore the seven married couples staring at us. We were too young and too ignorant to be going through a pregnancy and a birthing class. Nevertheless, Jamie had to do it, and I would not let her be alone. After time, we all began to bond and develop a tremendous amount of respect for each other. Everyone realized what a struggle it was for us to get this far.

During the "Mom Time," the dads and I sat outside talking about the babies' futures. The dads talked about pee-wee football, mutual funds and insurance. I talked about Shakespeare and Geometry. I was out of place, for sure, but I realized there is more to giving birth than nine months and a doctor. So much freedom was sacrificed, replaced with a huge amount of responsibility. The dads respected me and praised me for my humanity towards a friend, not to mention my maturity. I still just couldn't believe I was sitting around talking about babies. I wanted to be innocent again. I wanted to drive my car fast and go to parties, but more important responsibilities called me. I was maturing.

I was getting ready for school one morning when Jamie called me from the hospital. "Um, do you want to get over here?" she asked.

"It's only another sonogram. Besides, I can't miss class," I said.

"Well, I think you might want to get over here, 'cause I'm having the baby!" she shouted.

I ran out of the house and darted to the hospital. At the hospital, the nurse handed me scrubs and I entered her room. She lay there as I sat next to her.

"Well this is it," she said. "Nine months, and it's finally here." She grimaced with pain and moved her head back and forth. Doctors were in and out of her room every two seconds with medication. She was about to give birth. After a few hours of getting Jamie settled, she was fully dilated.

"Okay, here we go. When I say 'push,' you push," the doctor said.

She acknowledged him while grabbing my hands and nodding her head quickly several times. Jamie gave three pushes of strength and, with one final push, she breathed life into a new baby. The doctors cut the umbilical cord and cleaned the baby off. I sat in awe. Every possible human emotion struck me like a freight train.

"It's a boy," they exclaimed.

I smiled, and tears of joy ran down my cheek. No more fear, no more chores, just pure happiness. The baby was handed to Jamie, and she spent the first moments of the baby's life holding him in her arms. She looked up at me, and I looked at her.

"You did it, kiddo," I whispered in her ear.

The doctors left with the baby to run tests and weigh him. Jennifer and Ben came in with the birth certificate. "What's his name?" Ben asked. Jamie motioned for him to come closer, and she whispered in his ear. Ben smiled and went into a different room. I walked outside to get a drink.

I came back in a few minutes and saw the completed birth certificate. It read Blake Jonathan.

I smiled and cried. The doctors brought Blake back in. They passed Blake to me, and I held new life in my hands. I thought about the dads in birth class. Then I thought about Blake's future. His first steps, peewee football games, the first day of school and his first broken heart. All the dads' talk finally caught up with me. Jennifer and Ben looked at me and smiled. Tears rolled down their cheeks. I gave Blake to Ben and received a gracious hug from Jennifer. They were his parents now. They were his keepers. Jamie still lay there, crying but filled with delight. I went over to her and gave her a big hug.

"Everything okay?" she asked.

"Fine. Absolutely fine," I whispered, and kissed her softly on her forehead. I would never be the same.

Jonathan Krasnoff

Unstoppable

When I was fourteen, my life was pretty normal. I chilled with friends, worked to keep my grades up and played hockey. Everyone thought I was a shoo-in to be the goalie on the junior-varsity team when I started school in the fall. In fact, I'd attended goalie camp in Canada right before leaving for summer camp in late July.

It was my third summer at Camp Becket. We were about halfway through the session, and "Dad's Weekend" was about to start. I was psyched. My dad works a lot in Manhattan, and at home I was always on the ice—my dream was to play in the NHL one day—or hanging with my friends, so this weekend was one thing we always looked forward to.

On August 5, the day before my dad was supposed to drive up, I started feeling really weird. At dinner I didn't have much of an appetite, and I was totally freezing. I dug through the lost-and-found for a sweatshirt, then lay down on the Ping-Pong table until the rest of my cabin was done eating. I felt really achy and tired, as if I had a bad case of the flu. My legs felt like they were made of ice, and I couldn't stop shaking.

When I checked myself into the infirmary, the camp doctor told me I had a 102-degree fever. I puked my guts up all night. The next morning, I was so weak I could barely get out of bed. When I did finally make it to the bathroom, I passed out for a few seconds and hit my head on the sink. When I came to, I couldn't stop throwing up. As I was getting back into bed, the counselor on duty noticed two huge purple splotches on my stomach. She radioed the doctor, and two minutes later they'd started an I.V. of antibiotics and called 911. By the time the ambulance arrived, there were splotches all over my body and my skin was turning blue.

The trip to the hospital is a blur. All I could focus on was how cold I was. I had no idea that I was close to dying, or that halfway through the thirty-minute trip to the hospital, the ambulance had to pull over and wait for another ambulance that had life-support equipment.

I'd contracted meningococcemia, a type of rare bacterial infection called meningococcal meningitis that's usually fatal in the first thirty-six hours after you catch it. Even if it doesn't kill you, you've still got a huge chance of going deaf, having your organs shut down or being permanently brain damaged.

Meningococcemia can be spread through saliva, so I might have contracted it from sharing a water bottle on a hike two days before. People can be a carrier of the disease without getting sick. It's so rare that not every hospital has the equipment to treat it—including the one I was first taken to. The doctors in the ER put me in a drug-induced coma to help fight the infection and because my pain was so intense. Then they arranged for me to be airlifted to another hospital. By the time we got to the pediatric intensive care unit at the Baystate Medical Center in Springfield, I had no pulse.

Since my organs had stopped working, I was hooked up to all kinds of machines, including a ventilator that breathed for me. As a doctor explained to me later, the infection was burning me from the inside out. My parents, Gary and Nancy, my little sister, Olivia, and all my friends were constantly by my side, but I didn't know it.

I also didn't know that after two weeks in Springfield I was taken by ambulance to the burn unit at New York-Presbyterian Hospital in New York City. The infection had caused my blood to clot too much, and my veins were collapsing. Although my inner organs were getting better, gangrene was turning my hands and feet black. The doctors told my parents that unless my arms and legs were amputated, I would die.

During twelve operations over the next two months, while I was still unconscious, doctors removed layers of dead skin. By the time they'd gotten rid of all the gangrene, my knees, lower legs, lower arms and hands were gone. Skin was removed from my back and surgically grafted over where my arms and legs now ended.

In October, my condition was stable enough that the doctors decided to bring me out of my coma. I saw that my forearms and lower legs were gone before my parents told me. I was just so drugged up that I didn't care. Gradually, as I came out of sedation, my parents explained what had happened and showed me pictures of what the gangrene looked like. It was pretty intense—the skin on my legs was literally turning to ash. I felt lucky that I was still alive.

People who don't know me might think it's weird that I didn't fall into a huge depression or get pissed off about what happened. But sitting around thinking "Why me?" is just not my style. For one thing, I'm not into worrying about what other people think of me. (If I did, I probably wouldn't have been playing the bagpipes since I was five.) Playing hockey, you have to learn to deal with your injuries and get back into the game as soon as you can. I felt the same way when I knew my arms and legs were gone. "Okay," I thought, "I'll just get new ones."

My old hockey coach says I'm the only person he knows who could deal with this so well. Still, getting better was tough. I hated being poked and prodded and having tubes pulled out and stuck into me all the time. Sometimes I'd have "phantom pain": It felt as if my feet were still there and they *hurt*. But the worst part was definitely the "tank," a steel bathtub where burn patients go to have their wounds washed out. The nurses would peel off the bandages from my legs, arms and back and clean my wounds to help them heal faster. They said I was the loudest yeller they had.

Later that month, I was transferred—again—to Burke Rehabilitation Center in White Plains so I could build my strength back up and learn to get around. It was frustrating; for three hours a day I had to do sit-ups and push-ups and practice moving in and out of my wheelchair. Once I was fitted with prosthetic arms and legs, I had to learn to balance and stand and bend over and pick things up.

Now I'm grateful for all the exercises because I'm back to being really athletic, but at the time, I hated it. Every part of me was screaming in pain. Learning to walk was the toughest. I could bend the knees of my prosthetic legs, but they're not as flexible as real knees. Without feet, I couldn't feel the floor. It felt like I was levitating. My new hands were battery-activated, but every once in a while they'd freeze up.

When I got frustrated, I'd just stay by myself for a while until the feeling passed. But what helped me most was hanging out again with my friends. My parents got permission for them to spend the night with me in the hospital. We'd get takeout and watch movies. I knew my friends were relieved that I was alive and still *me*. I never tried to hide my scars from them. When I started joking about what happened and they saw I was okay with it, so were they.

On March 29, 2000, I was finally able to come home. My parents had moved my bedroom downstairs and had ramps built over stairs so I could get around easier. My medical costs were outrageous, but friends of our family held benefits to raise money for my bills and a wheelchair-accessible van. My dad's a show-business publicist, and a lot of his clients, including Christian Slater and Scott Wolf, pitched in to help. That was cool, but I don't want to be seen as "Nick the Angel" because of what happened. I'm still the same guy I was before I lost my legs and arms. I work out at the gym twice a week, I listen to Limp Bizkit and Korn, and I think Jessica Alba is totally hot.

I want to get back to my regular life, but it's tough when people don't treat me like a regular person. When I went back to my high school this fall, some kids weren't sure how to act around me. If some guys were making plans to see a violent movie, they wouldn't ask me to go. Girls would say *"Awww!"* and baby me—not think of me as someone to date. (Luckily, that's changing.) I'm also more independent than people think. I can write, eat with a fork, open doors, type on my laptop and even punch my friends. If little kids stare and ask questions, I just say something goofy like, "I misplaced my hands."

Joking around is how I deal with things. And yeah, I do have times when I get frustrated or discouraged. But I've always loved a challenge, and this is the ultimate one. I don't want anyone to feel sorry for me or think I'm helpless—I've just had to change some of my goals, that's all. The way I see it, nothing's impossible. I want to get into wheelchair racing and compete in the Paralympics. I'm learning how to drive, and this summer I want to travel abroad, maybe to New Zealand or Sweden. So I can't button a shirt yet—but hey, all in good time.

Nick Springer
As told to Stephanie Booth

The Long Journey Home

Conflict builds character. Crisis defines it.

Steven V. Thulon

I was like any other twelve-year-old. Girls had cooties. Nintendo and bike riding ruled my life. I had homework that I didn't always do. I won a few ribbons at track and field. I tried to stay up past my bedtime almost every night. I played baseball. I had a continuous craving for pizza. There was one thing that was different, though. I was really tired. I would come home and go to sleep at 4:30, get up and eat, and then go back to sleep until the next morning. My mom started thinking something might be wrong so she took me to our family doctor. He sent us for some blood work. We waited a week or so for the results. When the doctor's office called back, they wanted to do more tests. To this day, I don't know what they actually told my mom, but I just went to the hospital and they did their tests. After some more blood work, they came back and said they needed to do some other tests. One of them was a bone-marrow test. They took a big needle and stuck it into my lower back. I was out cold for the entire thing.

I honestly don't remember how people were acting around me during this time. I don't remember my mom or dad being upset or anything. I just thought they were normal tests they did for tired kids. The same night as the bone-marrow tests, I was admitted to the hospital. The next morning, the oncologist spoke to my mom and dad and told them that I had acute lymphoblastic leukemia.

I don't remember much of that morning—maybe it's better that way. The doctor and my mom and dad all came into the room, and the doctor explained to me that I had cancer. I just sat there and listened. I listened very closely. I didn't understand much until the doctor explained to me that I was going to lose all my hair. She said she was going to send a team of people to my school to tell all my classmates and my teachers that there was a student who had cancer. They said they would tell everyone that I wouldn't be feeling well and what they could do to help. They would tell them to treat me normally, she said, as if I wasn't sick. I was glad to hear about that because I was really scared about going to school with no hair. I didn't know what people would say or think. Looking back, I'm glad they did that.

I didn't really know what hit me. The next day I was getting lumbar punctures and massive doses of radiation. I had a full-blown transfusion. I received all this medicine and treatment in order to put me into automatic remission so they could begin chemotherapy. The first three weeks were brutal. The days I had treatment I'd come home and be so sick that I couldn't sleep. I'd be throwing up and couldn't eat anything. When I would eventually pass out from exhaustion, I would wake up in the morning and my pillow would be full of hair. That's when it started to hit me. I was really sick. When I would take a bath, I'd see chunks of my hair floating down the drain.

My mom took me to the barber to get my head shaved so it wouldn't look so bad. My older brother Matthew came along for support. After the barber had shaved my head, I looked in the mirror and suddenly got really sad. In an instant, my brother jumped into the barber's chair beside me and instructed the barber to shave his hair the exact same way. He didn't want me to feel all alone. It sounds silly but, by him shaving his head, it showed me that he loved me and he would do anything to make me feel better. That meant a lot to me.

My mom took me to the hospital every other day for the first three weeks. She took care of me because my dad had to work. She was always there for me. When my dad got home from work, he'd sort of take over and help out. Through all the chemo, I made a little friend named Brad Rowe. We went through everything together. We laughed. We cried. We played Nintendo. That made things a little easier for me.

The Sunshine Foundation came to us and offered me and my family a wish. They said they'd give us whatever I wanted. They said they didn't care what it was, just as long as it made me happy. I wanted nothing more than to meet Patrick Roy of the Montreal Canadiens. They set up this huge dinner and game and two-day trip. I was even going to sit in the team box during the game. Well, I wasn't too lucky there, either. The NHL strike took place and along with the players, my wish walked, too! The people from the Sunshine Foundation felt horrible. We ended up going to Disneyland instead. It was great!

The summer following my first batches of chemo, I went to a baseball camp because I was feeling better. I quickly realized I hadn't grown as much as the other kids. I couldn't run for as long as they could. I couldn't go all day like them. Finally, exhausted, I went to the coach to tell him I was sick and I just started crying. I thought he wouldn't, or couldn't, understand. It was brutal. I was embarrassed and frustrated because I couldn't do as much as the other kids. Through tears I told him I had cancer and that I wasn't able to go crazy all day long like the other kids. He said the most amazing thing to me. It has stuck with me ever since. He bent down beside me and told me, "Phil, God is taking care of you and keeping you here because he has something special planned for your life." Suddenly, I had something I didn't have a whole lot of before: I had hope.

My hope seemed to be built on sand, though. My friend Brad relapsed. He ended up in intensive care for a week, but eventually got out. I remember thinking everything was going to be fine. Then, a few weeks later one morning in class, my teacher pulled me aside and told me that Brad had died. I lost it. He had the exact same cancer that I did, and he *didn't* make it. I cried all day. I went to the funeral and didn't believe a minute of it. At thirteen, I didn't know what was going on with my life.

I was off treatment in January of my eighth-grade year. I actually had a few parties. Strange theme for a party ... but, man, did we celebrate "No More Chemo!" One party in particular was huge: my friends, both sides of my family, my brother's and sisters' friends, everyone. I continued to go for my checkups, and I got a pin that said, "I Beat Cancer!"

I'm eighteen now, and my life is just like any other teenager's. I hate exams. I play golf. I'm involved in my school. I do drama and help build stuff for tech. I help out with chaplaincy and all the masses. I have great friends. I will never forget, though, the difference my illness made in my life. I look at things differently now. I value my parents and their love instead of fighting with them. I get scared every now and then when I think that they won't be around forever so I have to be with them now. I do the family trips and dinners, and I am happy to be there. I love my brother and sisters. Yes, they sometimes drive me crazy, but I wouldn't trade them for the world. I am thankful for a school that teaches me lessons and friends who love me.

I think of what that baseball coach told me. Every day I try to figure out God's plan for me and try to live the life that I was graciously given a second chance with. I believe in the goodness of people. Every single one of us has a reason for being here. And anything is possible as long as you keep the faith and never, ever give up hope.

Phillip Thuss

Born to Win

Consult not your fears, but your hopes and dreams. Think not about your frustrations, but about your unfulfilled potential. Concern yourself not with what you tried and failed at, but with what it is still possible for you to do.

Pope John XXIII

The doctor called my mom and dad and me into his office. He said, "Jake, you have angiosarcoma, a very rare form of cancer. You have thirty tumors in your foot. In the last fifteen years, there have only been a few instances in the United States in which this form of cancer occurred only in an extremity. It is usually found in the internal organs, but for some reason yours started at your foot and spread to your ankle."

How could this be? During a basketball game—a summer league—I had come down wrong on my ankle. After limping around all month, I decided to get it checked out. School was starting, and I needed to be in top condition for basketball season. I thought at worst that I had fractured my ankle.

The doctor continued, "You really don't have a choice here. The biggest problem with this type of cancer is there is no cure. Chemo and radiation won't work. We need to perform a below-the-knee amputation."

I went home and went right to my room where I had a really, really good cry. I thought, *Why me? I'm only sixteen years old. I'm a good kid; I haven't done anything wrong in my life.*

That afternoon was the only time I felt sorry for myself. I thought about my grandmother, Baba—she had passed away a couple of years before—and how brave she was. She had diabetes. Because of complications, her leg was amputated. No matter how sick Baba felt, she always smiled and never complained.

I talked to God for a while that day. I said, "I'll try to be as strong as Baba was. If this means giving part of my right leg so I can keep my life, then I'm completely game, because I'm not about to lose my life."

The morning of the surgery I listened to a song from my favorite group, the Beastie Boys. I told myself to be strong, to just get it over with.

The first few days after the surgery were the hardest. I experienced phantom pains. Those really hurt. The brain doesn't understand at first that a body part is gone. I would wake up in the middle of the night having to scratch my toe, and I couldn't. This would go on for three hours—it was torture.

I was up on crutches right away. The next step was to get my prosthesis—an artificial leg. I'll never forget that day. The physical therapist told me that walking with my prosthesis would be difficult. I should expect it to take one and a half to two months to learn to walk without crutches. I looked at him and said, "You know what? I'm going to learn to walk without crutches in two weeks."

It ended up that I was half a week off. When I walked

into the therapy clinic, my therapist held up a basketball. He said, "Here, Jake, since you proved to me you could walk in record time, let's shoot a round."

I slowly walked outside to the court. I stood at the free-throw line, and he threw me the basketball. I threw it up and sunk it. You can't imagine the feeling when I heard the *swoosh*. I thought, *I've still got it. I'm still the same person.*

From then on, my progress just took off. A month later I learned how to jog. I was already playing basketball again, and during my free period at lunch, I was shooting baskets with my friends.

My dad took me to San Antonio to meet Thomas Bourgeois, the number-one pentathlete in the United States. A pentathlete is an athlete participating in five events at the Paralympics, elite sport events for athletes from six different disability groups. They emphasize the participants' athletic achievements rather than their disabilities. The Paralympic Games have always been held the same year as the Olympic Games. In Atlanta in 1996, 3,195 athletes participated.

Thomas won a bronze medal in 1992 in Barcelona and a silver medal in Atlanta in 1996. When we met up with him, I couldn't help but stare. Here was this professional athlete wearing shorts exposing his prosthesis—a black, robotic-looking device—and totally confident. He even had a sandal on his foot. And here I was wearing long pants trying my best to hide my leg.

After lunch, we went to the basketball courts. He and I played three college kids and beat them. I couldn't believe his moves. He made those guys look like little kids.

Thomas said, "Jake, it's unbelievable that in six months you are playing ball like this. You have a future in athletics." I went with Thomas to the Summer Nationals to watch him compete. To see all those athletes with prostheses was mind-boggling.

I ended up taking a clinic with Dennis Oehler, a gold-medal winner in the 1988 Paralympics. He puts on clinics for new amputees and teaches them how to run again. We started with a fast walk and then a jog. He told me to sprint like I normally would. I took off running. It was nine months after my leg was amputated, and I was sprinting. Tears filled my eyes—I felt like I was flying.

Dennis told me he had never seen anyone run so soon after an amputation. He entered me in the amateur one-hundred-meter race. I ran a fifteen-second hundred, which is pretty bad. But I finished the race and felt incredible.

I came home and told my parents I wanted to start running—but a sprinting prosthesis costs twenty thousand dollars. Luckily, Nova Care, the manufacturer, was so amazed with my progress that they sent me a leg for free.

I trained for the Nationals. I wasn't ready to compete with my old school team, but I got to train with them. The Nationals were awesome. This time I ran a 13.5-second hundred, qualifying me for the World Championships.

I went to the Olympic Training Center in California. Only U.S. Olympic and Paralympic athletes can train there. I worked really hard knowing I only had two weeks to get ready.

The World Championships were held in Birmingham, England. There were sixteen hundred athletes from more than sixty countries. My parents and sister came to see me compete for the first time. I made it to the semifinals, but once there I got totally blown away. I was just happy I was even there in the first place, with people who shared my philosophy. The feeling at those games—the spirit—was all about athletes from all over the world overcoming adversity and giving everything we have.

When I got back home, I tried out for the track team at my school and made the varsity squad. I think I'm one of the first amputees to ever run varsity track against non-amputees.

At the first race, as I lined up against two-legged strangers, I felt I had to break the ice. My dad told me, from the beginning, that people were going to act the way I act. He said to go into every situation with a positive attitude.

I looked at the other guys in my heat and said, "Am I at the wrong meet? I thought I was supposed to be at a disabled meet. You guys are going to kill me."

One guy said, "I've seen you in the newspaper. You're supposed to be fast. We heard about you. You can't pull that on us."

I thought if I could beat just one of them, I'd be happy. I ended up finishing fourth and beating three or four guys. They told me I was the fastest one-legged guy they'd ever seen.

My goal is to compete in the Paralympics this year. In the meantime, I train hard. I also go to the hospital and hang out with little kids. It's the greatest when I see a little guy, five years old, with his prosthesis, and I can lift up my pant leg and say, "Oh, look, I've got one, too!"

I am one of the lucky ones. My parents, coaches and friends supported me from the moment I was diagnosed. I met Thomas, who believed in me, and then Dennis, who taught me how to run. I'm going to see where my running takes me, but when that's over, I'd love to do what Dennis does—go out and teach young amputees how to run again. I also want to continue to tell my story to kids and adults who are suffering—anyone who's lost faith and thinks life is over—that if you look for something good to come from something bad, you'll find it every time. With the right attitude, you always win.

Jake Repp

Lumps

Never be afraid to trust an unknown future to a known God.

Corrie ten Boom

It's strange how it takes realizing your life will never be the same again to see how great each day really is. I'm fourteen years old, and I had been diagnosed with Hodgkin's lymphoma, a cancer of the lymph nodes.

Last winter, I made frequent visits to different doctors for several problems. I had a severe case of asthma and allergies and rashes on my legs. I had hip pains that kept me up at night. I was anemic, too. One afternoon, I went in to see my doctor about my hip pains and some swelling in my throat. We thought I had tonsillitis. My doctor took a few X rays and said everything looked fine. He looked inside my mouth and found a mild case of thrush, an infection, which he said would probably go away in a couple of weeks. When he felt my throat, he became concerned. I had several, hard-as-rocks lumps in my neck, chest and shoulders, where the lymph glands are. They weren't tender (if they were, that would have been because of a cold) and when I tilted my head, you could see lumps sticking out of my neck. He told my mother on the phone that night that he wanted me to be seen at Children's Hospital.

That night I went out to see a movie with my boyfriend at the time, Matt. I had a great time. I didn't even know that I was going to the hospital the next day. When I woke up the next morning, my mom told me to get ready. The whole way to the hospital, I had this weird feeling in my stomach, as if I were going up one of those tall roller-coaster hills.

It took us forever to find a parking space. When we made it inside, it didn't look like those hospitals in movies, all spic-and-span clean and wall-to-wall white. It was kind of warm and cozy, just like a hospital for small people should be.

When we went into the waiting room, a little bald girl with bright blue eyes and a smile walked out. I thought to myself, *Oh, how cute. I wonder what she is here for.* Then, I saw a boy from my school walk in who I didn't know very well. I knew he had cancer the year before. I knew his name was Matt, just like my boyfriend, and I knew that all the schools in the city we live in had heard about him and the disease he had. After he sat down, a little boy walked in wearing a black beanie hat. I eavesdropped on his conversation with his mother.

"Eric, wasn't it funny what Daddy told you to do this morning?" his mother asked.

"What did he tell me to do?" he responded.

"He said, 'Go upstairs, get dressed, brush your teeth and brush your hair!' Remember what you told him?" she asked.

"I don't have any hair!" Eric said with a smile.

Just then I realized where I was and why I was there. I was in the cancer clinic because of the lumps on my neck.

I knew from listening to my doctor's "Mmm-hmm"s and "Uh-huh"s that things weren't normal. After my mom filled out some papers, they finally called me in. This really pretty, blonde doctor named Jennifer felt around my neck, underarms, shoulders, stomach and pelvic area. She measured the lumps on my neck and wrote stuff down on a piece of paper.

She had this worried look on her face. "You have such pretty hair, nice skin and your weight is healthy. I'm worried about those lumps on your neck, though, Sweetie. We're going to have to do a biopsy on some of those lumps. It's a procedure where we make a small incision in your neck and take some out to do tests. I'd also like to do a bone-marrow test while we're at it."

I started crying and looked at her. "Am I going to die?" I asked.

"I doubt it," she said. "This cancer is 90 percent curable."

She gave me a hug and helped us schedule the biopsy. All the way home, my mom and I cried. When I got home, I called all of my friends and told them.

I went back to the hospital for my biopsy, and they put a bracelet on me and put me in bed to watch some movies while I waited. I watched *Ever After, Clueless* and the beginning of *A Bug's Life* before they came in to tell me what was going to happen. They gave me a Valium to relax me, which made me pretty sleepy. I tried to go to the bathroom and, when I got out of bed, I tripped because I was so dopey. My speech was slurred, too.

They hooked me up to an I.V. and rolled my bed down a large hallway and into a small, white room. There were several doctors in there, all wearing funny hats. They put a mask on me and told me to breathe deeply. It seemed like I blinked and then realized I was in the recovery room. It wasn't like in those movies where the people just automatically flutter their eyes and wake up to see lots of people around their bedside, looking at them with presents, teddy bears and balloons. Waking up felt like trying to bench-press five hundred pounds with my eyelids. And I wasn't so glamorous, either. I remember saying, "Ow . . . Oww . . . OWW!" Then I heard people talking about morphine to take away the pain. It did make me feel a little better. My mom helped me put on my clothes and they wheeled me out to my mom's car. I crashed on the couch as soon as I got home.

The next day I went to our school's Winter Ball and my boyfriend, Matt, dedicated the song "Let's Get It On" by Marvin Gaye to me, just to make me laugh. I didn't really dance that night because I was still tired and I was in a lot of pain, but I had fun.

A couple of days later, I went back to the hospital to see how the biopsy turned out. I had this feeling in my stomach. I knew I had cancer. I was right. I did have cancer. I burst into tears again because I knew my life would never be the same. I knew my hair was going to fall out; I knew I was going to have to endure chemotherapy; I knew all of it. And I just wanted to pretend I was dreaming.

I'm halfway done with my cycles of chemotherapy now and I'm not bald yet, but my hair is incredibly thin and still falling out. Matt and I broke up a couple of months ago. I was going out with this guy, Lucas, for a while but then he broke up with me. I'm okay with it, though, because there will be new romances. I will have new relationships. There's lots of life to live. I've told all of the people who I love that I love them. I wrote letters to those people I had stopped writing to. I've tried things I was once scared to do. I pretty much have a normal, fourteen-year-old teenage girl's life. I've been able to go to school pretty regularly except I'm not there a few Mondays a month. I just keep on saying to myself, "I'm a

fighter, not a victim of cancer." People have compli-
mented me on how strong I am. Now that I think of it,
maybe they're right.

Christina Angeles

Go for the Gold

*Be generous with your joy. Give away what
you most want. Be generous with your insights
and delights. Instead of fearing that they're
going to slip away and holding on to them,
share them.*

Pema Chödrön

I've had about seven surgeries already, and I am only
twelve years old. I was born without a chin, and I really
didn't have much cheekbones, so they redid those. My
ears were just skin, and right now the doctors are working on them. They're using ribs. Ribs grow back until
you're eighteen years old.

My mom told me what I had—Treacher Collins
Syndrome—when I was little. She never tried to keep it a
secret. She has the same birth defect as I do. She had to go
to a special school for the hard of hearing, and she didn't
want that to happen to me. I have a special hearing aid—
a headband—called a "bone conduction hearing aid" that
allows me to hear. I get to go to public school.

Mom and I went to different kinds of schools, but we

both know about being teased. I don't get teased much. But, if I do, I stand up for myself. I'll say, "It doesn't matter. You can make fun of me. Tomorrow it could be you." They usually stop laughing, and some even say they're sorry or they didn't mean it. I tell them to just not do it again. If someone has a problem with me, it's his or her problem, not mine.

I may not always fit in, but I try to stand up for what's right. I'm always trying to help someone else. I even postponed a surgery in 1995 because of the Oklahoma City bombing. I saw the bombing on TV and decided to do something.

I wanted to raise $20,000 to help the victims. My mom wanted to knock it down to $10,000, so I agreed. My mom asked my grandpa to help, and together they wanted to knock it down to $5,000. This time I said no—my goal was $10,000.

I planned a bowl-a-thon. To announce it, I made banners and started going out asking for sponsors. I got bored going house to house. I didn't raise very much money that way. So I told my mom I wanted to try car dealerships.

My mom and I walked into dealerships, and every time we went in, a salesperson said to my mom, "May I help you?"

She said, "No, talk to him."

I told the salesperson my plan and asked for his or her help. I don't think anyone said no. The car dealerships provided a lot of money.

Lots of people came to the bowl-a-thon, and we had a big banner for everyone to sign. The governor of Colorado, Governor Romer, also signed it. Then I flew to Oklahoma and handed the governor of Oklahoma, Governor Keating, a check for $37,000 and the signed banner. We made $27,000 over our goal!

I have raised over $87,000 for different causes since then, and my goal is to raise $100,000 by the time I am thirteen years old. Why do I spend my time raising money? I believe everyone can make a difference, and it doesn't matter how old you are, or who you are, or if you feel you are different, because everyone is different in one way or another. Some differences are on the outside and other people can see them, but some differences are on the inside.

Michael Munds

The Walk That Changed Our Lives

*It can be hard to break the friendship code of
secrecy and make your friend mad at you, but
you must do what you feel in your heart is right.*

Amanda Ford

The closer we came to the counselor's office, the more
obvious it became that this walk would be one of the most
important of our lives. It was one of the last days before
school got out for the summer, and eighth grade was coming to an end. My friends and I were all thrilled. Everyone,
that is, except our friend, Hannah.

It had started the previous summer, when Hannah had
begun to keep to herself a lot. Whenever we would go out,
she would insist on staying home by herself just to sit
around. In fact, a lot of changes had come over Hannah
ever since we had entered junior high. She obsessed
about her weight, her complexion and how unpopular
she was. She never seemed to focus on the good things
she had to offer; it was always about what she didn't have
or what she was lacking. We were all concerned that
something was very wrong, but at thirteen we didn't

exactly understand it or know what we could do to help her. Hannah seemed to be getting worse every day. She hated herself, and it was tearing our friendship apart.

Then one morning not long ago, Hannah came to school and told us she had almost committed suicide. She said she had thought about her friends and could not go through with it. We were in shock and had no idea what to do. Since she told no one else—not her parents or her sisters, just us—we tried to figure out what to do ourselves, feeling that no one else would understand. Though we didn't want to stop being there for her, we couldn't carry the burden by ourselves. We knew that if we made one wrong move, it could cost us our friend's life.

We walked into the counselor's office and waited for what seemed like an eternity until they called our names. We held hands as we walked in, each of us holding back tears. The counselor invited us to sit down, and we began to tell him about Hannah and all that had been going on. When we were finished, he told us that we had done the right thing. We waited as he called Hannah's mother. We were overwhelmed with a million questions. What would Hannah say when she found out that we had told? Would her parents be mad at her for not telling anyone sooner? What was going to happen?

When Hannah's mother arrived at school, she had obviously been crying and her face seemed full of questions. She began to ask about Hannah's behavior and what she had told us. It was awful to tell her how Hannah had been alone at home one day testing knives to see if they were sharp enough to take her life. We all cringed at the thought of not having her in our lives today.

We learned later that after we had gone back to class, Hannah had been called down to talk to her mother and her counselor. It turned out she was relieved and grateful that she didn't have to keep her secret any longer. She began counseling and has since gotten better. Since that day we are so grateful to see Hannah's smiling face, or even to simply be able to pass her a note in the hallway between classes.

If we had not taken that long, horrible walk to the counseling office, we may not have been able to share high-school memories with Hannah. I know now that when we took that walk, it gave us the ability to give her the greatest gift of all . . . her life.

Maggie McCarthy

For a Good Time, Call . . .

Sometimes I have the same dream. I'm running home from town on the road around Schultz Lake. It's dark and I'm scared. Somebody—I don't know who—chases me. I feel him shoot me in the back with a gun and I wake up.

I'd just started high school and was really excited. I dreamed about dating and proms and homecoming games. After two months, I noticed that the boys in my classes were treating me differently. At the beginning of the school year, they talked to me like anybody else; now they just ignored me. *I must be a nerd*, I thought. *It must be a character defect.*

One day, this senior, Chuck, stopped me in the halls. He was in student council and active in school. "You're such a nice girl," he said. "Do you know what they're writing about you in the boys' bathroom?"

Was he kidding? I didn't really believe him, and I didn't think about it too much. I kind of laughed it off. I was pretty self-assured; soft-spoken, but feisty. I had the normal ups and downs of growing up, but my family lived on a beautiful lake outside Duluth, Minnesota, and I was happy. Friends came over to swim, water-ski or ice-skate. I had a 4.0 grade point average and played piano and saxophone in the school band and jazz ensemble.

It can't be true. I'm not the type of girl that boys write that stuff about, I thought to myself. But two weeks later, another guy told me about the graffiti in the middle stall. The nicest stuff said I was a "slut." The worst stuff was obscene. I went to a guidance counselor and told her what I had heard. "Who do you think it could be?" she asked. I told her I had no idea—and I never did find out. The counselor told me the graffiti would be removed instantly. But it wasn't—it stayed in that stall for two years.

On the bus after school, the boys started teasing me. "Hey, Katy, can you come to my house?" they'd taunt. I usually just laughed. But as soon as I got off the bus, I felt degraded and embarrassed.

The graffiti got worse, scrawled on the door and both walls, carved with a knife or scratched into paint, or written in permanent ink. It was called the "Katy Stall." Most boys in school saw it, and most girls knew about it.

I went to two more guidance counselors and then the principal. He looked at me strangely, and he had an obvious where-there's-smoke-there's-fire attitude. "Boys will be boys," he told me. "Graffiti is a fact of life." He promised to remove it—but it never happened.

At school I tried to maintain the image that everything was fine, but when I got home I would cry. "What's wrong?" my mom would ask. "I had a bad day," I'd answer. I didn't want to tell my parents because I was used to solving problems on my own. But my confidence and self-esteem were shattering—and soon they were nonexistent. I felt afraid and helpless. Mostly, I felt voiceless.

To say I dreaded going to school is an understatement. I hated waking up. I didn't want to see anyone. I'd baby-sit every Saturday night and practice music any chance I

got. I'd play Chopin's "Preludes" because they were so
sad. I wanted a boyfriend badly, but didn't think I
deserved one.

My only good friend, Gini, told me, "Try to ignore it.
Just blow it off."

"It's not your name up there," I'd say. I was terrorized.

I finally told my parents, who got furious. They called
the principal to complain, but nothing was ever done.
Once, after school, I went into the bathroom myself and
snapped pictures. It made me sick. After two years, the
graffiti was still there.

Eventually, my dad gave the principal a twenty-four-
hour ultimatum, then called a lawyer. I called a program
that aided sexual-assault victims. After hearing my story,
the woman on the other line told me, "Katy, what's
happened to you is sexual harassment, and this can be as
emotionally damaging as physical assault."

Sexual harassment. I'd never used the words before,
and they gave me a chill. I now had a name for the nightmare. For the first time in two years, there was something
I could do to defend myself. I suddenly felt angry, feisty
again. I called the school board and asked for an apology
from the principal, as well as a letter explaining sexual
harassment to students and a new policy to teach the
issue in local schools. And I filed a complaint with
Minnesota's Human Rights Department.

It took time and paperwork, but the day came when my
parents and I faced the principal and a judge in a closed
meeting. A district attorney presented our case and, after
eight hours of negotiation, all my demands were met, plus
the school was required to pay a $15,000 settlement.

I thought it was over, but the next morning my story
was splashed on the front page of the *Duluth News Tribune*.
As a result, I was interviewed for many articles and
appeared on TV's *Donahue* and *Today*.

Then something else happened: I started dating Eric. He played on the football and hockey teams, but wasn't like the other guys. He didn't believe the graffiti. Because of him, the last few months of high school were every-thing I'd once hoped they'd be.

I wish it hadn't happened because I'll never be the same again. I still have a hard time trusting people. But if my story prevents one guy from sexually harassing a girl, or stops a girl who is harassed from blaming herself or helps her to take action, then maybe it will have been worth it.

Katy Lyle
As told to Mark Bregman

8

LEARNING DIFFICULT LESSONS

Experience is a hard teacher because she gives the test first, the lesson afterwards.

Vernon Saunders Law

What My Father Wore

What my father wore embarrassed me as a young man. I wanted him to dress like a doctor or lawyer, but on those muggy mornings when he rose before dawn to fry eggs for my mother and me, he always dressed like my father.

We lived in south Texas, and my father wore tattered jeans with the imprint of his pocketknife on the seat. He liked shirts that snapped more than those that buttoned, and kept his pencils, cigars, glasses, wrenches and screwdrivers in his breast pocket. My father's boots were government-issues with steel toes that made them difficult to pull off his feet, which I sometimes did when he returned from repairing air conditioners, his job that also shamed me.

But, as a child, I'd crept into his closet and modeled his wardrobe in front of the mirror. My imagination transformed his shirts into the robes of kings and his belts into soldiers' holsters. I slept in his undershirts and relied on the scent of his collars to calm my fear of the dark. Within a few years, though, I started wishing my father would trade his denim for khaki and retire his boots for loafers. I stopped sleeping in his clothes and eventually began dreaming of another father.

I blamed the way he dressed for my social failures. When boys bullied me, I thought they'd seen my father wearing his cowboy hat but no shirt while walking our dog. I felt that girls snickered at me because they'd glimpsed him mowing the grass in cut-offs and black boots. The girls' families paid men (and I believed better-dressed ones) to landscape their lawns, while their fathers yachted in the bay wearing lemon-yellow sweaters and expensive sandals.

My father only bought two suits in his life. He preferred clothes that allowed him the freedom to shimmy under cars and squeeze behind broken Maytags, where he felt most content. But the day before my parents' twentieth anniversary, he and I went to Sears, and he tried on suits all afternoon. With each one, he stepped to the mirror, smiled and nodded, then asked about the price and reached for another. He probably tried ten suits before we drove to a discount store and bought one without so much as approaching a fitting room. That night my mother said she'd never seen a more handsome man.

Later, though, he donned the same suit for my eighth-grade awards banquet, and I wished he'd stayed home. After the ceremony (I'd been voted Mr. Citizenship, of all things), he lauded my award and my character while changing into a faded red sweatsuit. He was stepping into the garage to wash a load of laundry when I asked what even at age fourteen struck me as cruel and wrong. "Why," I asked, "don't you dress 'nice,' like my friends' fathers?"

He held me with his sad, shocked eyes and searched for an answer. Then before he disappeared into the garage and closed the door between us, my father said, "I like my clothes." An hour later my mother stormed into my room, slapped me hard across the face and called me an "ungrateful little twerp," a phrase that echoed in my head until they resumed speaking to me.

In time they forgave me, and as I matured I realized that girls avoided me not because of my father but because of his son. I realized that my mother had slapped me because my father could not, and it soon became clear that what he had really said that night was that there are things more important than clothes. He'd said he couldn't spend a nickel on himself because there were things I wanted. That night, without another word, my father had said, "You're my son, and I sacrifice so your life will be better than mine."

For my high-school graduation, my father arrived in a suit he and my mother had purchased earlier that day. Somehow he seemed taller, more handsome and imposing, and when he passed the other fathers they stepped out of his way. It wasn't the suit, of course, but the man. The doctors and lawyers recognized the confidence in his swagger, the pride in his eyes, and when they approached him, they did so with courtesy and respect. After we returned home, my father replaced the suit in the flimsy Sears garment bag, and I didn't see it again until his funeral.

I don't know what he was wearing when he died, but he was working, so he was in clothes he liked, and that comforts me. My mother thought of burying him in the suit from Sears, but I convinced her otherwise and soon delivered a pair of old jeans, a flannel shirt and his boots to the funeral home.

On the morning of the services, I used his pocketknife to carve another hole in his belt so it wouldn't droop around my waist. Then I took the suit from Sears out of his closet and changed into it. Eventually, I mustered the courage to study myself in his mirror where, with the exception of the suit, I appeared small and insignificant. Again, as in childhood, the clothes draped over my scrawny frame. My father's scent wafted up and caressed my face, but it failed to console me. I was uncertain: not about my father's stature—I'd stopped being an ungrateful little twerp years before. No, I was uncertain about myself, my own stature. And I stood there for some time, facing myself in my father's mirror, weeping and trying to imagine—as I will for the rest of my life—the day I'll grow into my father's clothes.

Bret Anthony Johnston

The Graduation Speech

Jesse was well liked by everyone, so everybody anticipated what he had to say
As he walked up to the microphone, on graduation day.
For a moment he remained silent, as he peered at the faces
 from his senior class,
And then Jesse leaned into the microphone, and finally
 spoke at last:

"As your class president, I'm here to speak to you today.
I was up most of the night, considering what words that I
 should say.
I reminisced on school days, and all the many things I've
 done,
So many memories came to mind, but my thoughts kept
 me focusing on one."

And then Jesse held up a photo, and he moved it all
 around,
As everyone leaned to view it, and silence was the only
 sound.
You could have heard a pin drop, as Jesse placed the picture in full view,
And began talking of a classmate, that no one really knew.

"Charlie's life seemed meaningless, compared to yours and mine,
Because none of us understood him, we never took the time.
We saw only what we wanted to, that Charlie was not cool,
He was far from being popular, the butt of all our jokes in school.

"That's what we knew of Charlie, that much we decided on our own,
He simply wasn't worth our time, he was an outsider who deserved to be alone.
But you see Charlie had a passion, deep within he had a dream,
It was his one desire, to play for our soccer team.

"And of course that was ludicrous, it was totally absurd,
Charlie was no athlete, he was the senior nerd.
In gym class he was never captain, he was always chosen last,
He was the poster child for unpopular, he preferred history, science and math.

"And so some of us took it upon ourselves to keep Charlie from wanting to play,
For weeks we taunted him with insults, day after day after day.
We made sure that he wasn't welcomed, by anyone else on the team,
For whatever foolish reasons, we were set on destroying his dream.
And I'm here now to tell you, as your class president, I was wrong
I'm here to speak for Charlie, who couldn't be here, because you see he's gone."

Jesse paused just for a moment, to give time for his words
    to sink in,
As he looked about at the faces, of parents, teachers and
    friends.

"I'm not sure if all of you know it, I'm not sure if anyone
    cares,
But the reason Charlie isn't with us is a reason I feel I must
    share.
Cruel words they are definitely weapons, they destroyed
    Charlie's body and soul,
For all of the taunting and teasing left Charlie feeling out
    of control.

"And Charlie alone in a battle, gathered his weapons to
    fight.
He purchased some drugs from a dealer, his mother found
    his body last night.
Maybe it was only an accident, maybe Charlie wanted to
    die,
But no matter how it happened, we as his classmates
    know why.
For who in their lives hasn't been teased, or made to feel
    unbearable shame,
I'm certain that everyone in this room has endured some
    heartache and pain.
And maybe boys will be boys and girls will be girls, and
    we each have our battles to fight,
But no matter our justification, hurting Charlie was never
    right."

And then Jesse took Charlie's picture and held it firm in
    his hand,
And spoke to the photo before him, words unrehearsed
    and unplanned.

"If only I'd helped somehow, given you guidance to con-
 quer your dream,
If only a teacher, a classmate, if someone would have just
 intervened.
But I know I can never go back, I can never undo what has
 been,
For you will never receive your diploma, or ever play
 soccer again.
But deep in my heart I wonder, I can't help asking what
 if . . .
I would have reached out to you Charlie,
Would your school years have ended like this?"

Jesse stood lost in his thoughts, of a life that was ended
 too soon,
Until muffled coughs caught his attention, and nervous
 whispers began filling the room.
And then Jesse turned with a smile, before retreating back
 to his chair,
Teaching a valuable lesson, with his final words filling
 the air:

"I would like to introduce our valedictorian, he will be
 speaking today,
Please give him your full attention, please hear all that he
 has to say."
And then Jesse set Charlie's picture down, on the podium
 facing the crowd,
As the silence told Charlie's story, a message quite con-
 vincingly loud.

Cheryl Costello-Forshey

The Purse

My mother always has the Purse with her. The Purse contains a receipt for everything she has purchased that cost more than twenty-five cents since around 1980. The Purse also contains at least one dose of every conceivable over-the-counter medication, all expired.

If you need something, more likely than not, it can be found in the Purse. Tissues? In the Purse. Breath mint? But, of course. Tweezers, nail polish remover, nail clippers, needle and thread, pens, pencils, calendar, calculator, paper clips, tiny stapler—all in the Purse.

The Purse started out a relatively normal size, but over the years it has expanded to what seems like two feet in width. It is hopelessly, permanently open and overflowing. If you need something, virtually everything in the Purse has to be removed and examined in order to locate it, usually onto the nearest park bench or desktop. Many great discoveries are often found during such expeditions into the Purse, like pieces of paper containing long-forgotten locker combinations or telephone messages that should have been returned three or four weeks ago.

My mom just can't bear to not know what I am up to at any given moment. For example, when I get home from school, I have to download everything that happened during the day. Over the years, she has developed expert interrogation techniques that enable her to remove every tiny detail of a day's events from my brain. No detail is too small or too insignificant or too boring for her. And the same applies when she is telling you a story about something that happened to her.

I think my mother's mind is kind of like the Purse inside—all jumbled up with tiny artifacts and useless items. Most of them have to come out and be spread around before you get to something good or what you were looking for, but when she does get to that one valuable thing, it is as if you have just won the lottery.

When I first started hanging out with Heather, it was mostly at school or on the weekends. I don't know why I didn't tell my mom about her. I guess I just wanted to keep something private, or maybe I didn't want her to make a big deal about it, or maybe I was afraid my mom, with the Purse, would want to meet Heather. I think it was mostly that.

And so, every day I would come home from school and proceed to tell my mom what happened in each class, between each class, at lunch and after school. I would be urged to disclose what happened on the way to school and on the way home from school and up until the very second that I walked into the house. But every day I would conveniently leave out all details about Heather.

This went on for a few months and I knew my mom was starting to get suspicious, but I just couldn't tell her about Heather. I didn't want to admit it to myself, but I was ashamed of my mother. It made it worse that she prided herself on the honesty we shared, telling her friends that I could tell her anything and it would be okay.

Since I mostly saw Heather in groups, I would tell my mom that I was going to the movies with Katrina and

Steve and Trevor and Julian, but conveniently leaving out Heather. But one Saturday night I decided I wanted to see Heather alone. I wanted to go out on a real date with her. I had two choices: Either come clean and tell my mom about Heather, or lie. So I told my mom I was going to the movies with "some friends." I don't know why I thought this would work. She wanted to know which friends, what movie, what theater, who was driving, what time, if it was an R-rated movie, where I was going afterward, what time I would be home and whether or not I planned on buying popcorn. She left me no choice. I lied to her, and once I got started, I couldn't stop. I lied about things that didn't matter. I told her I was going to buy Red Vines when I knew I wanted Raisinettes, and I told her the wrong movie at the wrong theater. I told her I was going with Katrina and Trevor. I told her Katrina's mom was driving.

And so I left the house with a pit in my stomach. I wasn't good at this lying thing, and I felt guilty. I walked to Heather's house, and we caught the bus to the movies. I don't even remember what movie we saw, but the whole time I could only think about the fact that I had lied to my mom. We came out of the movie holding hands and, to my complete horror, my mom was standing there with the Purse. She had decided to take my sister to a movie and since she didn't want to intrude on me with my friends, she had chosen a different theater than the one I had told her, which of course was the wrong one because I had lied.

She didn't say anything, but if I had been paying attention, I would have been able to read the look of disappointment on her face. I was too busy worrying about her embarrassing me in front of Heather. All I could see was the Purse. I couldn't lie anymore, so I introduced my mom to Heather. My mom just stood there. She was in shock. I was in shock. And then I saw the look.

I guess I should have been relieved when she smiled at me, and then Heather, and invited us to dinner. It seems she had a coupon for Sizzler, they were having some sort of family dinner special for four, and my mom thought it was just perfect that we had run into each other. A coupon? What were we, homeless? I couldn't believe she suggested a coupon in front of Heather. And just when I thought things couldn't get worse, she started looking for the coupon. Oh no! Not the Purse!

At first I tried to stop her as she started to open the Purse. Then I realized there was no stopping her, so I tried to help. The Purse had to be completely unloaded onto a bench outside the theater. I was shuffling through the papers, trying to find the prized coupon, and I guess I was moving my hands too fast and I knocked the Purse. It flipped up in the air and as it did, I saw my life flash before my eyes, as if in slow motion, each one of those million receipts representing an important event. They ended up on the ground, spread about the theater, just as the movie next door was letting out. Crowds of people were stepping on all those papers.

That's when I lost it. The words came out in torrents, and I was powerless to stop them. "I can't believe you!" I yelled. "You are totally embarrassing me! Why do you have to carry all this crap with you all the time? Who cares about all these stupid receipts?" I picked up a Target receipt from the early 1990s. "Look at this," I said. "You bought T-shirts for Dad, and you got them on sale. Isn't that special?"

Heather looked on in shock. She grabbed me by the arm and pulled me to the side. "It's no big deal," she said.

"Yes, it is. I can't believe she's embarrassing me like that. She's so lame."

"Calm down," Heather replied. "It's okay. She was just trying to take us out to a nice dinner. I like Sizzler."

I couldn't calm down. Heather and I just stared at each other.

My mom and my sister were on their hands and knees picking up all those little pieces of paper and bits of string and lint-covered pills. I got down there and helped them. We left the theater and drove Heather home in silence. Other than hello and good-bye, my mom didn't speak to me for the rest of the weekend. I went to school on Monday, and Heather acted weird. I came home from school and walked in as usual. My mom was there, but she didn't say anything to me. Not even, "How was your day?" She just had that look of disappointment on her face. As long as I live, I will never forget that look.

I went up to my room to do some homework and play around on the computer. It was eerily silent. *Hey, this isn't so bad,* I thought. *I have a lot more time to myself.* But after a few hours, I began thinking about my day. I had gotten an A on an algebra test. It didn't seem to have any value until I could tell my mom about it. And I wanted to go down there and tell her about Heather. I wanted her to know how bad I felt. Worst of all, I had disappointed her. We had a good relationship and an honest one until I blew it. I lied. I was so disappointed in myself.

I finally got up the courage to go down there. She was sitting at the kitchen table with the Purse, sorting through all those receipts. Next to her was a *new* purse. A nice, flat, closable purse. She was transferring things into the new one. Just a few things. I sat there silently for a few minutes watching her sort. I noticed a restaurant receipt from Pizza Hut. I picked it up from the discard pile and noticed the date: August 26. My birthday.

"Hey, remember my birthday party last year?" My mom just looked at me. "You know, when I got the new skateboard?" Silence. More sorting. "I got an A on my algebra test." Silence. It was unbearable. I couldn't take it.

"I'm sorry. I'm really sorry. I didn't mean any of the stuff I said. I . . . I . . . miss you." She looked up from the sorting. There was a long pause. I was waiting for her to yell at me. I expected her to tell me how mad she was. I was ready for the worst, but all she said was, "How was your day?"

It's a few months later now, and that new purse, the one my mom was sorting, has become *the* Purse. And the next time Heather and I run into my mom and the Purse, I hope she has dinner plans in there somewhere.

Tal Vigderson

Friends to the End

Sometimes someone says something really small, and it just fits right into this empty place in your heart.

Angela, *My So-Called Life*

"Friends to the end!" Breana had signed the picture of us that hung on my bedroom wall. We were so happy the night it was taken, all confidence and smiles.

Breana's handwritten promise looped and curled with the joy we had shared. "Friends to the end"—and I was the one who ended it.

We had been friends for ten years, since the day I'd moved next door the summer before second grade. I was standing on the sidewalk watching the moving van being unloaded and there was Breana, straddling her bike beside me.

"That your bike?" She pointed at the pink bike my father was wheeling into the garage.

"Yes."

"Wanna ride to the park?"

"Sure."

Just like that, we became friends. We were next-door sisters.

Maybe if I could look back and say, "This is the moment our friendship ended," I could repair it. But there wasn't a dramatic split. I made one choice, one step, one rip at a time, until I had walked away from Breana and into my new life with my new friends.

I guess I could say that Breana started it. It was her idea that I try out for cheerleading. "You're the best dancer in our class and the best gymnast at the club. You'd be a natural."

"You're crazy," I protested, though I really did believe her and I did want to try out. I knew that Breana knew that. It was her job to talk me into it, though. That way, if I failed I could shrug it off with a "What did I tell you?"

I agreed to go for it when Breana promised to try out with me. She went to all the practices, learned the routines and spent two weeks in the backyard coaching me.

Breana was as excited as I was when I made the squad and more surprised than I was when she did, too.

The night of our first football game, Breana gave me a cross necklace that matched the one she had on. It was a great reminder that we were in this together, and we both shared our gratitude to God.

Our halftime performance was flawless, even the grand finale big lift. I jumped into my stance with Breana beneath me as my secure base. I posed on her shoulders and smiled for the flash of my father's camera.

It was this picture of us that Breana signed.

One afternoon after football practice, Drew Peterson caught up with us and asked me to the Homecoming Dance. My brain didn't know how to talk to a Drew Peterson. I could only nod. His blue eyes alone were enough to leave me speechless.

Breana was the one who finally spoke: "She'd love to!"

The night of the dance, Breana helped me do my hair and makeup and then left me with a hug. "Look for the heart. I'll be waiting up."

The heart. We had made those hearts for each other so many Valentine's Days ago that I don't remember when we started hanging them in our bedroom windows as a signal to meet at the back porch swing.

I shared everything with Breana after the first, second and even the third date. After that, I began to make up excuses. It was too late, or I was too tired. It wasn't like I was doing anything really wrong. It was just that I knew Breana wouldn't understand the kind of parties I was going to and the people I was with. Why did I have to explain myself to her anyway?

That stupid heart began to anger me. "Just grow up, Breana," I'd spit under my breath when I passed by her window after a night out with Drew.

Last night I didn't just pass by her window, I nearly passed out under it. I was losing my balance, and the next thing I knew, Breana was cradling my head in her lap.

She brushed my hair back out of my eyes.

"You are the real Miss Goody Two Shoes," I said, and burst into tears.

That's what Drew had called me at the party. "A toast to Miss Goody Two Shoes. She's too good to drink with the rest of us sinners," he had said, loud enough for everyone to hear.

My new friends lifted their drinks in a mock salute. "To Saint Jenny."

I laughed the hollow laugh that I had heard myself use so often during the last four weeks. Then I grabbed Drew's drink from his hand and gulped it down. They all hooted their approval.

The alcohol's harshness shocked me. I couldn't breathe and when I finally gasped in air, I went into a coughing spasm. My stomach rolled. I needed help. I grabbed for Drew, but he dodged my reach.

"I guess some people just can't handle their liquor." He pointed at me, and they all snickered. Standing in the center of their ridicule, I suddenly wanted nothing more than to be the person they were accusing me of being.

These were my new friends? They laughed *with* me if I did what they did but *at* me if I didn't?

"Please, Drew, I want to go home."

"Sure thing," he said, much to my relief. He wasn't such a bad guy. Tomorrow I would talk to him. I knew I could make him understand about his friends and these parties. After all, he had said that he loved me.

Drew took my hand and led me out the door to the sidewalk. He turned me towards home. "Go play with your dolls. Call me when you grow up."

I stumbled the six blocks to home. It wasn't until I saw the heart in Breana's window that I knew I had made it, but not without taking a spill on the porch and making the rude comment to Breana.

The next morning came fresh and new, but just a little too early for me. I struggled out of bed and cleaned up for the day. I put on my cross that Breana had given to me. Faith renewed, I fastened the chain with a sense of joy. I was starting over.

I flung open my curtains and hung my old Valentine's heart in the window. I wanted it to be the first thing Breana saw. I could hardly wait for our reunion on the back porch swing, to be together again.

Looking across at her bedroom, I almost expected to see Breana smiling over at me. The last thing I expected to see is what I saw. The heart was gone. Her window was empty.

I walked through the house and out to our swing in a fog of shock. There the shock turned to pain. On the swing cushion was half of the heart from her window. Breana had written just two words: *The End.*

I sank into the swing as torn apart as the heart I held on my lap. The faded heart turned deep red where my tears dropped on it. It had taken me too long to see the truth. I was too late.

I was crying and gasping so I didn't hear her approaching. But I looked up and saw Breana standing over me. I wiped my tears and nodded.

Breana sat down. She placed the other half of the heart beside the one in my lap. On it were the words: *Friends to.*

I studied the pieced-together heart for a moment before grasping what it meant. Hope started to fill me, and I began to cry.

"Friends to the end?" I finally managed to ask.

"Yes." Breana smiled and gave the swing a little push start with her foot. "Friends to the end."

Jenny Michaels
As told to Cynthia Hamond

I'm Sorry . . .

I'm sorry for all the times I lost my temper
For the times when I was rude
For all the gifts that were given
And never received thank-yous.

For all the love you've given me
And I haven't given back
For all the times you were patient
A virtue that I lack.

I'm sorry for all the people
To whom I was so cruel
To all the people I laughed at
I acted like a fool.

I couldn't see past your imperfections
I couldn't see past my pride
Your feelings I trampled all over
On my high horse I would ride.

I'm sorry for all the times I lied
For the people I hurt along the way
Not a day goes by that I don't regret it
And I'd take it back any day.

The only person I cared about
Was me and only me
And now I'm truly sorry
I only wish I could make you see.

I'm sorry for everything I've done
For all the people I let down
I'm only asking for a second chance
So I can turn things back around.

I know that it's a little late
My deeds can't be undone
I realize now that I was wrong
And I'm sorry everyone.

Teal Henderson

A Different View

At fourteen, fifteen and sixteen, with our bodies changing and maturing, the way we looked was the most important thing in the world to us. Obvious flaws were tragic. A pimple could prove fatal. My friends and I strived for perfection. Guys started paying attention, and girls were trying to outdo each other.

In high school, my friends and I were on the gymnastics team, and our bodies became even more important to us. There would be no fat, no bulges, only muscle. We would do grueling repetitions of a variation of the sit-up called a jackknife. Hands behind your head, legs straight, you'd bend in the middle bringing your knees up to your face—brutal but effective.

On the weekends, we would go to the beach in our bikinis, proud of our washboard stomachs. We were strong, but we had to be in order to negotiate all the moves required of the parallel bars. We looked good and had the bodies we wanted. God forbid anything would interfere with that.

We had no tolerance for anyone who appeared different. We would be critical to the point of cruelty to others, and even to ourselves, if we strayed from the path.

One summer day, all my friends were at my house swimming. It was hot, and we were enjoying some time away from the sweltering gym. One of our favorite things was to take tumbling runs off the diving board.

At one point I was running from the patio back to the deck of the pool. In between was an expansive stretch of lawn. It was summer and bees and butterflies were all over the place. I felt myself step on something and instantly a hot burning sensation ran up my leg. I had stepped on a bee, and while it was dying under my foot it stung me.

My head started to whirl, and I instantly started to feel sick. That night, I began to run a high fever and my leg and foot were red, hot and swollen. My uncle, who is a doctor, came over and gave me a shot of adrenaline, some Benadryl and put me to bed. He said I would be fine in the morning—I think all doctors are required to say that.

The next day I felt a little better, but my leg and foot were very swollen. I couldn't walk; I could barely stand. When my foot started to go numb, everyone became more concerned. My foot was not getting good blood supply, and I had red striations running up my leg.

I had to go into the hospital, and my leg had to be in traction as if it were badly broken. I couldn't move or exercise, and all I could do was think about how soft my middle was becoming. That depressed me more than any concern over my leg.

That would all change when I heard the word "amputation" being used. Were they kidding? This was just a bee sting! Apparently, my foot was still not getting the blood supply it needed, and it was bluish in color. They would have to accelerate their course of treatment if I was to avoid surgery.

Never before did I have such great appreciation for my

foot. And walking seemed like a gift from the gods. Less and less would I want to hear from my friends who were visiting to talk about gymnastics and who was wearing what. More and more I anticipated visits from other kids on the ward, who were quickly becoming my friends.

One girl came to visit me regularly. Every time she came, she brought flowers that she had picked from right outside my window. She knew that I couldn't go outside to enjoy them myself, or even stand next to my window to see them. She was in remission from leukemia and felt compelled to come back and encourage everyone on the ward. She still had no hair, and she was swollen and bloated from medications that she had been taking. I would not have given this girl a second glance before; I now loved every inch of her and looked forward to her visits.

Finally, I was improving, and soon thereafter I went home. I was on crutches, my leg was still swollen and my foot felt more like a useless piece of meat on the end of my leg, but I was walking, and I had my foot! That funny-looking, shriveled little thing at the end of my leg was my pride and joy. I had new appreciation for my legs, and even my thighs, which I had always looked at with disdain before.

When I would go back to the hospital for physical therapy, I often saw my friend. She was still visiting people and spreading good cheer. I thought if ever there was an angel on this Earth, it had to be her.

My perspective changed that summer. I had newfound appreciation for my body, my health and the struggles others have with theirs. Sure, I still wanted to look good, but it would never be with the same kind of obsessive snobbery.

Years later I learned that my friend from the hospital had died and I was very sad. But I knew that any time anyone would think about her, their hearts would still be uplifted. Mine always is. I only wish I knew where she was buried . . . I would bring her some fresh flowers that I would pick, from just outside my window.

Zan Gaudioso

It's Just the Way We Are

We hold on to things the tightest,
when we are forced to let them go—
We always want things a certain way,
when we know they can't be so.

Dreams always last the longest,
when they are furthest from our reach—
And the lessons we can learn the most from,
are often the very ones we teach.

The grass is always the greenest,
when it lies on the other side—
And the truths we preach to others,
are often those we can't abide.

We hold fast to the things in a storm,
which are most likely to blow away—
And yet we neglect to wear sunscreen,
on a bright and sunny day.

We spend our time trying to see things,
when perspective is one thing we lack—

And we never appreciate what we've got,
until we can't get it back.

We expect the whole world to give us a break,
and yet ironically we'll find—
That when others come asking the same of us,
we tell them they're out of their mind.

We tell everyone what's wrong with this world,
and we do nothing to make it right—
We complain about families falling apart,
and yet do nothing to keep them tight.

We preach about loving our neighbors,
and we teach children right from wrong—
But we never set good examples for them,
when real chances come along.

We complain about not having enough time in our lives,
to do what we must do—
Yet if we were given more hours in the day,
we'd use up all that, too.

We desire to be close to all those we love,
yet all too often look on from afar—
And when it comes to the truth do we want to change,
or remain forever as we are?

Kristy Glassen

My Greatest Teacher

*Do not think of your faults; still less of others'
faults. Look for what is good and strong and try
to imitate it. Your faults will drop off like dead
leaves when their time comes.*

John Ruskin

It seems like a lifetime since I returned the hat, but it
was only seven years ago. I returned it to Dave, who had
taken it from a lost-and-found box at school.

It was a common plaid English cap, but for me, it was a
special hat. I hid behind that hat for three years. It hid my
pain. During the three years I wore that hat, I never took
it off when there was another person in the room. Even
now, I remember the agony, the pain, the self-hate—the
isolation.

I wore the hat because of a hair transplant I got when I
was twenty years old. A hair transplant is a lengthy
process. Over the course of a year, I visited a plastic surgeon once a month. At each visit, he transplanted hair
from one region of my scalp to another, which is a nice
way of saying he drilled holes in my head and replaced

the empty pits with hair grafts taken from other parts of my head.

"Before you know it," he said, "the hair will be hanging in your eyes." I clung desperately to that hope, which supported me until it slowly dissolved, leaving me alone with a self I hated.

Even now, it is hard for me to believe how far gone I was. I was "done," as I sometimes say. I was like one of those clowns who has painted himself into a corner—I had nowhere to turn.

Day and night I walked around with that hat on, afraid to let people see me without it. I remember the absolute loneliness I felt while sitting in the plastic surgeon's office after he had drilled holes in my head. I could feel the drill against my head, hear and feel the tendons and skin ripping. I smelled the skin burning from the drill. I even felt the drill against my skull—when it would move no longer.

I gradually realized that the hair transplant wasn't working the way I thought it would.

I began to have fantasies about dying because I never thought I could be happy again. I didn't want to commit suicide, but each night when I went to bed, I prayed that my life would end. Sometimes I lay in bed wishing I were dead. I even imagined myself as a corpse, leaving the world and its troubles behind.

One day I found myself in a deep place. My sense of body or self had faded away. There was darkness all around, and I felt as though I barely existed. Gradually, I realized I wasn't alone: A presence was there in the darkness with me. I recognized that this presence was connected with God and that it was loving.

I expressed my suffering and lack of understanding to the presence because I wanted to know why I had to suffer so much. It assured me that *if I was honest and sincerely tried*, it would show me.

After that experience, I started to come out of my depression. After three years, however, I still wore my hat.

In the summer heat, I wore the hat to hide my head, and since I thought a hat looked weird with a T-shirt, I wore a jacket. I thought my head would be less noticeable with a hat on it and the hat less noticeable with a jacket. I smoked a lot of marijuana in order to forget why I wore the jacket. One deception after another, designed to hide from myself.

After three years, I knew it was time to stop wearing my hat. I began to go for walks at night without my hat. In the darkness, no one could see me, and I could gradually learn to feel comfortable without it. Feeling the night breeze on my head was a new sensation. I felt elated and scared at the same time. I felt I was alive again.

Last year at my nephew's high-school graduation party, I remembered my high-school graduation party. There was a picture taken of me with my two best friends. Afterward, we told everyone about the law firm we would have someday. It would be called Elliott, Zachary and Harrington.

Although we were best friends, we were always competitive with each other. Because of that, I felt I could never let my guard down or show them my vulnerable side. I couldn't bear to let them see me after I flunked out of college and started losing my hair. I thought people liked me because of the image I presented. Now, I was depressed and insecure. The image was shattered. Since I didn't have it all together, I thought they would laugh at me.

So I moved away and didn't answer their phone calls. When they came over, I didn't answer the door. When my best friend, Ted, finally came over, I told him I didn't want to see him anymore.

"Bill," he pleaded, "what's wrong? Are you depressed?"

"I just don't want to see you anymore," I replied without looking at him. I never saw him again.

That night at my nephew's graduation party, I felt it was time to see Ted. After all this time, I could explain to him what had happened.

I hesitated. What if he were a rich and successful lawyer with a beautiful wife, big house and Mercedes? Could I handle that? After all, I lived in a mobile home. What if he saw I wasn't the hotshot anymore? Maybe *he* was the hotshot now. Even though the hat was gone, I realized I was still hiding.

I called the only Zachary in the phone book. It was his sister. "Hi," I said. "I'm an old friend of Ted's."

"I don't know where he is," she replied. "You know about the trouble?"

"Trouble?" I asked. "What trouble?"

"He started having problems his second year in college..."

I hung up, and the terror made its way from my stomach to my throat. Although it was after eleven o'clock at night, I jumped in the car and drove to the house where he grew up.

Ted's mother explained about Ted. He had been diagnosed as a schizophrenic his sophomore year in college— six months after I had refused to see him anymore. He was in and out of hospitals during the time I had been wearing my hat.

That night when I got home I called Ted at the institution. "Ted, this is Bill Elliott."

"Yes," he said very matter-of-factly. After all those years, I expected more recognition or surprise in his voice.

"Bill Elliott," I continued. "I was your best friend in high school."

"Yes," he said simply.

"Do you remember me? I smashed up your dad's car. Remember?"

"Yes. You were known as 'tenacious,'" he said. "I have to go now." It was the voice of a robot. It was the same voice that Ted joked with in high school, but now he wasn't joking.

Ted had been a good student and athlete. While I had always just tried to get by, Ted had tried to excel.

"What happened at school, Ted?" I asked.

"I didn't finish." Although his tone of voice hadn't changed, I could sense his shame.

"Are you married?" he asked.

"No."

"Are you in trouble?" he asked, concerned.

"No," I said, remembering all I had been through. "Not anymore." I could feel his relief. Here he was, in a mental institution, and he was worried about me.

"Do you have a good heart?" he asked.

"Now I do." The tears began to run down my face.

"Good," he said with finality and approval. For some reason, it really mattered that he approved of me.

"Ted, may I come to see you?"

"No, don't come here."

"May I call you again?"

"I would prefer you didn't." I could hear the shame. He was ashamed of his condition. "I got to go now," he added. There was a finality in his voice. If he had hung up then, I don't think I would ever have been able to reach him again.

"Ted, I have to tell you something," I said, as I started to cry. "You were my best friend. You're still my best friend. Do you remember the last time you came to see me at my sister's house?"

"Yes, I remember."

"I didn't want to see you because I was ashamed of myself. I was losing my hair and was really depressed. I didn't want anyone to see me that way."

"Well, I have to go."

"Ted, may I call you again?"

"Yes," he said, and he hung up.

Ted had been my competitor in high school, and even though it had been twelve years, I had carried on an unconscious competition with him that for years had existed only in my mind. Now, Ted and I had arrived at the same place, the place where the most important question is, "Do you have a good heart?"

William Elliott

9

EATING DISORDERS & DEPRESSION

*W*hen it gets dark enough you can see the stars.

Lee Salk

Starving for Control

My junior year started off great. I was going out with my first boyfriend, I was an honor student and school-work seemed pretty easy. I was always busy after school, with voice lessons, dance class, play practice and auditions. I loved having so much going on in my life. I felt like I could handle anything.

In October of that year, I got the best news—I had landed a role on an HBO show called *The Sopranos*. We had shot the pilot episode the previous June, but now I learned that it was going to be a full series. Filming didn't start until the next June, after school let out. I didn't think things could get better, but that left room for things to get worse.

Just two weeks after I found out about *The Sopranos*, my boyfriend broke up with me with no explanation. I felt like my life was over. I cried for days, moping around. I didn't want to go to dance class, and I didn't even want to go to school. I wondered why he'd broken up with me and began to fear that it was because I wasn't as pretty or as skinny as the other girls we knew, so I put myself on a small diet—"just to lose five pounds."

I also got involved in even more activities at school. I joined a repertory dance team and a singing group and helped with my school's fashion show. I did my studying at night, after my activities. My parents were worried: They'd always said that if my grades started to slip, I would have to leave "the business"; still, I reassured them that I was used to taking on a big load.

But in January, for the first time, I felt like things were spinning out of control. My extracurriculars began to interfere with studying. I drove myself crazy trying to decide which activity took precedence. I couldn't spare any extra minutes to think about dieting, so I made what seemed like a great plan. Each morning I'd wake up early to exercise and then choose a menu for the day. Diet and exercise seemed to be the only parts of my life I had complete control over.

I was losing weight and getting tons of compliments from friends and family, which pushed me even further. I severely restricted my calories and woke up earlier and earlier to get extra hours of exercise in. If I didn't work out, I couldn't think about anything else until I did. I began to actually fear food and crave exercise. I was completely miserable, but strangely, I felt I *had* to do it. Instead of me being in control, this compulsion was controlling me.

I started to fall asleep in school and at practice. My grades were slipping, and my friends started asking me why I brown-bagged my lunch all the time and never wanted to go out to eat with them. I made excuses, telling them I didn't like the cafeteria food and that I needed to stay behind and catch up on work during lunch period. I didn't go out on weekends anymore—that was when I caught up on my sleep. I, the social butterfly, was becoming someone I wasn't, and I didn't know why.

Not too long after that, my parents commented that I was getting too skinny. I told myself that they were just being parents and ignored it. I knew I didn't look good, but I wouldn't look in the mirror because I didn't want to see what was happening to my body. I *had* to exercise and plan my meals. It was so horrible. A normal life didn't exist for me anymore. Happiness wasn't an option. There were no options.

I knew exactly what my best friend meant when she kept asking me, "Is everything okay?" but I couldn't admit my problem. I told her I was dancing too much, and the weight loss had "just happened." The kids in school were cruel. They said I looked "disgusting" and laughed at me. They seemed almost *glad* to see me in such a bad state. Maybe it was because I was becoming successful in my career. Even some of my close friends took part in poking fun. This hurt me so much. I didn't want to be around the kids from school anymore. I was on my own.

While getting ready to go out with my parents one day, I stepped in front of the mirror. As I stared at my reflection, I couldn't believe what I saw: Hollow, sunken eyes, ringed with large dark circles, belonged to what was barely a body. My bones stuck out, and some ribs were visible. I was emaciated. I had lost my breasts, my legs were tiny and I had grown hair all over my body (this commonly happens when you are underweight). I felt like a ghost.

During that car ride, I kept thinking that if I ended my life, this all would go away. That suicide had even crossed my mind scared me more than anything had yet, and I began to cry. I told my parents that I didn't want to live anymore, that I couldn't handle it. My dad pulled the car to the side of the road, and my parents cried, too, asking me what was wrong. Finally, I blurted out, "I have an eating disorder. Please get me help!" It was so difficult, but it was the best feeling in the world to finally say it. They admitted they had secretly suspected this all along, but, like myself, had never truly believed that I could have an eating disorder. Then my parents told me they couldn't be prouder that I'd told them and that they were going to help me get better.

The next day I had an appointment with a psychiatrist and a nutritionist, both of whom I started to see twice a week. About a month into therapy, I got used to the idea that I needed to gain weight. Putting on weight was harder than I thought it would be, but I was trying. Saying "I gained a pound!" isn't always praised in our society, but at that time it was the best news I could give anyone. My parents were very supportive during all of this, and many of my friends were also amazing. I think a major part of my recovery was regaining my happiness, too.

When June rolled around, I couldn't wait to start filming the first season of *The Sopranos*. I had just turned seventeen, and I was feeling good. But when I went for my costume fitting, the people on the set were disappointed. I wasn't the same girl who had auditioned for the part. Though I had gained some weight, I was still very, very thin. They pulled my mom aside and voiced their concern: I didn't look healthy, and they were worried that I wouldn't be able to handle the long hours of filming. In short, if I didn't gain some weight back, I would be replaced.

It was a shock—but it was more incentive for me to get better. I hung around the craft services table and truck to get little snacks between takes, and I continued to see my nutritionist and therapist.

Eventually, we all agreed that I was strong enough to be on my own. Today, my life is pretty much back to normal. I have returned to my regular clothing size, and instead of exercising every day for hours at a time, I go to the gym about three or four times a week, working out with a trainer or doing my Tae-Bo video—just to be healthy. No foods are off-limits. I make a conscious effort to eat the right foods for energy and good health, but I will not diet. I find myself enjoying life even more now that food isn't always on my brain.

Jamie-Lynn Sigler

[EDITORS' NOTE: *The following are some resources for eating-disorder support and education. Eating disorders are serious and even deadly if left untreated. If you or someone you know is suffering from an eating disorder, it is important to talk to a professional as soon as possible. The following are some resources that will help you find the information and support you need.*]

Bulimia/Anorexia Self-Help Hotline: 800-448-3000

Eating Disorders Awareness and Prevention (EDAP): 800-931-2237, *www.edap.org*

Eating Disorder Recovery Online: *www.edrecovery.com*

Just One of Those Days

"This is the worst day of my life,"
she says casually
as she has a million plus times before.
She slams the door of her room,
blocking the outside world,
the chaos,
and her parents.

Everything is always going wrong
and there's nothing she can do.
"Leave me alone!"
she yells,
not really talking to anyone in particular.
She draws in a deep breath.
She inhales her troubles,
her sorrows, her secrets.

She exhales nothing—
all of her feelings stay locked inside.
She keeps them close until they consume
her soul slowly—bit by bit.
Her angry music blasts loudly,

heard down the street.
But she doesn't care.

She is only concerned with her troubles,
and she can't seem to get them out of her mind.
They stay there eating away her other thoughts.
Jumping onto her bed and burying her head
    into her covers as deep as they can go,
she looks back on her day, sighs,
    and gets ready for tomorrow.

Jenny Sharaf

Suffering in Silence

I am standing in line at the pharmacy with my mom waiting to have my prescription filled. What brought me here was more than my mother's old Mercury Sable. What led me here has spanned the course of my lifetime. A series of blackened days each exactly like the one before it has led me to this place.

This morning after waking up for about the fourth time, I finally forced myself out of bed. I felt nauseous at the prospect of another day. Here I am fifteen years old, a time of life when most kids race to greet the dawn, and yet I try my best to sleep the time away.

Slowly I move toward my mirrored bureau feeling as though I'm walking through Jell-O. Each step is a deliberate effort, although my body is young and healthy. I often wish that life came with a conveyor belt that I could just step on and ride to get where I need to go.

As I reach the bureau, I stare into my reflection in the mirror holding one hand upon the bureau's cold hard edge, while running the other through my long pile of misspent hair. Each strand seems to go its own way, determined to defy me. What I see in my reflection disturbs me. I don't see that young girl with potential who my parents say I am; rather, I see ugliness and imperfection. I wonder what I did to deserve this face which causes me so much pain. I'm not deformed by nature's standards. I have two eyes, a nose, and a mouth, yet it must be this hideous face which causes others to reject me.

Other girls my age are surrounded by friends and laughter. I walk alone through the halls of my school wishing I could be them. Wishing I could be mostly anyone but me. What secret do these other girls share that I'll never understand? It's tough to be an outsider watching life as others live it, and I wonder when it is going to be my turn.

Most days sleeping seems a less painful way to spend the hours than living. My dreams are my only escape. If I could, I'd love to, oh-so-neatly, slip into the shoes of one of those my age who smilingly surround me. What does it feel like to laugh out loud or unconsciously dance your way through a day?

I believe in reincarnation, because I must have done something awfully wrong to deserve this punishment. I am unworthy of the happy times that others get to be a part of so effortlessly.

And I am angry at a God who would allow me to suffer this way. I am angry at my parents, and so I say things to them that I regret only moments later. Foolishly, I rant and rave over things that they can't help. "Why do we have to go out with another family for dinner tonight? I just want to be alone," I cry. I hate being subjected to another child my own age that my parents are force-feeding me to spend time with in an effort to create a perfect social life. Is it that they want me to be happy, or do they really only want themselves to be happy? I hate my parents, and I love my parents so much that each of my defiant outbursts is followed by self-hatred over the pain I am causing them every day.

I worry that life will never be any different for me. I'm frightened to the point that I sometimes wonder what the point is. Is there really any reason to make my bed, or clean my room, or even shower? Sure it will make my mom happy, but it won't change anything for me. Is outward appearance all that life is really about? If I can just hold it all together, keeping a smile on my face and a clean room, at least maybe then my parents could be happy. They would think I'm fine and normal, but I would know I'm not. I would still feel this awful pain inside me.

I feel alone in depression, as it separates me from everyone around me. I feel freakishly different, in my own world. And when I step outside my world it always ends in pain. A simple two-minute conversation with a peer gets twisted through my mind endlessly throughout the day . . . throughout the weeks. Why didn't I say this or that? Why did I say this or that? What did they mean when they said this or that? If only I could have done it or said it differently. Regret, frustration, depression, this is my routine. It's not friends I see walking towards me as I enter my school's cafeteria; rather, I see an endless series of confrontations with the enemy. They do not understand me. I do not understand me.

All this led to my visit with Dr. Katz. And now I am standing at my mom's side as she is having my prescription filled. She taps her fingers nervously on the counter as we wait, and I again feel guilt for the pain I've caused her.

Dr. Katz and I talked for precisely fifty minutes earlier today in his dreary little office. He sat across the room from me, while my mom waited uneasily out in the hallway. I tried to form a feeble smile as the door closed between us so that she wouldn't worry about me. I guess it's too late for that.

Dr. Katz listened to me speak, while closing his eyes and nodding his head slowly in a rhythmic fashion. I wondered if he really heard my words, or if he was just taking a quick nap at 120 bucks a pop. When he'd heard enough from me, or it was nearly the end of our allotted fifty minutes, he opened his eyes and began to speak.

He told me that he believes I am suffering from depression, and I rolled my eyes at his brilliant deduction. He then went on to explain that it is not my fault, and in my head I wondered how he knew that I believe that it is all my fault.

He asked me if I have ever heard of something called a "chemical brain imbalance." I shook my head. He explained to me that this is what causes my depression and that there are medications that can correct it. He asked me if I have ever heard of Obsessive-Compulsive Disorder or OCD and I again answer no. He told me that this disorder sometimes accompanies depression, manifesting itself as different obsessive compulsions. In my case, he said, it causes me to replay social situations over and over again like a broken record. I was struck by the fact that I've never even listened to a record, only CDs, but I got the point.

And so that's why I am standing here with my mom, waiting for the pharmacist to fill my prescription. For the first time I feel sort of hopeful that something can lead me back to life. The pharmacist casually looks my way as he counts out the tiny yellow pills, and I wonder if he feels sorry for me. I wonder if he thinks I'm crazy.

Then the gray-haired old lady who works the register rings up my sale, and I stare at the tiny bottle that might hold hope for me. I look forward to my next visit with Dr. Katz, hoping that maybe our sessions together will quiet something that is currently screaming inside of me. And I wonder how many other kids are out there who are suffering in silence just like me.

Ruth Greenspan
As told to C. S. Dweck

[EDITORS' NOTE: *Clinical depression is a serious illness that can affect your grades, your relationships with friends and family members, and your behavior in all areas of your life. Some of the signs of depression include:*

* *A change in appetite and sleep patterns*
* *Loss of interest or enjoyment in usual activities*
* *Prolonged sadness*
* *Withdrawal from friends*
* *Feelings of worthlessness*
* *Lack of energy*
* *Poor school performance*

As many as 15 to 20 percent of teens have experienced serious depression. If you are concerned that you or someone you know may be suffering from depression, we encourage you to talk to your school counselor or an adult you trust. Treatment for depression can include therapy and/or medication. The following are some helpful resources.]

Youth Crisis Line: 800-843-5200, *twenty-four hours*

Info Line: 800-339-6993
General information and referrals.

Teen Line: 800-TLC-TEEN

Cookie-Cutter Hands

It started a few years ago—the cutting. My boyfriend had just broken up with me, and my mother disappeared. She left a note—that was it—and then was gone.

On the outside I was your typical high-school freshman. I was in the popular group. Older boys liked me, and I earned straight A's. I was told to be grateful, to rejoice that I didn't have to keep a job after school and that I could attend a private college back east after graduation. I was told that everything was going to be okay. I was told to smile, and not to think about Mom or stress out over school. I was told not to care. Except, the problem was that I *did* care. I cared about Mom leaving and my boyfriend dumping me, and not being able to talk to anyone. I cared that my dad was always working and that I was always alone. I cared about everything—and I felt so alone.

On the inside I was tormented by feelings of angst, loneliness and self-loathing. My mother's leaving confused me. I was ashamed and humiliated over my breakup with my boyfriend. In a sense, I felt dead. It was as if I went to school mummified. No one knew that my insides were rotting away, slowly.

I never talked about these feelings with my friends. Why would I? What would they say? How would they react? I was happy and fun to hang out with at school, and nothing was ever wrong. I grew up in a neighborhood where the grass was always cut and sixteen candles on the cake justified a shiny new car.

Somehow, even though I was suffering, I couldn't feel it. I wanted to feel the pain that I could not understand. I wanted to reshape the crooked emotions into a neat little line that stretched across my right arm, a line that curved around my ankle, a line that liberated the caged ghosts screaming inside me. The razor was like a tool, a wrench used to tighten the screws on my innards and keep them in place so that I didn't have to cry in public or talk about my pain or feel alone.

With every red beaded line, I would sigh in calm relief. I didn't cry when I was hurt or upset. Instead, I cut. The complex emotions leaked from my flesh in the form of blood, rather than from my eyes in the form of tears. Anytime I felt empty or stressed or confused, anytime I looked in the mirror—hating myself and my cursed reflection—I would cut. I would cut just to bleed, to know that I was still breathing, to feel my heart race and my nerves stir.

My secret kept me safe. I became addicted to a pain that didn't hurt, but instead felt nice. I sought refuge in the shower with my cookie-cutter-like razor, making imprints on my soft flesh: circles and lines, hearts and stars. I was steady with my razor. The whole world seemed to blur and slow down, and the cuts left me calm as I watched the crimson tears drip onto the white shower tiles.

I hid my scars under designer blouses with long sleeves. Sometimes I let them show.

"Darn cat," I would say if anyone asked. "Darn friggin' cat."

My addiction to self-mutilation lasted all through high school. No one knew that there was a war going on inside of me. I was really good at hiding it. Sometimes I flirted with the idea of pressing the razor harder into my wrist to make the whole world stop. I never did, though, thank God. Instead I got caught.

After four years of hiding my cookie-cutter hands and neatly sliced arms, my father finally noticed my self-inflicted wounds. I couldn't use the same excuse with him. He knew we didn't have a cat.

I felt naked showing my father my scars. I didn't want to share them with him. I was angry with him for being so unaware, for letting my mother leave and for abandoning me with my pain. He scrutinized the red marks under my sleeves and the scabbed lines beneath my socks. And then he cried. My father had never cried before. I cried, too, and at that moment, I snapped. I suddenly realized how unhappy I was. I wasn't happy at school, and I wasn't happy after cutting myself. Cutting had been a release, an ephemeral exhale, a brief hope that I could make it hurt enough to release the pain, so that I could smile again, and that my smile would be for real. I wanted to make myself bleed and then watch myself heal. I wanted to be in control of the wounds inflicted in order to see the pain I felt inside, and, yet, I realized at that moment that I wasn't in control of anything.

I started seeing a doctor and learning how to express my emotions and make my pain tangible. I wrote in my diary and played the guitar. I talked to my father and my friends at school. I talked to my new boyfriend. I tried to get out of the house as much as possible, exploring nature and the other side of the window. I took in the air and relaxed. Slowly, it became easier. Slowly, my addiction lessened, and I was okay. It was hard, but I grew stronger each time I faced my pain. I realized that for the past four years, I had been walking through shadows without taking the time to look up at the purple jacaranda trees that cast them.

Kelly Peters
As told to Rebecca Woolf

[EDITORS' NOTE: *I know how scared you are and I know you think it's different for you, but I promise if you reach out and ask for help, it will come. Here are some resources for you, so that you don't have to face what you are going through alone.*]

National Mental Health Association Help Line: 800-969-6642

United Way Crisis Help Line: 800-233-4357

Numb

The sharp edge of the razor cuts my skin easily.
I'm numb to the pain,
Numb to the blood,
Too numb to realize what's happening,
To realize what I'm doing.
One cut follows another,
And another,
Till I can't stop.
The razor falls from my hand,
Blood drips down my arm,
Tears roll down my cheeks.
What have I done?

Jessica Dubose

10

DEATH
& DYING

*It is only when we truly know and understand
that we have a limited time on Earth and
that we have no way of knowing when our
time is up that we will begin to live each day
to the fullest, as if it were the only one we
had.*

Elisabeth Kübler-Ross

This Too Shall Pass

While compiling this book we were touched with sadness by the passing of two teenage girls who were readers of our *Chicken Soup* books. We, too, learned the hard way that suffering and death touch each and every one of us. None of us are able to go through life without suffering from life's hard lessons, including the hardest lesson of all—the death of someone we love and care about.

While working on *Teen Love: A Journal on Friendship*, we sent a permission agreement to a girl who had sent us many wonderful poems. A week or two later we received a letter from her mother. She explained to us that her daughter, Teal Henderson, had passed away on May 11, 2000. She went on to say that both Teal and she loved the *Chicken Soup for the Teenage Soul* books and that her daughter would have been so thrilled to know that we were considering her poetry for publication. Because Teal loved to write, her mother felt blessed that she was left with even more memories of her through the many stories and poems her daughter had written.

Her mother shared these special words about her daughter saying, "She embraced life fully, almost fearlessly, as if she knew her time here would be short.

She was our sunshine and though we no longer bask in her light, we'll always feel the warmth of her love."

We did include some of Teal's poetry in *Teen Love: A Journal on Friendship,* and are including more of it in this book. As you will see, Teal was an amazing writer and she seemed to somehow sense the preciousness of each moment she was alive. We remain deeply touched by Teal's poetry and by her mother's incredible courage and generosity. We thank her for sharing with us her daughter's beautiful poetry and a mother's unending and unconditional love.

Shortly thereafter we received another sad letter about one of our readers, Ailie:

> My daughter, Ailie, was killed in an automobile accident on March 3rd. I bought her Chicken Soup for the Teenage Soul *about three weeks before she died. SHE LLLLLLLOVED YOUR BOOKS!! She was so thrilled when I handed it to her that she hugged me harrrrd!! ("I love you, Mama!" I can hear her voice. . . .)*
>
> *I find her everywhere on our computer. She loved your Web site and writing. She sent you poems, she gave advice to others on your Web site and asked for advice as well. She truly loved all that you stand for. She was becoming a strong, proud woman, and you can take responsibility for a lot of that!*
>
> *I wanted to share this with you so you know how special you were to her, as she was the heartbeat in my chest.*
>
> *Every morning she would come in my room and ask if I wanted to read her new poem. I loved them all.*

Bonnie was kind enough to share with us a poem she had written to her daughter before she died.

I Have an Angel

I have an angel with me,
inside of my head,
even when she is not near.

She came from me,
and she resides with me,
and in me every moment of my living.

From the moment she emerged she owned me,
heart and soul.
She brings me my greatest joys,
and my most unholy sorrow.

And we are linked spiritually,
and physically.

She has the greatest beauty I have ever seen.
The poets have written of the likes of her . . .
golden hair, and eyes of the sea,
a heart capable of capturing the soul,
of anyone or anything that comes near.

She grows even as I watch,
and when she is grown,
she will be a power to behold:
strong, beautiful and powerful in spirit,
graceful, delicate, charming and funny.

She captures your eyes, but wait until
you feel the pull of her true self—
you can fall, you know!

Everyone who knows her has fallen,
and she has only just begun . . .
My smiling Angel,
my smiley,
my Ailie.

Bonnie Gainor

She also shared a poem that Ailie wrote to her mother
in response:

Mother

I have a mother,
and she's very sweet.
During the fun times,
she always tickles my feet.

When I'm down,
or drowning in self-doubt,
all I have to do is call her name,
and she will let me out.

We have been there for each other,
always through thick and thin.
When there is a secret that I didn't know,
she would let me in.

She will never leave my heart,
no matter what she does.
She's my one and only,
she's my one true love.

Ailie Anna Amalia Pearson

While compiling this book and thinking about the sadness that some of the stories expressed, I wondered if some of it was too depressing for teenagers to read. There is so much about death and illness in these pages, and I thought that perhaps it is best for teens not to think about these things. What made me change my mind was the passage, "A time for every season. A time to live and a time to die. A time to laugh and a time to cry."

I also thought about a story my aunt told me when I was a teenager and went through the death of a loved one. Soon after she told me this story, my aunt passed away unexpectedly.

A woman lost her last living relative to old age, and she was devastated. She went to a wise man and asked him if he could bring her relative back to life. He told her he could, but he needed to make a special potion and she must bring him the ingredients. She eagerly agreed. He listed strange ingredients, all of which she brought back faithfully.

Finally, he said, "The last thing you must bring me is a grain of rice from a family that has suffered no losses and has lived in constant happiness." The woman eagerly set off to look for such a family. It sounded easy enough to her. She looked in all the houses in the village and the surrounding villages, but found no one who had never suffered the pain of losing a loved one. She went out to look in the rest of the country, but still found no one who could help her. I must leave no stone unturned, *she thought. She traveled across the world and asked at every house, but found no family that fit the wise man's description.*

Finally, exhausted and discouraged, she returned to her village and told the wise man, "There is no family in the world that has not lost a dear one. Please, tell me there is another way to complete the potion." The wise man replied, "Not one family in the world has escaped the pain of losing a loved one.

The potion cannot be made. All families have suffered like you do now, and their pain has passed. So will yours."

Our thoughts and prayers go out to both Teal's and Ailie's families and to all of our readers who have suffered the loss of a loved one. There are no words to express the honor we feel when a mother or a friend chooses to share their deepest feelings and experiences with us. This is true generosity of spirit because it is done in hopes that you, the reader, will come away a better person. This compassion is the fire that drives us; it is the reason and the heart of all that we do.

Kimberly Kirberger

Seize the Day

Just a moment in this lifetime,
Just a tragedy ahead.
Not knowing where each turn will lead,
Within seconds we might be dead.

Live each day to the fullest,
Do not stop to wonder why.
Do everything your heart desires,
In dreams, reach for the sky.

Surprises at every stop sign,
With its share of wrong ways and dead-ends.
Statistics don't help you with the future,
They only tell you where you've been.

With so many people among us,
There are no certainties.
And all it takes is just one person,
To reroute history.

Don't waste one single moment,
How very precious that they are.
What seems a long way off,
Is really not that far.

Teal Henderson

Some People Come

Some people come into our lives and quickly go.
Some stay for a while and leave footprints on
our heart, and we are never, ever the same.

Flavia Weedn

A good friend of mine passed away on December 26 because of a deadly combination of a debilitating type of muscular dystrophy and meningitis. The day before the visitation at the funeral home, I stepped out to Wal-Mart after work intending to purchase a sympathy card to mail to his bereaved parents. I must admit that I was shocked and disappointed at the time—and I remain that way now—at the decided lack of relevance, originality and simple, heartfelt kindness that greeted me in that card aisle. The birthday cards were as amusing as usual, and those bearing congratulations were brightly colored and encouraging, but those few cards on the bottom row, claiming to offer "Deepest Sympathy," left a lot to be desired. Real pain and genuine condolences seemed to be buried under layer upon layer of trite, meaningless, talentless poetry and camouflaged by pastel watercolors of birds, berries and hackneyed, if somewhat beautiful, sunsets.

It appeared to me that even the purveyors of the greeting card, the all-purpose wordsmiths who have given us a poem and a painting for all occasions, cannot find the words to express what someone feels when a loved one dies.

The card I ended up selecting showed a blue-tinted sand dollar half-buried in a rippled sand dune of a similar hue, while a scripted font declared, "Wherever a beautiful soul has been . . . there is a trail of beautiful memories." I was, in a word, delighted when I found it, hidden behind one claiming that "time heals all wounds"—the poetry it contained did not make me cringe, the art was simple, and it contained no uneducated, condescending assurances that the grief would, eventually, pass and that life would go on as usual. I was especially pleased that the writing on the inside was small and condensed and provided for two very nearly blank surfaces on which I could inscribe a personal note.

And yet, nearly a week after Kevin's death, those blank surfaces remain blank, and the card still sits on my desk. I have not, thus far, found the heart or the words to write that personal note. The visitation, funeral and interment have come and gone. I have spoken personally to Kevin's parents and expressed my sympathies. And I have shed many tears on many shoulders on several different occasions.

But I simply cannot bring myself to prepare the card. It's honestly not because I don't know what to say because words, or a lack thereof, are not something I generally struggle with. It is simply that I just can't decide which stories to share in a card about beautiful memories.

What to say to the people who knew and loved him best? I don't think I can tell them about anything of which they are not already aware. While I'm certain that stories of his courage and compassion would be appreciated, I'm also confident that they would be somewhat redundant. They're aware, I'm sure, of his sharp wit and his intense hatred of pity, and they've seen that animated smile of his time and time again.

And so the card sits.

Should I tell them of the time I pushed Kev's wheelchair through a friend's neighborhood, and he kept telling me that, having been a passenger in a small vehicle under my command on an only slightly bumpy sidewalk, he pitied my future passengers in an actual car? Should I tell them of the code in which Kevin and I used to speak, much to the annoyance of those with whom we ate lunch every day and about how we used to laugh at their frustrated faces? Should I tell them about the day I knew he was going to confess his undying love for my best friend, and I didn't warn her out of a promised loyalty to him, and then how I accidentally walked in on the whole scene, far too late to save either of them from deep embarrassment?

There are, however, some memories that taint the sweet ones and turn our relationship somewhat bittersweet in retrospect. I long very much to tell his family about all the times I got frustrated with him because he couldn't do very much for himself and so relied on me for help, and about the time when, faced with two jobs and a pile of homework, I actually told him that I didn't have time for him. I want to tell them about how I fully intended to pass up what ended up being my final opportunity to see him, a friend of five years, at his Christmas party just days before his death, to spend the evening with my boyfriend of one month. I don't want to burden his hurting family, but I want somebody to know that Kevin had an amazing way, even in the last few days of his life, of reminding everyone of what was important and what wasn't.

And so the card sits. I can see it from where I am right now, tucked lightly into the envelope, accompanied, of course, by a stamp and my new pen. And yet, accessories notwithstanding, it is blank.

Goethe, a nineteenth-century German writer and scientist, once commented that the things that matter most must never be at the mercy of the things that matter least, and although I can't say for sure whether or not Kevin was aware of that insight, I wish I could show his parents the many ways his daily life embodied that principle. There were a great deal of things in his life that certainly could have mattered quite a bit more—the fact that he couldn't walk or even use his arms very much, the fact that he couldn't speak as clearly as he would have liked, the fact that he couldn't play catch with us at lunch or have a regular romantic relationship with a girl or even hand over his own money while making a purchase or do any of the other things that we all take for granted—but somehow they weren't the things that mattered most to Kevin because he knew, better than any of us, what was important.

Instead of growing to loathe the elevator that he was forced to take instead of the stairs at school, he named it "Otis" and let us all ride in it with him. Instead of dwelling on his inability to communicate orally, he developed a great love for the Internet and produced "Your Daily Laugh," a daily e-mail newsletter of jokes and stories designed to encourage and brighten everyone's day. And instead of growing bitter and unhappy as his condition worsened, he grew to love and worship the God who had made him the way he was.

Kevin knew that it wasn't time that was important; it was how that time was spent that would matter in the end. He was aware that it wasn't the number of relationships that one was involved in that was meaningful, but rather the quality of those relationships, and so he worked hard to maintain the friendships that were so important to him, often in spite of great difficulty or distance. He knew that forgiveness was important, because he was aware that time wouldn't always wait for things to just work out. Every day was a struggle for him, but he compensated by watching *The Simpsons* and reading every *Calvin and Hobbes* treasury that was ever compiled, because he knew that if you can't laugh, the days are just too long.

Not everyone has had the pleasure of knowing someone with an attitude that positive. For those of us who have, however, our lives have been touched in a tremendous way. We know that life is too short to have the things that matter most be at the mercy of the things that matter least. We know how to live—now—and most of us are willing to let you in on the secret. Seize the day. Watch *The Simpsons.* Name an elevator. And laugh a little.

And to Kevin, the one who informed me with the biggest smile I have ever seen on anyone's face that everyone gets to walk in heaven, I hope you're enjoying those cartwheels. You earned every one of them.

Lauren Anderson

My Guardian Angel

When I was fourteen years old, I met two people who would change my life forever. During the summer before ninth grade, I was at the beach with my friend, Nick, when he introduced me to his best friend. His name was Lee. We were instant friends. There was something about his smile that stayed with me for the rest of that weekend. We started talking to each other online, and then on the phone. We just clicked.

Over the next few months, I found myself falling in love with Lee. I don't know how or why it happened, but it did. By the time football season rolled around in mid-October, Lee and I were dating. Going out to eat after home games was a tradition for cheerleaders and football players at Central. And since I was a cheerleader and Lee played football, that's usually where we ended up on Friday nights. One night I was sitting with Lee eating my usual chicken fingers when this short, kind of pudgy kid walked in and strolled right over to our table.

"Meghan, this is Dan Welch," Lee said to me.

The kid looked at me with bright-blue eyes, smiled the biggest, whitest smile I'd ever seen and said, "Hey, what's up?"

Little did I know that this was the beginning of the most important friendship I'd ever have in my life, and that I would grow to love that smile (not to mention that laugh) and depend on it to get me through some of my worst days. Dan made me laugh, made me cry, picked up the pieces when my life seemed to fall apart, and always managed to keep me smiling. We had staring contests that I *always* lost and wrestling matches that I usually won. He paged me when my favorite songs were on the radio and didn't care when I sang at the top of my lungs to them in his car.

For about a year, the three of us spent as much time as we could together. They were my life. Lee and I had our ups and downs, but no matter how many times Lee and I fought or saw other people or made each other mad, we always found our way back to each other.

Then at the end of August 1999, my heart was broken. Dan and Lee were going off to college. And even though they were only going forty-five minutes away to Boston where they would be roommates at Northeastern, I thought I was going to die without them.

But it wasn't as bad as I thought it would be. My parents didn't mind the phone bill too much, so I got to talk to them every day, and we talked online, too. They came home every weekend. On one of those weekend nights, they called me from Lee's house to tell me they were coming to pick me up so I could go play Lazer Tag with them. As much as I wanted to go (I had been bugging them for a while now about going with them), I had to tell them no since I had to get up early the next morning. I was on my way out the door to the mall when the phone rang at 7:45. The last person I expected to hear from was Nick, who had gone with them. He sounded different, kind of shaken up. He told me they were just waiting for the game to start so I thought nothing of it. When I got home from the mall I found out he'd called again, right after I had left. I thought that was odd, so I called him back. As soon as he opened his mouth, my body turned to ice.

"I have bad news, Meg . . . Lee and Dan were in a car accident tonight on the way to Lazer Tag."

I almost dropped the phone. This was not happening to me. Not to the two people I loved most in the world. I wouldn't believe it.

"No, Nick, I don't believe you. You would've told me when you first called . . . no, you're lying! How could you lie about something like that? I hate you!"

Right before I hung up, I heard Nick yell, "I'm coming over right now . . . wait for me. . . ."

I went downstairs, still shaken, and waited by the door. I expected to see the three of them come up my steps laughing at how "gullible" I was. But when Nick walked up alone, I knew he had told me the truth. I could see it in his face.

"Nick, please tell me they're okay . . . they have to be okay! Nick, tell me!" I didn't know what I was saying; I could barely see straight I was crying so hard.

"Lee's in the ICU in Boston. I don't know if he's gonna be okay or not. No one would tell me anything."

"And . . . what about Dan?"

No answer.

"Nick, tell me he's okay!" I yelled.

"I can't, Meg. . . ." Nick got very quiet and looked down. "Dan didn't make it. I'm so sorry, Meg . . . I'm so sorry. I was going to tell you earlier when I called you before, but I couldn't tell you . . . not like that, not on the phone." Nick was struggling for words, and I was struggling for breath.

"No!" I collapsed against him, crying. He pulled me into his arms and just hugged me. One of my best friends was dead, and my boyfriend was in intensive care. It was too much.

Nick got me into the living room and told my parents the details. Lee and Dan had been following Nick and a few other people in Dan's father's Blazer. Dan had lost control of the truck, and it crashed into the guardrail, flipping over and throwing them out. They didn't have their seat belts on. Nick had called me from the side of the road on his cell phone. He told me later that he had needed to hear my voice; he had needed to know that at least one person he cared about was okay.

Somehow I made it through that night. I went to see Lee at the hospital, and his mom told me he'd be okay. He had a broken cheekbone, a dislocated shoulder and some other injuries, but he would be okay. He didn't know about Dan yet, and everyone was worried about how to break the news.

I spent the next week in a daze, just going through the motions. Nothing mattered to me anymore. I cried myself to sleep every night, and even cried throughout the day. How do you go on without your best friend?

Telling Lee about Dan was the hardest. His parents told him, and he didn't believe it at first. Eventually he realized it was true, and when he did all he could do was cry and hold my hand. I didn't know what to say, so I stayed pretty quiet when they told him. It was a sad moment for all of us and a life-changing one for Lee.

It's now been almost a year and a half since Dan's death. Lee is fine now, physically, but emotionally we're both scarred for life. There is a part of us that will always be missing, a place in us that will always have Dan's name on it. I've been to his grave countless times, and I talk to him every night. I would give anything to have my best friend back. Nothing and no one will ever take his place. But I know he's watching over me. He once promised me that he would always be there for me and that he'd never let me down. I know Dan, and I know that he'll keep that promise forever.

Meghan O'Brien

And Then I Tell My Story

My mom and I fought all the time. She worked full-time as a waitress, so she expected me to take care of Kimmy, my six-year-old sister, and to clean the house. This one day I was frustrated, and I didn't want to do the dishes. I asked her, "Why do I have to do everything?"

My mother dragged me outside and put me in the car. She looked at me and said, "You know what AIDS is, right?"

"Yeah, I know what that is. I heard about it on TV," I muttered.

"I have AIDS; Kimmy and I both have AIDS. We have AIDS, Maria, and I can't fight with you anymore. I need you to help me." Then she went back into the house.

I remember sitting there stunned. I didn't know what to do. I didn't cry; I was just so scared.

Just the week before I had seen the AIDS quilt on television. I saw names of people who had died from the disease. I thought, *This doesn't relate to me.* And I had switched to cartoons. I was only twelve years old, after all.

Now, the two people I lived with and loved had AIDS. My mom had been infected through a blood transfusion before my sister was born. This was back in the early 1980s when they didn't check blood supplies.

My mom did not want me to tell anyone because she was afraid of people's reactions. After she told our church leaders, they asked her not to bring Kimmy back to Sunday school. She had gone to her church for support and instead found out they were afraid they would catch the disease.

So we kept it a secret and moved around a lot. I didn't have many friends, and that was really hard on me. My days were spent going to school, coming home to take my mom and Kimmy to doctor's appointments, paying bills, grocery shopping, cleaning the house and taking care of them at night. I got frustrated sometimes not having a normal teenager's life. I wanted to do normal things, but this was my mom and sister. It felt right to be there with them.

After a while, I became less frustrated. For the longest time, every birthday I would wish for a cure, for them to be okay and not die. My wish changed as they got worse. I started praying to God, "Please, God, take them, and don't let them go through a lot of pain." Life became more about loving the time I had with them and preparing myself for their deaths.

Mom and Kimmy went to the hospital more and more. I wanted to be with them, so I slept in a chair at the hospital; sometimes I was given a cot. Every time they went to the hospital I was sad and scared, wondering if they were going to die.

Eventually, we contacted the AIDS Foundation. They were wonderful. They had counselors who came to the house. I could talk with them; they understood what I was going through. At fifteen years old, I finally had a support system and friends.

My last two years of high school I was home-schooled.

It was too hard to go to school every day. The hospital stays were becoming more frequent and longer. The teachers knew about my situation and helped me with my assignments.

Kimmy passed away three years ago in the hospital. She was thirteen years old. I got a lot of support from the AIDS Foundation, but I did have to sign papers and make final arrangements. Mom didn't want to do it. She was too sick, and it made her too sad.

After Kimmy was gone, my mom quickly got worse. She had a brain infection and couldn't talk. Nurses taught me how to change her catheter and take care of her at home. They came to check on her every morning.

The day came when Mom didn't recognize me anymore. She mostly slept—she was on heavy pain medication. One night she was breathing really hard. I slept next to her all night, fearing the worst.

She died the next morning. Thank God, the nurse happened to be there. Otherwise, I think I might have lost it.

I stayed at the house by myself for a month. I wanted to; I needed the time alone. I started packing things and had a garage sale. My friends from the AIDS Foundation were there for me helping any way they could.

These same friends are now my family. One very good friend—Kimmy's counselor—is like a big sister. She invited me to stay at her house. I've lived with her for two years.

I'm still sad. I miss Mom and Kimmy every day. But I'll be okay. I have a lot of friends and a lot of love. I'm in community college now, and I love school.

I don't think AIDS will ever leave my life. It's part of who I am. I want to help educate as many people as I can. I participate in all of the Foundation events. I speak to students at colleges, high schools, middle schools and elementary schools to educate them about AIDS prevention. Many schools are afraid to tell kids to wear condoms or practice abstinence. When I speak I tell them, "You really need to protect yourself. Don't be fooled. Just because someone doesn't look sick, he or she could still be infected. Don't assume your boyfriend or girlfriend is all right. And don't think it can't affect you." And then I tell my story.

Maria Piñedo

[EDITORS' NOTE: *For more information on AIDS and HIV or if you would like to get involved in AIDS/HIV education and prevention efforts, the following are some helpful resources.*]

Teen AIDS Hotline: 800-234-4TEEN

National AIDS Hotline: 800-342-2437
Information, referrals, support, twenty-four hours.

Youth Crisis Line: 800-843-5200
Twenty-four hours. Bilingual.

I Wonder as I Wander

I wonder as I wander
Out under the sky
Why do people I care about
Always have to die?

Are you happy where you are,
Wherever that may be?
I wonder as I wander,
Do you still think of me?

Is it nice up there in heaven?
For I know you made it there.
Are the clouds made out of marshmallows?
Do you know that I still care?

I look up at the winter sky,
And shed a single tear.
I think of all the days gone by,
I'll always hold you dear.

I wonder as I wander
Out under the sky
Why do people I care about
Always have to die?

Hilary Begleiter

The Death of a Friend

I have had a rare anemia my whole life, which requires me to go to the hospital every four weeks for a blood trans-fusion. Every four weeks I spend two days in the hospital with nothing to do. I know some of the kids who go to the hospital regularly, and sometimes we visit each other's rooms. Only problem is, most of these kids are much younger than I am, and I can't really relate to them. I accept this fact and try to make the best of it every time I go.

During a routine visit sometime after my fifteenth birthday, my favorite nurse asked me if I had met Greg, a new patient about my age. I told her I hadn't but would like to, so she led me to his room. My life would never be the same.

His room was full of silver balloons, games and sport drinks. Greg was a boy with tan brown skin and curly black hair. He had a controller in his hand and was play-ing Nintendo. After we were introduced, he asked me if I wanted to play. I love video games so I gladly accepted his offer. I immediately noticed a neon yellow bag hanging from his I.V. pole. I asked him what it was and he told me it was chemotherapy for his leukemia. I had never really talked to someone with cancer before so I was intrigued to hear the details of the disease. We exchanged information about each other while playing Nintendo and, by the time we were done, I felt as if I had known him for years.

We were friends from that day forward. Whenever I was admitted to the hospital, I would ask if he was there. If he had just left the hospital, the nurses would always tell me Greg had asked about me. Finally, Greg's foster mom suggested to my dad that we take our friendship outside the hospital walls. So Greg started visiting me at my house, and our bond grew even stronger.

Greg's appearance changed from time to time because of the chemotherapy. His thick, curly black hair would come out, and he would look like a ripe peach covered with fuzz. Sometimes he would lose large amounts of weight and become skinny like a toothpick. The physical changes would never affect his character, though. He always kept his upbeat attitude, and he never showed any signs of fear or sadness.

Earlier this year, Greg's condition took a turn for the worse. His doctor told him that he had to come to the hospital every day for antibiotics, potassium and platelets. Since Greg's foster mom lived a good hour from the hospital, the daily hospital visit was going to pose a problem. Greg's foster mom was trying to find him a foster home closer to the hospital, so my dad applied to become a foster parent so we could take Greg under our roof. We lived less than a mile from the hospital so we thought it would be perfect. Unfortunately, the foster-care people didn't see my father as financially stable enough, and Greg ended up staying with a Russian couple who already had two foster kids.

I brought my Sony Playstation along with me when I visited him during his daily four-hour stays at the hospital. One time when I was keeping him company, I asked about his prognosis. He told me, "They've tried everything there is to try, and I might die." I couldn't believe how honest he was with me.

He was really thin, just under one hundred pounds, but I felt confident that he would be all right. After some strong antibiotics and other medications he was taking, he eventually did get better. He packed on a few pounds, grew some hair, and soon we were back to hanging out and playing video games together. We went to see *The Matrix*, which Greg decided was his all-time favorite movie. We were at the apex of happiness, and things couldn't have been better. Then, *bam!* Like a sniper's bullet, Greg was suddenly hit with a nasty infection. The chemo had affected his immune system, making him vulnerable to bacteria that was looking for a place to set up shop. Greg was once again hospitalized and bedridden. I prayed for him every time I visited.

First he lost his ability to play video games, then his ability to speak, and finally he started to slip in and out of a coma-like sleep throughout the course of the day. This continued until one Sunday night, when I went upstairs to visit Greg after receiving my blood transfusion. As I entered his room, a great sadness hit me as I saw him lying in the small bed covered in pink blankets. His eyes were closed, and every breath he took seemed as though it may be his last. He had about six tubes connected to him and four machines all around him. I wanted to push the button on the machine that administered morphine because he appeared to be in tremendous pain. I felt scared because he didn't look as if he would recover. I took his hand, which was as cold as ice, and said a prayer. I prayed for divine action and for Greg's soul to do whatever it needed to do, even if that meant going back to the other side. My dad then came to take me home, so we said our good-byes and headed back to the house. I got a good night's sleep, but the next day we got a call and found out that Greg had passed away about two hours after we left.

Knowing Greg changed my life. Greg's struggle with leukemia made me realize that no matter how bad I feel sometimes, there are people who have it worse. Even though I have to go through life with a blood disease, Greg's death taught me to be thankful for what I have rather than sad for what I do not.

Cassius Weathersby III

Timeless Friendship

Growing up, I often found myself living with my grand-mother for indefinite periods of time while my mother was in and out of treatment centers for drug and alcohol addiction. My parents divorced when I was two. My father (my custodial parent), being a firefighter, had to be away for twenty-four-hour shifts. This was when I stayed with my Gram. I was old enough to somewhat understand what was going on with my mom but still young enough to see it as an opportunity to spend as much time as possible with my grandma. To me, it was an endless slumber party, full of Tile Rummy, staying up past my bedtime and playing with the boy across the street, Matt Luke.

Matt was three years older than I, but we were always able to find something to do together. In the winter, we would sled on the giant hill behind my grandma's house. In the summer, we enjoyed games of tag and hide-and-seek with the other neighborhood kids. Boys didn't yet have cooties, nor were they creatures to be admired. Life wasn't that complicated. I didn't see him as a boy, but as a friend.

On the days I was at my grandma's, I would casually sun myself on the porch, waiting for Matt to notice I was there and saunter over. If it was just the two of us, we'd sit and chat for a while then gradually make our way into the house so we could race each other down the stairs— our favorite pastime. We'd sit, we'd run, we'd lie on our stomachs. Stair races became a very creative—and competitive—event. However, they never lasted long. My grandmother would eventually chase us off the stairs (something about ruining the carpet; grandmothers are funny that way) and into the living room, where we would settle down with a quiet game of bingo.

No one has the perfect childhood, and Matt and I were certainly no exceptions to that rule. Even now, I couldn't tell you exactly what his problems were; we never discussed them in detail. I just knew they existed. There was no need to tell each other sob stories. Words weren't necessary. Just being able to sit there in mutual understanding was enough.

Inevitably, time moved on, and both of us grew older. I was living with my grandmother less and less, and eventually Matt moved away from the house across the street. Time passed, and our friendship became virtually nonexistent.

My thoughts drifted to Matt only occasionally, as my life became occupied with the endless hassles of middle school, and eventually high school. What had once been a thriving friendship had been reduced to a few faded photographs in a dusty album under my bed.

Then, less than a month after my seventeenth birthday, I found myself in a position I had dreaded all my life: preparing for the funeral of my beloved Gram.

Her passing wasn't sudden; she had been in and out of the hospital for some time. But to me it never seemed quite real. Not until I was faced with the harsh reality of looking into the now forever-closed eyes of the woman who had been my best friend.

During the visitation, I was thanking the other mourners for coming when I saw Matt's Aunt Kathy coming over to me. Kathy and her family had lived in the house that once belonged to Matt, and she, too, had become like a daughter to my grandmother. A flash of Matt came to my mind and I said more to myself than to her, "I wonder if Matt knows."

She put her hand on my shoulder and said, "Andrea, I honestly don't know. I haven't talked to him, and I know he is in school, but I'll try and call."

I didn't hold out much hope of seeing him at the funeral. I hadn't spoken to him in almost ten years. So when I walked into the church that night and saw Kathy sitting alone, I wasn't surprised.

Near the end of the service, there was a time for sharing memories about my grandmother. Many people spoke. Clutching the microphone, voice shaking, I did my best to share a couple of the countless memories I had of her. Then at the end, a voice rose from the back of the sanctuary. The words will forever remain engraved in my heart.

"Ahem . . . well, I don't know if Andrea remembers me . . . but I'm little Matt Luke. . . ." He went on to tell a beautiful story about the times the three of us had shared, and how my grandmother had always felt like a grandmother to him.

After the service, I buried my face in his chest and cried. No words were spoken. They weren't needed. The connection had been restored. This was a boy, now a man, whom I had not seen nor spoken to in ten years. He had found out about the funeral the night before. He had his own commitments—school and work—but he came anyway because he knew it was important to me. Knowing that he had put his life on hold to be there for me still brings tears to my eyes.

Matt and I have only talked a handful of times since the funeral, but he is a constant presence in my heart. He is not only a friend, but an angel sent by my Gram at a time I needed one most.

Andrea Wellman

Grandma's Words of Wisdom

The little girl's grandma lies dying in bed,
She stands nearby listening to what is said.
Her eyes hold tears she tries hard not to show,
Her grandma smiles, for there isn't much she doesn't
  know.

"Sweetheart, don't you worry at all about me,
Forever you will hold me in your memory.
I have lived to a rather ripe, old age,
Compare it to a storybook, each day has a new page.

"You will end up facing challenges, don't give up hope,
Just use your heart to make decisions, and you will always
  cope.
One must be strong to live with successes and strife,
I know this now from my experiences in life.

"You'll have many choices you'll have to make,
And yes, dear, many times your heart will break.
Despite the pain and tears, your heart will always heal,
Never give into temptation, don't let yourself steal.

"Listen to my words, my dear child, they are true,
These are the things when I was your age I wish I knew."
With a slight smile and a squeeze of her hand,
Grandma hoped she helped the little girl to understand.

She kissed her grandma gently as she slowly closed her
    eyes,
And with Grandma's wisdom in her heart, she said her
    last good-bye.

Heather Deederly

Smiles in My Heart

One of my first memories is of my Gramma cuddling with me in the rocking chair in her kitchen. She would sing in my ear and call me Dolly, and tell me how much she loved me, her first-born grandchild. Whenever I stayed overnight, she would give me a bath with warm, white bubbles and then wrap me in the fluffiest towels she had. She made me feel safe.

She would peel the skin off apples, cut the apples into little pieces and sprinkle cinnamon and sugar on them because that was the way I loved them. She let me put as many different kinds of sprinkles and syrups on my ice cream as I wanted. She would buy root beer when I was coming to visit and always made sure the glass was at least half-full of foam because that was my favorite part. And then she would refill it again and again until I was full of root-beer foam. She made me feel special.

I remember sitting on her bed watching her get ready to go out and being amazed by her rituals. She smelled of Dove soap and Noxzema cream. She wore a red shade of lipstick that came in a green tube. On Saturday nights she would wash her hair in the kitchen sink, twist her hair into little waves, and hold them together with bobby pins so that in the morning she would have curls in her hair. She was beautiful.

Her voice was warm and made me feel safe, like fireplace fires and hot chocolate on snowy days. Her laugh was strong and clear; when she laughed with me the rest of the world didn't exist. I felt like I was the only thing she cared about. In the same way, her tears when I was sad made me feel like I would never be alone. She yelled at me once when I was mad at my mom. When I went storming out the door, all she said was, "I love you."

She let me ruin those tubes of lipstick when I'd play dress-up in her clothes and shoes. She taught me how to play bingo, and when I sat with her, staying up way past my bedtime, playing with her in a smoke-filled room of old ladies, I felt so cool. When I was seventeen, I knew she was dying. I would spend the night at her house, and she would still wait up for me to get in, half-asleep and snoring on the couch. When she lay dying in her hospital bed, she called me to come to her from where I stood hiding in the corner, and though her grip was weak and her lips pale, she held my hand and kissed me. She was dying, yet she comforted me.

She passed away four years ago. Sometimes it feels like it was yesterday. Entering her house, I sometimes expect to find her sitting at the table. There are times when it occurs to me that I have skipped thinking of her for one day or that I have misplaced the sound of her laugh or the healing of her touch, and it frightens me. I thank God when I remember. I thank God when I am able to cry because that means I have not forgotten her. I thank God that she was my Gramma, and I will always love her.

Sara Tylutki

Let's Go Dancing in the Rain

Spring break of 1999 was perfect—I got to spend the entire time with my friends just vegging and hanging out. Of course, there was that English project due the day I got back, which I put off until the Sunday before. I was sitting at my computer furiously making up an essay when my little sister walked in from softball practice eating a snow cone and laughing with a sticky smile.

"Whatcha working on?" she asked lightheartedly.

I smiled at her appearance and told her that it was just an English essay. I turned back and continued clacking away. From behind my shoulder she tried to start a conversation.

"So . . ." she began. "You know a kid in your grade named Justin? Justin Schultz?" She licked at a drip on her snow cone.

"Yeah, I know him," I replied. I had gone to elementary school with Justin. He had to be the greatest guy I knew. He never stopped smiling. Justin had tried to teach me to play soccer in the third grade. I couldn't get it, so he smiled and told me to do my best and cheer everyone else on. I'd kind of lost touch with him in the last year, but I told my sister yes, anyway.

"Well," she said, trying to keep her messy snow cone under control. "His church group went skiing this week." She paused to take a lick.

Lucky guy, I thought.

My sister swallowed the ice chips and continued, "So he went skiing and today he died."

I felt the blood drain from my face in disbelief. My hands froze on the keyboard, and a line of Rs inched across the screen. My jaw slowly dropped as I tried to process what she'd said. *Breathe,* something in my head screamed. I shook my head and whipped around to look at my sister.

She was still innocently munching on her snow cone, staring at it determinedly. Her eyes rose to mine and she leaned back, a little startled. "What?" she asked.

"Y-you're joking, right? Who told you that? I don't believe it. How? Are you sure?" I spit out a long string of questions.

"Claire," she stopped me. She began a little slower this time. "A girl on my softball team was house-sitting for them. Justin's parents called her today and told her, and she told me. Sorry, I didn't think you knew him." She sat very still waiting for my response.

Every memory I had of Justin flashed through my mind. I inhaled slowly. "No. No! NO!" I tried to scream. No words came out. I sat up clumsily and shakily ran from the room with my sister behind me yelling, "Wait! I'm sorry . . ."

I called one of our mutual friends right away. She told me between sobs that no one knew why he died. The thirteen-year-old was as healthy as a horse. He fell asleep on Saturday night in the hotel room, and when his room-mate tried to wake him up Sunday morning, Justin wasn't breathing. I didn't want her to hear me cry, so I quickly got off the phone.

I went to school the next day and put on the same strong mask. The principal gave an impersonal announcement about Justin's death that morning and almost immediately I could hear sobs throughout the classroom. That was the worst week of my life. I tried to be a shoulder for others to cry on, but inside I was the one crying.

On Wednesday evening my friend gave me a ride to Justin's viewing. What surprised me when we walked into the room was that Justin's parents weren't crying. They were smiling and comforting everyone. I asked them how they were holding up, and they told me that they were fine. They told me they knew that he wasn't hurting now, that he was with God and would wait for them in heaven. I cried and nearly collapsed. Mrs. Schultz stepped forward to hug me, and I cried on her beautiful red sweater. I looked into her eyes and saw her sympathy for a girl who'd lost her friend.

I went home that night with a deep sadness in my heart for Justin. I wrote a letter to him that I planned on giving him at his funeral. In the letter I wrote to him about how sad everyone was, how much we missed him, how wonderful his parents were and the things he'd never get to do on Earth. I closed it with:

> *Somehow I've always believed that once in heaven, tangible things really don't mean that much anymore. Well, before you get too used to your new life, take these things with you. The smell of grass thirty minutes after it's cut. The feel of freshly washed sheets. The heat of a small candle. The sound a bee makes. The taste of a hot Coke just poured and swirling with ice— hot, but partially cold. The feel of raindrops on your soaked face. But if you take nothing else with you, take your family's embrace.*

I paused and stared into my candle. I rearranged my pen in my hand and continued writing. *Tell you what, Justin. When I die, let's go dancing in the rain.* I smiled through tears and slid my letter into an envelope.

The next day was Justin's funeral. At the last minute, my ride had to cancel because of a schedule conflict, and I was left to sit alone in my house crying. I glanced down at my letter and smiled, "How am I going to get this to you now, Justin?" I laughed through my tears and kept crying.

Sometimes strange thoughts pop into my head, as if from somewhere else. Sitting on my bed fingering a tissue, one of those thoughts told me how to get it to him. *Smoke is faster than dirt.* I was startled by this, but after thinking about it, I realized I was to burn the letter, not bury it. I cried for an hour as I carefully burned the letter. I'd burn a corner, then blow it out under the running water in the sink, afraid of the flames. Eventually, the letter was gone and the white smoke streamed from my window. I waved it away and prayed to God that Justin would someday read my words in the smoke.

That night I dreamt about death and awoke at 2:38 A.M. to hear rain tapping on my window. Rare are the visible words from heaven, but those precious raindrops were my answer. I had told Justin that I wanted to go dancing in the rain. The slow rhythm on my window told me that Justin had heard me. In that moment, I knew that he felt no pain and that we would see each other again. And on that day, we will go dancing in the rain together.

Claire Hayenga

When Tomorrow Starts Without Me

When tomorrow starts without me, and I'm not there to see;
If the sun should rise and find your eyes all filled with
    tears for me;
I wish so much you wouldn't cry the way you did today,
While thinking of the many things we didn't get to say.
I know how much you love me, as much as I love you,
And each time you think of me, I know you'll miss me,
    too;
But when tomorrow starts without me, please try to
    understand,
That an angel came and called my name and took me by
    the hand,
And said my place was ready in heaven far above,
And that I'd have to leave behind all those I dearly love.
But as I turned to walk away, a tear fell from my eye,
For all my life, I'd always thought I didn't want to die.
I had so much to live for and so much yet to do,
It seemed almost impossible that I was leaving you.
I thought of all the yesterdays, the good ones and the bad,
I thought of all the love we shared and all the fun we had.
If I could relive yesterday, I thought, just for a while,
I'd say good-bye and kiss you and maybe see your smile.

But then I fully realized that this could never be,
For emptiness and memories would take the place of me.
And when I thought of worldly things that I'd miss
    tomorrow,
I thought of you, and when I did, my heart was filled with
    sorrow.
But when I walked through heaven's gates, I felt so much
    at home.
When God looked down and smiled at me, from His great
    golden throne,
He said, "This is eternity and all I've promised you,
Today for life on Earth is past but here it starts anew.
I promise no tomorrow, but today will always last,
And since each day's the same day, there's no longing for
    the past.
But you have been so faithful, so trusting and so true,
Though there were times you did some things you knew
    you shouldn't do.
But you have been forgiven and now at last you're free.
So won't you take my hand and share my life with me?"
So when tomorrow starts without me, don't think we're
    far apart,
For every time you think of me, I'm right here in your heart.

David M. Romano

Wherever You Go

Happiness is a perfume you cannot pour on others without getting a few drops on yourself.

George Bernard Shaw

I loved Katrina right away. There was no way you couldn't. She was new to our school, but she didn't seem shy or nervous at all. She smiled at everyone, even on the first day of class. Unfortunately, we only got to enjoy that smile for the first three days of school. Our teacher informed us that Katrina had leukemia and would be in the hospital for a bone-marrow transplant. I had no idea what that was, but it sounded scary, so some of my friends and I decided to go see her in the hospital. She had just moved to a new town and didn't even get a chance to make friends with anyone yet. We wanted to keep her company. That's how we came to know Katrina and how much fun she really was.

It was a little awkward at first because we didn't know her, but when she started telling us about her hospital adventures we were all laughing, and before we knew it, we had been there for almost three hours. She told us about the kid in the room next to her who would get up and pull the fire alarm for absolutely no reason. And sure enough, while we were sitting with her, the fire alarm went off. We all laughed when nobody flinched, and the hospital staff just went about their duties like nothing was wrong. She told us how her mom would sneak in Chinese food for her. And how much she missed her animals: a pony, pigs, a ferret, a mouse, a rat, two hamsters, a cat, nine dogs, two chameleons and a snapping turtle. Later, her mom told me that her favorite thing to do was to go to the Humane Society and adopt the most ugly or abused animal. She always managed to take it home and make it beautiful.

Once she was released, we spent a lot of time together. She came over to my house, and we had many sleepovers. She had lost all her hair during her chemotherapy treatments so she was always wearing a hat of some sort to cover her head. For her first school dance, she bought this yellow hat that had blonde braids hanging down from it. She loved it. At the dance, Katrina danced all night long and never stopped. She was having the time of her life. Suddenly, she took off her yellow hat and started twirling it by the braids and throwing it into the air. I don't think I ever saw her laugh so hard.

She was hopeful that she would eventually be able to play sports again so she went out and bought some running shoes that were two sizes too big for her. She told me she'd be able to fit into them as soon as she was able to run again. Her optimism was contagious.

Soon we got the news we had all been waiting for: Her cancer was gone. The doctors told her she was in remission. She could live her life once again. She began to gain weight, which looked good on her. She had been so tiny when I first met her. Her legs and wrists had always looked so fragile. Now she was looking stronger by the day. She had always told me she hated being short, but even I was surprised when she came to school in four-inch heels one day. She was so proud of those shoes. She kept walking up to people and saying, "Finally! I'm taller than you!"

One night I came home from school to a message from Katrina on our answering machine. She told me to call her right away when I got home. It sounded like she was crying. I knew there was something seriously wrong because she never cried.

She started crying when she heard my voice. "My cancer is back," she sobbed. They were the most terrifying four words anyone had ever said to me. I didn't know what to say. My heart felt like it stopped. She told me that her lymph glands had been getting swollen lately, so her mom took her to the doctor. When they tested her, they found out the cancer was back. We were both crying. She told me I was the first person she called because I was her closest friend. That made me cry even more. She was scared, and she didn't want to die. She told me how much fun she was having lately. I told her I was there to fight with her. There was no way I was going to let her go.

We visited her as much as we could. We gave her cards and this huge wall print that everybody at our school had signed. Her room looked like a gift shop after a while. She told me the cards and gifts really helped her to stay hopeful.

I heard that her family was having financial problems. I thought of ways that we could help them. Our whole eighth-grade class got together and came up with ideas. Our first fundraiser was a dance. At least half the high school came, and we had a donation jar there that was full by the end of the night. People paid to get in, and we found a DJ who put on the music for free. Katrina came to the dance, and she had a blast. We took the leftover baked goods we were selling there and had a bake sale the next day.

We thought of "Hats On for Katrina Day" because she always wore hats. We had the students and staff at our high school pay to wear a hat all day during school. We raised a lot of money because hats are not allowed at our school, and everybody likes to wear them. It was a huge success. We also had a whopper feed, a raffle and a basketball game between the seniors at our school and the staff. We ended up raising over $4,500 for Katrina and her family. When they found out, they were thrilled. It felt good to be able to help them.

Soon enough, Katrina was released from the hospital to her home. She was being cared for under hospice, which meant that a nurse would come out to the house to care for her because there was nothing more the hospital could do. When I heard this, I was really sad and scared. Her parents told us she had anywhere from a few weeks to a few months to live. I was in shock.

On April 5, Katrina woke up and told her mom that it was time for her to go to heaven. It was time for her suffering to finally end. She started coughing and couldn't breathe very well so her mom took her to the hospital right away. Katrina died at ten-thirty that night. Katrina had told her mom that if she didn't make it she wanted to be cremated. Her mom had asked her why, and she had said, "Because you move around a lot, and I want to go with you wherever you go."

The next day at school, my friends and I were talking about Katrina and the good times we had with her. All of a sudden everybody got really quiet. People always say that whenever that happens it means an angel is flying over. I hope it was Katrina. And if it was, she's going to be real busy. We move around a lot, too.

Kari Fiegen

11

GROWING UP

*There is always one moment in childhood
when the door opens and lets the future in.*

Deepak Chopra

Somewhere in the Middle

A journey lies ahead
for all teenagers today.
A journey to adulthood,
our youth to kiss away.

But as we go we find ourselves
at a truly awkward stage.
We're partial, unripe, sketchy and crude
at this tender age.

We're old enough to make a choice
yet still young in many ways.
Too young to pack our bags and go,
too old to want to stay.

Young enough for fun and games,
too old for carefree lives.
Young enough for hopes and dreams,
yet for reality we strive.

Old enough for heartfelt pain,
too young to find the cure.

Too old for childish ways of past,
too young to be mature.

Old enough to fall in love
and give our hearts away.
But, still too young to understand
just why we feel this way.

We're trusted, loyal, proud and true
yet scolded, sneered and scorned.
Between the role of adult and child,
we are somewhere torn.

Like an uncompleted work of art,
we're awkward, unsure, half-baked.
But be patient please
for we're on our way
to becoming something great.

Liza Ortego

Losing Becky

I didn't see it coming, the day I lost my best friend. Becky and I were eating our bag lunches at some benches out by the school tennis courts. We were alone; our other friends weren't with us, which was unusual in those days—we almost always ate lunches in a group, the eight of us—so this should've tipped me off. It's true that Becky had been acting strangely for the past few weeks, alternately ignoring me and snapping at me. When I'd asked her what was wrong, she'd said, "Nothing!"

"Then why are you acting so weird?"

"If I'm so weird, maybe you shouldn't hang around with me."

So I was glad today to be hanging out with her, just the two of us, like old times. We'd been best friends for almost two years. We'd met soon after we started the seventh grade and quickly fell into being best friends in that mysterious way friends sometimes do. We'd shared countless phone calls and school lunches and sleepovers. We'd spent many weekends together, laughing gut-strengthening laughs, playing records and the radio; I played piano while Becky sang in her light, high voice. We shared lots of inside jokes and goofiness, like our hilarious games at the tennis courts. Neither of us were any good at tennis, so as we hit the ball wildly off the mark, we'd yell to each other, "It's still going!" laughing helplessly and scrambling to retrieve the ball, no matter how many times it had bounced.

But today at the tennis courts, neither of us was laughing or even smiling. And suddenly, I realized that this lunch alone together had been planned. Becky wanted to talk to me.

"You wanted to know what was wrong," Becky said. Her tone was overly kind and condescending. "For awhile now, we've felt you haven't been having a good time with us." Why was she saying "we"? I had a sinking feeling. She was right about my not having a good time lately hanging out with our friends. Really, they were Becky's friends, and I hung around with them for her sake. They were nice enough girls, but I didn't have much in common with them. They liked Top-40 music, which increasingly bored me. They thought the music I liked was too weird. During lunch, they'd chat on and on about thirteen-year-old boys, gymnastics, TV shows and how stupid the popular girls were. More and more, I'd tune out their chatter, daydreaming about the bands I liked, feeling profoundly bored by Becky's friends—but not by Becky. I endured my boredom because of her. Besides, there was a certain security in having these girls to sit with at lunch, having them if you wanted them.

Becky went on with her speech: "I want to be . . . popular." Her voice was quavering and ruthless. "You don't seem to want to, but we feel it's important." I couldn't believe I was hearing this. They'd gone on and on about what lame idiots the popular girls were. But what Becky had to say next sent my world spinning. "We think maybe you ought to have lunch with some other girls from now on."

"But who?" I asked, panicking. I couldn't think of a single person. It suddenly sank in that I no longer had a best friend.

"What about those older girls? You seem to get along with them," she suggested with a trace of what sounded like jealousy. It was true that I did get along with some of the older girls—like Lisa, who we'd met in an after-school creative-writing workshop, who wrote strange, impassioned poems, and who'd loaned me a tape with some equally strange, impassioned songs on it, songs I listened to over and over again. The older girls were more interesting than Becky's friends. But at that moment, all I wanted was for Becky to say we were still best friends. I felt like no one could possibly want me around.

The next day at noon, I put my books in my locker, grabbed my lunch, slammed the locker shut, then headed automatically for Becky's locker as I had every day for what seemed like forever. Just as I saw her—small, thin girl with shoulder-length black hair—I remembered. She saw me, and we both stood frozen for a moment. Then I made myself turn and walk in the opposite direction. It was like a divorce.

At first, I wandered around school close to tears all the time—in class, in PE, everywhere. But I did start getting to know some of the older girls better. I began to eat lunch with them, to sit with them during free period. We talked about the music and the movies we liked, and I found myself having fun. No longer did I have to tune out—I wasn't bored anymore. I still missed having a best friend. But by the time I got to the ninth grade, I had many friends and several close ones—and a number of them had also been dropped by their previous cliques for being "too weird." They liked the same music I did, and some of them even went to see live bands. Soon I was going out, too, and my whole world seemed to open up.

Becky and I were never friends again, although I still talked to her from time to time at school. Sometimes I tried to tell her about the fun I was having, but she didn't seem to understand. She and her friends hadn't become any more popular than when I was part of their crowd. I didn't know whether that continued to matter to her.

She apologized to me one day in the school lunchroom for the way she had treated me. "I can't believe I did that to you!" she said. But I told her I had long since realized that she had done me a favor. I had found my true friends, friends who could really understand me, friends I could be completely myself with, while the pain of Becky's rejection has become a distant memory.

Gwynne Garfinkle

Something I Couldn't See

I used to joke that the first person I ever met, after my parents, was Ellie Oswald. Ellie was the daughter of our next-door neighbors, and our mothers introduced us before we were a month old; for most of my life, I couldn't remember a time when Ellie and I hadn't been friends.

We went to the same school, and we spent nearly all our free time with each other. We put together jigsaw puzzles, dressed up, played house (one of the reasons I liked Ellie was that she would always agree to be the man), and ran around the golf course that our street dead-ended onto.

We told each other everything, and we knew each other so well that we could communicate without speaking. In fifth grade, her seat was two rows ahead of mine, and sometimes when Mrs. O'Hara wasn't looking, Ellie would glance back and ask questions or tell me things with her eyes: *Doesn't Brad Bentley look cute today? Why is social studies so boring? Do you want to play four-square at recess?* So certain and familiar was my friendship with Ellie that, in an odd way, I never thought of it; it was just my life.

It was around fifth grade that Ellie and I went from being girls who had existed on the periphery of our elementary school's social scene to being the ones everybody wanted to be friends with. I still can't entirely account for this. One day, we were just hanging around with each other, watching TV and drinking root beer in her parents' room; the next day, we were being flooded with invitations to birthday parties and were the ones other girls wanted to be partners with in gym or sit next to on the bus. Our classmates asked about our opinions, laughed at our jokes and confided their problems in us.

But being popular wasn't easy—honestly. At lunch, girls would cram around the table where we'd chosen to sit, and when we finished our lunch and stood, they'd all stand, too. If two girls got in a fight at a slumber party, I'd be called on to settle the dispute. And I always felt the press of my classmates' wishes for attention from me. I wanted to be nice to everyone, but sometimes it felt exhausting.

It was around eighth grade that my classmates began rebelling—girls and boys fooling around with each other, shoplifting, smoking cigarettes. Such activity made me distinctly uncomfortable. Ellie and I had both always done well in school, and I valued my teachers' approval. And I definitely didn't want to get into trouble with my parents. Plus, it all just seemed unnecessary. Cigarettes smelled bad and made you cough, and why would I hide somewhere, covertly puffing away, when there were so many other things I was interested in?

But I could feel how my lack of interest in misbehaving began to separate me from my friends—including Ellie. If a bunch of us were spending the night at Gina's house and some boys were going to sneak in after Gina's parents went to bed, I'd purposely go to sleep early. Then, the next morning, the other girls would have a new, shared

point of reference that I was outside of. I couldn't understand my classmates' rush to act older; we had the rest of
our lives to be old, but so little time left to be young.
When I tried to talk about this with Ellie, she would
simply say, "Things are changing, Caroline." I wanted to
say that they didn't have to change—that we didn't need
to be at the center of things, that it would be okay if it was
just us again—but I could never force the words out.

One Saturday in October, I was at the grocery store
with my mother when I ran into a classmate named
Melissa. She pulled me aside and whispered, "Is Ellie
okay?"

"What?" I said.

"From last night."

I swallowed. My heart was pounding. "What happened
last night?"

"You don't know?"

Melissa wasn't someone I particularly liked, and it
embarrassed me to have to ask her for information about
my own best friend. "No," I said. "I don't know."

"Well, I guess Gina's parents are out of town, and she
had a party and everyone was drinking, and Ellie fell
down the steps and cut her forehead. I heard she had to
get stitches." Melissa squinted at me. "I can't believe you
don't know this."

It was difficult to absorb all the information at once—a
party? Ellie falling? Stitches? How had I not known about
this? Had I not been invited to other parties? Since when
had Ellie been a drinker?

When I called Ellie, she sounded subdued and defen-
sive. "It wasn't a party," she said. "It was just a few people.
And I didn't have to get stitches. I didn't even go to the
hospital."

"Do your parents know?"

"No, and don't tell your mom or she'll tell mine."

"But something really bad could have happened," I said.

"But it didn't," she replied. "So chill out."

That was the moment, those were the words—*so chill out*—that made me know for certain that things between us had changed dramatically and permanently. And sure enough, Ellie soon made some excuse to get off the phone. I had lost her.

As popularity had once suddenly been bestowed upon me for no apparent reason, it was just as suddenly snatched away. Girls who had hung on my every word barely acknowledged me in the halls; several times, when I passed by a cluster of them, conversation would stop. The truth was, I might even have been relieved by this shift except for the fact that this time I didn't have Ellie to keep me company. For most of ninth grade, I was alone. I still saw Ellie in class, but whenever the teacher or another student said something that reminded me of her and I glanced over, her gaze was averted, her eyes somehow deadened. I heard that she started smoking pot. She also stopped making honor roll and began going out with an older guy named Dave who'd been kicked out of our school.

Throughout most of high school, I was incredibly lonely. It wasn't until college that I made friends with people whom I felt the true sense of connection I'd once felt with Ellie. So maybe it's surprising that when I look back, I don't regret any of it. I spent much of high school studying, and it paid off when I got into my first-choice college. I focused on what interested me, like the books we read for English class, and I joined the track team, and today I still love to read and to run. Ironically, my decision not to do things that made me uncomfortable, like drink and smoke and lie to my parents, caused me a lot of discomfort. But it was a manageable discomfort; there was something true in it. I can honestly say that the consequences of being yourself are never worse than the consequences of not being yourself.

As for Ellie, the last time I saw her was the summer I graduated from college, when I ran into her at the mall. I knew she had gone to community college then dropped out to work, and soon after, became pregnant. It surprised me to see that she was pregnant again. "When are you due?" I asked.

"September." Her voice was flat, and her skin was pale and pasty.

I was afraid to ask anymore. I was pretty sure she wasn't married.

"What's going on with you?" she asked.

"I just graduated," I told her. "And I'm going to London for an internship."

"That's great," she said, and again, there was no enthusiasm in her voice.

I wanted to look at her and tell her with my eyes, *It will be okay for you, too, Ellie! I remember how smart and strong and fun you were. I know that you can put your life together again.* But every time I looked at her, she was looking away—staring hard at something I couldn't see.

Caroline Smith

My Grandma Told Stories

When I was young, my mother was going to Florida to visit my grandmother. I begged her to take me with her. "I'll take you, but remember," my mother warned me, "Grandma is sick."

I had seen plenty of sick people before, so I figured it wouldn't be a big deal. Besides, by the time we got to Florida, my grandma would probably be okay. Then we would have fun just as we used to. I remembered how important I had felt the summer before when my grandma carried me on her shoulders down the streets of St. Petersburg.

My mother and I took the train to Florida. She brought a bag of cherries along with us. It was a huge bag, but instead of giving me a handful to eat, she gave me the whole bag to hold. After I ate my first handful, I looked at her, but she didn't say anything. Although she sat next to me, she seemed far away, immersed in her own thoughts, as she vaguely looked out the window. I took another handful, and still she didn't say anything. She didn't even notice. My mom let me eat all the cherries I wanted, but when I looked down at my new shirt and discovered cherry stains on it, I was afraid I'd get in trouble. When I told my mom, she said it was okay, and she patiently wiped at the stains with a cold, wet rag.

We took a cab from the train station to my grandma's house. I got more and more excited as we approached. Grandma was a great storyteller and her stories made me feel special whenever she told them.

"Grandma, tell me a story," I'd say, and she would always begin the story, "Once upon a time there was a boy named Billy . . ." Every story started with a boy named after me. When I arrived at her house, my first words were going to be, "Grandma, tell me a story."

When I got to Grandma's house, she didn't come out to meet me. Even after I ran up the steps, she still didn't come out to meet me. I went into her bedroom. In a moment, I was changed forever, because what I saw in that room wasn't my happy-go-lucky grandmother. It was a crumpled body, thin and drawn.

That night as I lay in bed, I heard my grandma moaning in pain. It had the same effect on me as someone running fingernails across the blackboard. I just wanted it to stop. It continued all night.

The next morning, I asked my mom if I could leave because it hurt too much to see Grandma that sick. She sent me home that afternoon on the plane. A few weeks later, my mother came home and asked me if it was all right if Grandma came to live with us. I said yes, but in reality I never wanted to see my grandmother again.

Although my grandma lived with us for the next few months, I never went into her room. She couldn't get out of bed. I didn't have to see her. Every so often, when I walked past her room, I could see her with her back turned toward me. Sometimes her backside showed from under her nightgown and I saw how wrinkled it looked with her back and bony pelvis showing through her hanging skin. I felt ashamed because I didn't think I should see this side of my grandmother.

One day, my grandma called to me as I walked by her room. I didn't want to go. Her voice struck an intimate and familiar cord inside me. It was a voice I couldn't disappoint. I followed the voice as though in a daze. In her room, I didn't look at her. I just looked at the floor and told myself that this wasn't my grandmother—it just couldn't be.

I was about to run out of the room and leave it forever when she spoke, "Once upon a time there was a boy named Billy . . ." I followed her words to that place beyond words and crumpled bodies, to that place of recognition and recollection: ". . . and little Billy loved his grandma very much. . . ." I raised my head and looked at my grandmother. Although her crumpled and dying body hadn't changed, I could now see behind her appearance. I went into her room every day after that until she died, and every day she told me another story about a boy named Billy.

William Elliott

Where the Locks Click Open

Nobody can give you wiser advice than yourself.

Cicero

Flipping to journal entry number seventy-nine, I smile knowingly at the subtle change in voice I can't quite explain and note with mixed irony that the entry has the same digits as the year of my birth. Since my first weekly journal assignment in the second grade, I've taken my journals more seriously as an exercise for myself. Rereading them shows me the peaks and valleys, the good and the ugly. It's enlightening to read about my childish obsessions, the arguments with friends that now seem trivial, and the ones that still carry their salty sting. It may only be ink on paper, but it's my loves and hates and sighs. When I'm not writing in my diary, I find myself out of touch with reality, unwilling to see it in my own words and handwriting.

Journal entry seventy-nine was written when my best friend held her hands out and shoved the sight of two tormented wrists into my face. I wrote about a stumbling dimness in her eyes as I looked from her wrists to her face, searching for some kind of explanation or answer. "Who did this to you?" tumbled out of my mouth. "I did," she replied. I grabbed her hand, careful not to touch the bruises and fine lines and knots of dried blood. Her eyes lowered to the ground, unable to withstand the pain of my blunt eyes. I was only thirteen then, barely a teenager, and my best friend since childhood had been hospitalized for attempting to commit suicide. The shared silence we'd become comfortable with as best friends was broken that day. Noise screamed in my ears—always the incessant yet not verbalized question of "Why, WHY? *WHY?*" She had a constellation of reasons, but I know now that she never could have given me one I could come to terms with. In that period of darkness where an unbridgeable gulf separated me from her, the mirror of my own self-evaluation shattered piece by piece, and fragile shards of my naïveté and beliefs fell to the ground.

I wrote about gliding through a pins-and-needles dream where numbness overwhelmed my body and emotions. Her deep pain translated into my own, and I felt as if her experience became my own first brush with death. In the face of all this adversity, the complexities of our lives intertwined even more strongly than before. Through her dimmed and lifeless eyes and through my numbed voice in the form of senseless words on an unde-termined page, I began to see with a wider perspective on life and death.

A lot of what happened that day and the months that followed are a blur. For a long time, it remained an untouchable subject tucked away somewhere deep and dark in never-never land. Today, looking back on that particular entry and the entries that followed, I can trace a distinct change in tone and voice. What Peter Pan always dreaded happened to me overnight—I grew up. Even though I sometimes feel a pang for the return of my idealism and innocence, I know now that what I gained instead was more precious—an affirmation of love and strength.

Writing in my journal has provided clarity in my life; it brings me to a place undisturbed where I can collect my thoughts while staying in constant repair with reality and myself.

Stephanie Hsu

Rolling Down Summer's Hills

Every human being on this Earth is born with a tragedy, and it isn't original sin. He's born with the tragedy that he has to grow up. A lot of people don't have the courage to do it.

Helen Hayes

We run through the August night with only fireflies lighting our way, feeling the freedom of time that only children of summer ever know. The echo of our laughter sails through darkness, while we chase each other in tag. Soon we become silent, hunting through the tall, damp grass punctuated only by the beating of our hearts.

A hand pierces through the night, grabbing me. Our two bodies fall entwined into a huddled mass of legs and arms with her gaining the upper hand because I let her. She pins me down upon my back, her hands holding mine outstretched upon the moist grass. Straddling my chest with her knees, I sense her head slowly growing ever nearer. We're so close that I can feel the ins and outs of her breath upon my lips. She covers my mouth with her own and I am lost in the newness of my first kiss.

Before I can speak or think, she pulls away. Running off, she leaves me there dazed. That was how the night ended; this is how it began.

It's the summer of my thirteenth birthday, and I'm enjoying these majestic Pocono days. Our cabin overlooks the endless rolling hills carpeted by sweet-smelling grasses and black-eyed Susans. My younger brother Mikey and I climb to the highest point and then, lying down on our sides like two bowling pins, we close our eyes rolling wildly down to the bottom. It's a dizzying sensation to feel the world spin around and around this way. Sometimes I lose control and go careening off into some unplanned foreign destination.

And so it is when I first see Carly, hanging out among the other girls at Lake Wallenpaupack. I didn't know then that I'd go careening off sideways and smack straight into her world.

She hangs with this group of thirteen-year-old girls who've teamed up more out of convenience than common interest. Her long black hair falls in waves against her pale white skin, and she has this unique ability to smile at me with her eyes.

My posse looks like an odd assortment left over in some thrift-shop clearance box. First off, there's me. I had a major growth spurt this summer, and my limbs feel way too long. It's weird to suddenly tower over your own mother, the person you've looked up to your whole life. Now a good three inches taller than she, I can easily pat her on the head. Yet no matter how much I eat, my pants hang low on my gangly, 105-pound frame. Everything is changing around me and inside me. I can't even count on feeling comfortable in my own skin, which is now riddled with acne.

Then there's my ten-year-old brother, Mikey. He hasn't found any other kids his age around, and appears to be going through severe Nintendo withdrawal. It's my responsibility to watch out for all four fast-moving feet of him. We make an unlikely pair. Although only three years come between our ages, almost two feet separate our heights.

Finally there's Ron, who's fourteen, a full year older than I and so much more wise in the ways of the world. He shoves his Mets cap low on his head to shield his eyes from the sun and any parent's watchful gaze. In his left ear he sports a fake diamond stud, which denotes the coolness he envelops.

Ron and I sit on the dock, dangling our feet in the water's edge, while Mikey floats carelessly in his black inner tube. Once in a while we have the nerve to dart our eyes over to the girls who are taking turns diving into the water in their bright bikinis, giggling and trying to peek over at us as well.

Ron shares his experiences with women and I wonder how much of it is really true, but I listen closely just in case it is. Some of his stories are funny, and others are just really gross, but I tuck all of what he tells me safely away in the annals of my mind for future reference.

My only other experience hearing about sex was back in health class, and there it seemed like such a crude joke. There was this one jerk in the back of the room who'd laugh whenever the teacher mentioned anything sexual. He was the same guy who'd repeat over and over that there was going to be a "teste" on Monday and then die laughing at his own wit.

At home, my parents speak in strictly medical terms. The way they tell it, the whole thing sounds more like a painful procedure for wisdom teeth removal than a pleasurable experience. Here, sitting on the dock with Ron, it seems a lot more real. I watch Carly in her red two-piece. Her shining black hair reflects the noonday sun, and I wonder what it would be like to kiss those peach-colored lips. So far it's taken all the courage I can muster just to say hi as we pass each other every day at the lake.

Soon, night falls and Dad calls us around the dinner table to have an informal family meeting. He says he wants to talk about our "future." The cabin is hot and noticeably un-air-conditioned. The sweat on the back of my legs causes my skin to stick to the vinyl-covered dining chairs.

My dad sits at the head of the table with his elbows resting on the yellow Formica. He hasn't shaved since we arrived here, and the gray stubble on his cheeks and chin make him look old. My mother sits at the other end of the table still wearing the same swimsuit she wore earlier today down by the lake. She pulls the seat of her suit down over each thigh, fidgeting more than her usual calm demeanor allows. Mikey sits lazily dipping his Oreo cookies into a large glass of milk and then sucking them down over his wet lips.

My dad tells us he's been laid off from work—straight out with no beating around the bush. I can't say I'm shocked; we all saw the writing on the wall. Dad's a tex-tile man, and the industry is dying. I know this because I've heard the hushed conversations between my mom and dad. With most labor now going overseas, there's just not enough work to keep the U.S. sewing factories alive. It's not as if Dad has a profession where he can just slip comfortably into a new opportunity. Finding another job at forty-six years old is rough.

Mikey just keeps sucking down his cookies. He's too young to understand that there is no magic that will make everything better, and that Dad doesn't have all the answers.

In between frantic thoughts, I hear Dad saying some-thing about our home; using words like "scaling down" and "tightening belts." All I keep wondering is, *How is this going to affect me? Will I still be able to afford to go to the movies with my friends, or will I be left at home? And where will my home be?* I hear Dad saying something about our horrendous taxes and the possibility of moving to a smaller apartment.

I want to grab him and yell, "Stop! Don't you know you're ruining my life? I can't move . . . this is where all my friends are . . . this is where I go to school. We had a deal, remember? You would take care of me, and I would never have to worry about these kinds of things, because I'm just a kid."

And then this feeling gives way to a sickening rush of guilt for being so selfish. I look over at my parents who seem small and vulnerable. Who are these pathetic imposters whose words change everything for all of us, and how should I react to these strangers that I love so much? Should I lie and tell them everything will be okay? And is that what they need to hear, or is that really what *I* need to hear? I suddenly feel like the parent.

That night I run out to play tag with all those kids whose lives are still unchanged. I run through the night hoping to knock the wind out of myself—running to forget about my dad or maybe to stumble onto an answer that will save us. That's when Carly's arm reaches out to grab me. She kisses me, and I forget for one moment about all the uncertainty.

Then she's gone, and I lay there in the pitch-black darkness with my head spinning the same way it did when I rolled down those long summer hills. I feel that same dizzying disorientation lying there alone in the darkness, and I realize that sometimes there are no real answers, and life goes on.

C. S. Dweck

Tough Stuff Resources

800-SUICIDE: 800-784-2433

Al-Anon/Alateen: 800-344-2666
For friends and family of people with drinking problems.

Alcoholics Anonymous: *www.alcoholics-anonymous.org*

Befrienders International: *www.befrienders.org*
International referral service for suicide prevention.

Boys Town National Hotline: 800-448-3000
Bilingual suicide prevention hotline for boys and girls.

Bulimia/Anorexia Self-Help Hotline: 800-448-3000

Center for Substance Abuse Treatment: 800-662-HELP

Child Help USA: 800-422-4453
Twenty-four-hour child-abuse hotline. Telephone counseling and referrals.

Children of the Night: 800-551-1300,
www.childrenofthenight.org
Rescuing children from street prostitution.

Covenant House Nineline: 800-999-9999
Crisis line for youth and parents. Referrals throughout the U.S.

Eating Disorder Recovery Online: *www.edrecovery.com*

Eating Disorders Awareness and Prevention (EDAP):
800-931-2237, *www.edap.org*

Gay, Bi or Questioning Teens: *www.outproud.org*

GED Hotline: 800-626-9433
Twenty-four-hour information on how to take the GED.

Homework Hotline: 800-527-8839
Twenty-four hours. Closed in summer.

Kid Save: 800-543-7283
Information and referrals for kids in crisis.

Missing Children Hotline: 800-222-FIND

Narcotics Anonymous: *www.na.org*

National AIDS Hotline: 800-342-2437
Information, referrals, support. Twenty-four hours.

National AIDS Hotline (Spanish): 800-344-SIDA

National Child Abuse Hotline: 800-422-4453
Twenty-four hours. Crisis intervention, information and referrals.

**National Mental Health Association Help Line:
800-969-6642**

National Runaway Switchboard: 800-621-4000

RAINN (Rape Abuse & Incest National Network):
www.rainn.org
National Sexual Assault Hotline: 800-656-HOPE
Free. Confidential. 24/7.

Teen AIDS Hotline: 800-234-4TEEN

United Way Crisis Help Line: 800-233-4357

Victims of Crime Resource Center: 800-842-8467
Monday Through Friday, 8:00 A.M.–6:00 P.M.

Youth Crisis Hotline: 800-448-4663

Yellow Ribbon Project: 303-429-3530, 3531, 3532,
www.yellowribbon.org
Helps prevent teen suicide.

More Chicken Soup?

Many of the letters, stories and poems that you have read in this book were submitted by readers like you who have read *Chicken Soup for the Teenage Soul* and the other *Chicken Soup for the Soul* books. In the future, we are planning to publish *Chicken Soup for the Teenage Soul IV, Chicken Soup for the Teenage Soul on Love and Relationships, Chicken Soup for the Teenage Boy's Soul* and *Chicken Soup for the Teenage Christian Soul.* We would love to have you contribute a story, poem or letter to one of these future books.

This may be a story you write yourself, or one you clip out of your school newspaper, local newspaper, church bulletin or a magazine. It might be something you read in a book or find on the Internet. It could also be a favorite poem, quotation or cartoon you have saved. Please also send along as much information as you know about where it came from.

Just send a copy of your stories or other pieces to us at this address:

Chicken Soup for the Teenage Soul
P.O. Box 936
Pacific Palisades, CA 90272
e-mail: *stories@iam4teens.com*
Web site: *www.iam4teens.com*

Supporting Teenagers

With each *Chicken Soup for the Teenage Soul* book that we publish, we designate one or more charities that are doing important work for teens to receive a portion of the profits that are generated. We are making a donation to the following charity:

Soup and Support for Teachers and Teens

Soup and Support for Teachers and Teens gives teachers the opportunity to use the *Chicken Soup for the Teenage Soul* books free of charge along with a guidebook called *101 Ways to Use Chicken Soup in the Classroom.* If you would like to know more about this program and find out ways you can help or be a recipient of this program, contact:

Soup and Support for Teachers and Teens
P.O. Box 999
Pacific Palisades, CA 90272
phone: 310-573-3655
e-mail: *soupandsupport@iam4teens.com*

Who Is Jack Canfield?

Jack Canfield is a bestselling author and one of America's leading experts in the development of human potential. He is both a dynamic and entertaining speaker and a highly sought-after trainer with a wonderful ability to inform and inspire audiences to open their hearts, love more openly and boldly pursue their dreams.

Jack spent his teenage years growing up in Martins Ferry, Ohio, and Wheeling, West Virginia, with his sister Kimberly (Kirberger) and his two brothers, Rick and Taylor. The whole family has spent most of their professional careers dedicated to educating, counseling and empowering teens. Jack admits to being shy and lacking self-confidence in high school, but through a lot of hard work he earned letters in three sports and graduated third in his class.

After graduating college, Jack taught high school in the inner city of Chicago and in Iowa. In recent years, Jack has expanded this to include adults in both educational and corporate settings.

He is the author and narrator of several bestselling audio- and videocassette programs. He is a regularly consulted expert for radio and television broadcasts and has published numerous books—all bestsellers within their categories—including more than twenty *Chicken Soup for the Soul* books, *The Aladdin Factor, Heart at Work, 100 Ways to Build Self-Concept in the Classroom* and *Dare to Win.*

Jack addresses over one hundred groups each year. His clients include professional associations, school districts, government agencies, churches and corporations in all fifty states.

Jack conducts an annual eight-day Training of Trainers program in the areas of building self-esteem and achieving peak performance. It attracts educators, counselors, parenting trainers, corporate trainers, professional speakers, ministers and others interested in developing their speaking and seminar-leading skills in these areas.

For further information about Jack's books, tapes and trainings, or to schedule him for a presentation, please contact:

The Canfield Training Group
P.O. Box 30880 • Santa Barbara, CA 93130
phone: 800-237-8336 • fax: 805-563-2945
e-mail: *speaking@canfieldgroup.com*
Web site: *www.chickensoup.com*

Who Is Mark Victor Hansen?

Mark Victor Hansen is a professional speaker who, in the last twenty years, has made over four thousand presentations to more than two million people in thirty-three countries. His presentations cover sales excellence and strategies; personal empowerment and development; and how to triple your income and double your time off.

Mark has spent a lifetime dedicated to his mission of making a profound and positive difference in people's lives. Throughout his career, he has inspired hundreds of thousands of people to create a more powerful and purposeful future for themselves while stimulating the sale of billions of dollars worth of goods and services.

Mark is a prolific writer and has authored *Future Diary, How to Achieve Total Prosperity* and *The Miracle of Tithing*. He is the coauthor of the *Chicken Soup for the Soul* series, *Dare to Win* and *The Aladdin Factor* (all with Jack Canfield) and *The Master Motivator* (with Joe Batten).

Mark has also produced a complete library of personal empowerment audio- and videocassette programs that have enabled his listeners to recognize and better use their innate abilities in their business and personal lives. His message has made him a popular television and radio personality with appearances on ABC, NBC, CBS, HBO, PBS, QVC and CNN.

He has also appeared on the cover of numerous magazines, including *Success, Entrepreneur* and *Changes*.

Mark is a big man with a heart and a spirit to match—an inspiration to all who seek to better themselves.

For further information about Mark, please contact:

Mark Victor Hansen & Associates
P.O. Box 7665
Newport Beach, CA 92658
phone: 949-759-9304 or 800-433-2314
fax: 949-722-6912
Web site: *www.chickensoup.com*

Who Is Kimberly Kirberger?

Kimberly is an advocate for teens, a writer for teens, a mother of a teen, and a friend and confidante to the many teens in her life. She is committed to bettering the lives of teens around the globe through her books and the outreach she does for teens on behalf of her organization, Inspiration and Motivation for Teens, Inc.

Kim's love for teens was first expressed globally with the publication of the bestselling *Chicken Soup for the Teenage Soul*. This book was a true labor of love for Kim, and the result of years of friendship and research with teens from whom she learned what really matters. After the success of the first *Teenage Soul* book, and the outpouring of hundreds and thousands of letters and submissions from teens around the world, Kim went on to coauthor the *New York Times* #1 bestsellers *Chicken Soup for the Teenage Soul II* and *Chicken Soup for the Teenage Soul III*, *Chicken Soup for the Teenage Soul Journal*, *Chicken Soup for the Teenage Soul Letters* and *Chicken Soup for the College Soul*. Kim's empathic understanding of the issues affecting parents led her to coauthor the recent release *Chicken Soup for the Parent's Soul*.

In October 1999, the first book in Kim's *Teen Love* series was released. *Teen Love: On Relationships* has since become a *New York Times* bestseller. Her friendship and collaboration with Colin Mortensen of MTV's *Real World Hawaii* produced the much-loved *Teen Love: A Journal on Relationships* and *Teen Love: On Friendship*. She recently released *Teen Love: A Journal on Friendship*.

Her nonprofit organization, Soup and Support for Teachers, is committed to teens and teachers having available to them inspiring and supportive reading materials.

When she is not reading letters she gets from teens, Kim is offering them support and encouragement in the forums on her Web site, *www.iam4teens.com*. She also enjoys nurturing her family, listening to her son's band and hanging out with her friends.

For information or to schedule Kim for a presentation, contact:

I.A.M. 4 Teens, Inc.
P.O. Box 936
Pacific Palisades, CA 90272
e-mail for stories: *stories@iam4teens.com*
e-mail for letters and feedback: *kim@iam4teens.com*
Web site: *www.iam4teens.com*

Contributors

Some of the stories in this book were taken from previously published sources, such as books and magazines.
These sources are acknowledged in the permissions
section.

Most of the stories were contributed by readers of our
previous *Chicken Soup for the Soul* books who responded
to our requests for stories. If you would like to contact
them, you can reach them at their e-mail addresses provided below.

Lauren Anderson is currently studying English and Women's Studies at
the University of Waterloo in Ontario, Canada. She can be reached at
lk_anderson@hotmail.com.

Christina "Chrissi" Angeles is a high-school student in California. She finished chemotherapy and radiation in late 2000. "Lumps" was written to get
everyone to live life to the fullest, because you never know when it will be
gone. Chrissi can be reached at *skittlechrissi@aol.com.*

Analise Antone presently attends college as a soon-to-be English major. Her
passions are reading, writing, psychology and all things performance-related.
"Reaching Mom" was her first short story, as well as her first publication. She
can be reached at *AnaliseAntone@aol.com.*

Natalie Atkins is a college student in South Carolina. She is majoring in
English with a concentration in Creative Writing, and both works for and sub-
mits to her annual campus literary magazine. Her story is dedicated to Daniel,
Ray and Kunkel.

Hilary Begleiter is a high-school junior in Des Moines, Iowa. She wants to
dedicate this poem to her grandfather, grandmother and Frank. She hopes it
can help comfort those who have had to deal with the death of a loved one.
You can reach her at *moonandstars80@hotmail.com.*

Rachael Bennett is an aspiring poet in California. She has written for several
private organizations and hopes one day to write a book on teenage depression. This particular piece has been dedicated to both of her mothers, as well
as her dad. She can be reached at *CABabyBlueEyes@aol.com.*

Tiffany Blevins is a seventeen-year-old full-time student and soon-to-be full-
time mother from Springfield, Ohio, who enjoys writing poetry and short
stories. She can be reached at *SugarFrostedQt@hotmail.com.*

Iris M. Bolton is the executive director of The Link Counseling Center's National Resource Center for Suicide Prevention and Aftercare (*www.thelink.org*). She is the cofounder of the North Atlanta, Georgia Chapter of the Compassionate Friends. She also founded the Survivors of Suicide Support Groups in metro Atlanta, and the S.O.S. Support Team, providing home visits to the bereaved. She authored *My Son . . . My Son, a Guide to Healing After Death, Loss, or Suicide,* a book about the survival of her family in the aftermath of the suicide of her son. She is married to Jack Bolton and is the mother of four sons.

Jennifer Braunschweiger is a writer living in New York City.

Danielle Collier is a freelance writer and published fiction writer. She has a B.A. from Columbia University and an M.F.A. from the Iowa Writers' Workshop. Her story is dedicated to her parents and brother. She can be reached at *booxbabe@yahoo.com.*

Jessica Colman is in the James Madison College at Michigan State University. She would like to dedicate "A Most Precious Gift" to her family, with special thanks to her brother, Zack, who has shared every aspect of their parents' divorce and without whom it wouldn't have been as easy. She can be reached at *Tedebear81@aol.com.*

Cheryl Costello-Forshey is a writer whose poetry can be found in several of the *Chicken Soup for the Soul* books, as well as in the books, *Stories for a Teen's Heart, Stories for a Faithful Heart* and *A Pleasant Place.* Cheryl can be reached at *costello-forshey@1St.net.*

Tiani Crocker is a single mom who resides in Bellingham, Washington, with her son, Zion. She attends college part-time and works part-time. Her story is dedicated to her brother whose love inspired it.

Jennifer Dalrymple-Mozisek lives in Dallas, Texas. She graduated from the University of Texas at Austin with a B.A. in English. Jennifer would like to dedicate "Our Song" to the memory of her mother, June Rae Dalrymple-Stanton, and to her father, Michael Anthony Mozisek. She can be reached via e-mail at *jenmoz@aol.com.*

Heather Deederly is a nineteen-year-old residing on Vancouver Island, B.C., Canada. She's taking a course on freelance writing, following her dream. She thanks God and the events in her life for her motivation. She also thanks her mother and sister for their encouragement to pursue her dreams, and her best friend and fiancé, Colin, for giving her strength, courage and always being there for her. She can be reached at *Hezz_17@hotmail.com.*

Jennifer Deyo is a student at Mankato State University, Minnesota, and plans to obtain a degree in Elementary and Special Education. She loves helping others and working with children. Her story is dedicated to Sally Tillema and her family for never giving up on her. Her story was written to help other teens who may be in abusive relationships to believe in themselves. She can be reached at *deyo_jenny@hotmail.com*.

Garrett Drew is an aspiring freelance writer. His passions include his close friends, music and writing. This story is dedicated to those who mean the most to him: Mom and Dad, Beth, Rachael, David, Jennifer and Donny.

Jessica Dubose is a junior in high school. She is an introverted dreamer and writer. Her father, who died in March 2000, continues to be her inspiration as he watches and guides her from heaven. She can be reached at *XOjessicazy@aol.com*.

C. S. Dweck is the author of I.A.M. 4 Teen's "Little Voice" column. His writing has appeared in such publications as *MH-18 Magazine, Real Kids, Real Adventures #12* and *The Market Guide for Young Writers, 6th Edition*. He aspires and perspires to have his own book published. Reach him by e-mail at *dweck@ptdprolog.net*.

Kari Fiegen is a sixteen-year-old honor student from Dell Rapids, South Dakota. She enjoys writing poems and short stories, reading and playing sports. She believes that you should live life to your fullest every day and set high goals. Kari dedicates her story in loving memory of Katrina Marie Jenema.

Monique Fields is a reporter for the *St. Petersburg Times*. She has written about education and children's issues for seven years. She lives with her husband, Kenneth J. Roberts, in Clearwater, Florida.

Kristine Flaherty is a fifteen-year-old sophomore in high school. She plays basketball for her school team and enjoys writing, reading, listening to music and getting together with friends in her free time. Her story is dedicated to her dad. She can be reached by e-mail at *kteen76@hotmail.com*.

Bonnie Gainor is the mother of Ailie Pearson. She can be reached at *smiley@smileysday.com*.

Gwynne Garfinkle lives in Los Angeles. Her poetry, essays, fiction and music reviews have appeared in such publications as *The American Voice, Big Bridge, Loca* and *The New Times*. She is the author of a book of poetry, *New Year's Eve* (Typical Girls Press). She can be reached at *gwynnega@aol.com*.

Zan Gaudioso is a freelance writer whose stories have appeared in newspapers and magazines across the country. She has also contributed stories to *Chicken Soup for the College Soul, Chicken Soup for the Parent's Soul* and *Chicken Soup for the Teenage Soul III*. Zan's career path has been varied and eclectic, from surgical nurse to business owner, sign-language teacher to publicity coordinator for the Academy Awards. Zan is currently enjoying life as a writer and lives in Pacific Palisades, California with her fiancé Robert and their dog Delilah. She can be reached at *Zannie1@aol.com*.

Kristy Glassen is currently a junior at Penn State University majoring in Elementary Education. She looks forward to publishing her book, *Most of the*

Questions, Some of the Answers, about college life in the next couple of months. Her second book, *When Life Comes Our Way,* will follow. All of Kristy's writing is for those who have the courage to keep reaching for their dreams, no matter what the cost. She can be contacted at *keg157@psu.edu.*

Cynthia Marie Hamond began writing three years ago. Her stories have been published in several books and magazines. This is her sixth in the *Chicken Soup for the Soul* series. Her story "Goodwill" from *Chicken Soup for the Kid's Soul* was seen on the *Chicken Soup for the Soul* TV series. You can reach Cynthia at *Candbh@aol.com.*

Claire Hayenga was born in Forth Worth, Texas. Since then she has lived with her mother, father and younger sister in four different locations in the area. The arts greatly interest Claire, who is sixteen years old.

Teal Henderson is no longer with us. She died shortly after her seventeenth birthday. She embraced life fully, almost fearlessly, as if she knew her time here would be short. Her parents say that she was their sunshine and, though they no longer bask in her light, they will always feel the warmth of her love.

Krysteen Hernandez is a fifteen-year-old sophomore in high school in Redondo Beach, California. She has been writing poems for about a year and has written about various subjects. She can be reached at *HellZLiLAngeL637@aol.com.*

Stephanie Maria Hsu wrote her essay in high school in 1996. She is a graduate of the University of Virginia '01, where she received the Distinguished Student Award and was a Jefferson and Echols Scholar. She is a geographical mutt and plans to continue her wanderlusting ways as she pursues her dream of working in the Third World. She is a management consultant in New York City. She can be reached at *smh2b@alumni.virginia.edu.*

Bret Anthony Johnston is currently a Teaching-Writing Fellow at the Iowa Writers' Workshop. His work has twice been honored in the *Atlantic Monthly,* and has appeared in such magazines as *Glamour, Mid-American Review, Southwest Review* and *Shenandoah,* where one of his stories received the 2000 Jeanne Goodheart Prize for best fiction of the year. His stories have been anthologized in *Patterns of Exposition 16ed* and *Scribner's Best of the Fiction Workshops 1999.* He can be reached at *Bretjohnst@aol.com.*

James A. Kisner, author of *Sweet Dreams and Tender Tears,* writes poetic stories based on true-life events. His poetry reflects his life and the lives of those who read his Internet pages and submit their stories to him. For information on his Web pages and books, e-mail him at *POPPYK1@aol.com.*

Traci Kornhauser is a high-school student in Melbourne, Florida. She enjoys sketching and would like to make a career in fashion design. This story is her first to be published, and she hopes to continue writing in her spare time. She dedicates this story to M. K.

Jonathan Krasnoff is a junior at Kansas State University in Manhattan,

Kansas. He is majoring in Public Relations and Print Journalism. Jon hopes to attend law school after graduation. This story is dedicated to the bonds of true friendship. He can be reached at *jdk9569@ksu.edu* or by writing to P. O. Box 1415, Manhattan, KS 66505-1415.

Hawon Lee lives in New Zealand with her parents and two sisters. A writer from an early age, she hopes to become a professional writer one day. Hawon dedicates "Help Me" to all victims of child abuse, especially her friend whom she based this poem on. She can be reached at *bluesmurfz@hotmail.com.*

Kara MacDonald has written poetry since the age of eleven. She dreams of publishing her entire book of poems before she sets out for a career as a novelist, playwright and songwriter. Her writing has never before been published. She would be thrilled to hear from you at *CGLENN7127@aol.com.*

Maggie McCarthy is currently a senior in high school. Maggie loves to write and gets her inspiration from her family and friends. This story is dedicated to her beloved friends who have always helped her follow her dreams, and to all the people like "Hannah"—may they find the hope, faith and courage to live each day.

Meghan O'Brien is a high-school student from Lawrence, Massachusetts. Most of her writing, including this story, is dedicated to the memory of her best friend, Dan, who died in a serious car accident in October 1999. She is also published in the book, *In-Between Days,* a compilation of poems from The International Library of Poetry. She can be reached at *AngEL8926@aol.com.*

Liza Ortego is a seventeen-year-old high school senior from Tioga, Louisiana, who enjoys cheerleading, student government and participating in service clubs. She is active in her youth group at church and loves writing, reading and playing the piano. Liza can be contacted at *LizaLo11@aol.com.*

Amanda Parmenter is a part-time student majoring in Technical Theater. She completed an apprenticeship with the Omaha Community Playhouse, where she still volunteers. She has been fortunate to travel many places and looks forward to many more adventures as she matures. In her spare time, Amanda enjoys reading and writing. She can be reached at *Mandrat@aol.com.*

Susan K. Perry is a social psychologist and author of *Catch the Spirit: Teen Volunteers Tell How They Made a Difference,* as well as a bestseller called *Writing in Flow,* and other books. Her many articles have appeared in such publications as *Seventeen, Teen, USA Today* and *Psychology Today.* Her Web site is *www.BunnyApe.com.*

Tyler Owen Phillips graduated from Westlake High School in Thousand Oaks, California, and is currently in the U.S. Army, stationed in Germany. He likes to surf and skateboard and is in a band called "The Six Pack Lady Killers," which won first place last year in a European Battle of the Bands. Tyler can be reached at *Jazzsoda3@hotmail.com.*

CONTRIBUTORS 339

Kate Reder is an English major at Wesleyan University in Connecticut. She wrote her story when she was in high school back home in San Francisco.

Jenny Sharaf lives in Southern California and is currently a junior in high school. She hopes to one day pursue a career in journalism. She works at I.A.M. 4 Teens, Inc. reading letters that come from teenagers all over the world. She has also worked on *Teen Love: On Friendship*. Her poetry has been published in *Teen Love: A Journal on Friendship*, and she hopes to have more of her poetry published in future books. She would like to thank her friends for making the world a lot more fun. She can be reached at *jenny4@hotmail.com*.

Caroline Smith is a writer living in the Midwest.

Lisa Teller is a writer and mother of three young boys in upstate New York. Her poetry has been published at *www.passionsinpoetry.com*, under the pseudonym, Lia Fail. Lisa also enjoys writing children's stories that rhyme and aspires to publishes them. She can bed reached at *iamirish@worldnet.att.net*.

Phillip Thuss is currently in his second year of university majoring in business. After college, he would like to work in the business end of the entertainment industry. He has talked about his experience with cancer to many people in hopes that it may help to comfort them in their own time of need. He can be reached by e-mail at *pthuss@hotmail.com*.

Sara Tylutki is a public-relations specialist and freelance writer in central New York. She has contributed several human-interest articles to central New York newspapers. "Smiles in My Heart" is dedicated to the memory of her grandmother. Sara can be reached at *stylutki@hotmail.com*.

Eva Unga is a writer for *Woman's World* magazine.

Tal Vigderson lives in Los Angeles and is currently managing director of Icebox.com. He previously worked as an entertainment attorney representing talent, production companies and new media clients. He has had past careers in photography, entertainment-marketing research and teaching. Tal likes to travel and enjoys tennis, writing, hiking and photography. He can be reached at *TOV3@aol.com*.

Jackie Waldman, author of *The Courage to Give*, is the cofounder of Dallas' Random Acts of Kindness Week. An expert on volunteering and service organizations, Jackie has appeared on numerous TV and radio programs, including *Oprah* and was profiled by CNN as one of their "Heroes of the Millennium." She lives in Dallas, Texas, with her husband, three children, and Johnnie and Frankie—their beloved dachshunds.

Cassius Weathersby III is a recent graduate of Beverly Hills High School and now attends Santa Monica College in Santa Monica, California. He has always had a passion for video games, and his career plans include designing new video games and systems. In his first year of college, he discovered his ability to communicate ideas in writing. He can be reached at *Broham1@aol.com* or 369 S. Doheny Dr., Box 371, Beverly Hills, CA 90211.

Andrea Wellman is a class of 2001 graduate from west Michigan. She will be attending a private college for her undergraduate studies in Journalism, Theater or Education. This story is dedicated to her departed grandmother and the people who have always believed in her. She can be reached at *TigrLily44@hotmail.com.*

Jessie Williams is a Music Performance major at Coe College in Iowa. She is involved in Coe College Women's Tennis, Student Senate, Tri-Delta sorority and Mu Phi Epsilon. Along with writing and music, she enjoys spending time with friends at school and spending summers at home in Colorado with her mom and puppy, Abigail.

Sarah Woo is a fourteen-year-old high-school student. She has been writing ever since she was seven and also loves singing, acting and playing volleyball. "That Warm Night" was her first poem, written when she was thirteen. Sarah can be reached at *swoozers@hotmail.com.*

Rebecca Woolf is a freelance writer and photographer who has written for *Chicken Soup for the Teenage Soul II* and *III, Teen Love: On Relationships, Teen Love: On Friendship, Teen Love: A Journal on Friendship, 19* (the popular UK magazine) and more. Keep your eyes out for Rebecca's first solo book of poetry titled, *Through Broken Mirrors: A Reflective Memoir.* Rebecca is the program director and newsletter editor for Lead the Star, a creative company devoted to inspiring creativity and strength of identity in young adults. To reach Rebecca, please e-mail her at *rebeccawoolf@leadthestar.com.*

by William Elliott. ©1996 William Elliott. Published by Quest Books, an imprint of Theosophical Publishing House.

Starving for Control. Seventeen magazine/Jamie-Lynn Sigler ©October 2000.

Just One of Those Days. Reprinted by permission of Jenny Sharaf. ©2001 Jenny Sharaf.

Suffering in Silence. Reprinted by permission of C. S. Dweck and Ruth Greenspan. ©2001 C. S. Dweck and Ruth Greenspan.

Numb. Reprinted by permission of Jessica Dubose. ©2000 Jessica Dubose.

This Too Shall Pass. Letter excerpt reprinted by permission of Shari L. Henderson. ©2001 Shari L. Henderson.

I Have an Angel; Mother; and letter. Reprinted by permission of Bonita L. Gainor. ©2000 Bonita L. Gainor.

Some People Come. Reprinted by permission of Lauren Anderson. ©1999 Lauren Anderson.

My Guardian Angel. Reprinted by permission of Meghan O'Brien. ©2000 Meghan O'Brien.

I Wonder as I Wander. Reprinted by permission of Hilary Begleiter. ©1999 Hilary Begleiter.

The Death of a Friend. Repinted by permission of Cassius Weathersby III. ©1999 Cassius Weathersby III.

Timeless Friendship. Reprinted by permission of Andrea Wellman. ©2001 Andrea Wellman.

Grandma's Words of Wisdom. Reprinted by permission of Heather Deederly. ©1999 Heather Deederly.

Smiles in My Heart. Reprinted by permission of Sara Tylutki. ©1997 Sara Tylutki.

Let's Go Dancing in the Rain. Reprinted by permission of Claire Hayenga. ©1999 Claire Hayenga.

When Tomorrow Starts Without Me. Reprinted by permission of David M. Romano. ©1993 David M. Romano.

Wherever You Go. Reprinted by permission of Kari Ann Fiegen. ©2000 Kari Ann Fiegen.

Somewhere in the Middle. Reprinted by permission of Liza Ortego. ©1999 Liza Ortego.

Losing Becky. Reprinted by permission of Gwynne Garfinkle. ©2001 Gwynne Garfinkle.

Something I Couldn't See. Reprinted by permission of Caroline Smith. ©2001 Caroline Smith.

Where the Locks Click Open. Reprinted by permission of Stephanie Maria Hsu. ©1996 Stephanie Maria Hsu.

More Great Books...

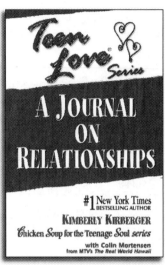

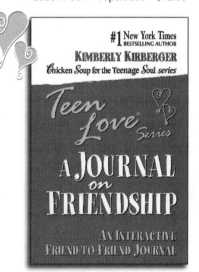

Just for Teens

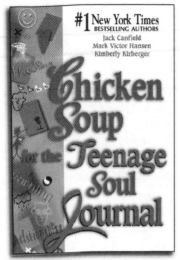

Code #6374 • Paperback • $12.95

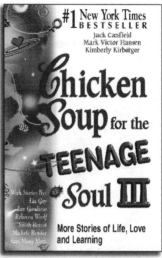

Code #7613 • Paperback • $12.95

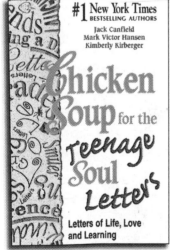

Code #8040 • Paperback • $12.95

Code #7028 • Paperback • $12.95

Also Available in Quality Paperback

A Cup of Chicken Soup for the Soul
Chicken Soup for the Baseball Fan's Soul
Chicken Soup for the Cat & Dog Lover's Soul
Chicken Soup for the Christian Family Soul
Chicken Soup for the Christian Soul
Chicken Soup for the College Soul
Chicken Soup for the Country Soul
Chicken Soup for the Couple's Soul
Chicken Soup for the Expectant Mother's Soul
Chicken Soup for the Father's Soul
Chicken Soup for the Gardener's Soul
Chicken Soup for the Golden Soul
Chicken Soup for the Golfer's Soul
Chicken Soup for the Jewish Soul
Chicken Soup for the Kid's Soul
Chicken Soup for the Little Souls
Chicken Soup for the Mother's Soul, Vol. I, II
Chicken Soup for the Nurse's Soul
Chicken Soup for the Parent's Soul
Chicken Soup for the Pet Lover's Soul
Chicken Soup for the Preteen Soul
Chicken Soup for the Single's Soul
Chicken Soup for the Soul, Vol. I-VI
Chicken Soup for the Soul at Work
Chicken Soup for the Soul: Christmas Treasury
Chicken Soup for the Soul Cookbook
Chicken Soup for the Sports Fan's Soul
Chicken Soup for the Surviving Soul
Chicken Soup for the Teenage Soul, Vol. I, II, III
Chicken Soup for the Teenage Soul Journal
Chicken Soup for the Teenage Soul Letters
Chicken Soup for the Teenage Soul on Tough Stuff
Chicken Soup for the Unsinkable Soul
Chicken Soup for the Veteran's Soul
Chicken Soup for the Woman's Soul, Vol. I, II
Chicken Soup for the Writer's Soul
Condensed Chicken Soup for the Soul
Sopa de Pollo para el Alma, Vol. I, II, III
Sopa de Pollo para el Alma de la Madre
Sopa de Pollo para el Alma de la Mujer
Sopa de Pollo para el Alma del Adolescente
Sopa de Pollo para el Alma del Trabajador
Sopa de Pollo para el Alma del Cristiano